Bureaucracy in Crisis

Bureaucracy in Crisis

Three Mile Island, the Shuttle Challenger, and Risk Assessment

Maureen Hogan Casamayou

Westview Press

BOULDER • SAN FRANCISCO • OXFORD

Copyright © 1993 by Westview Press, Inc.

Published in 1993 in the United States of America by Westview Press, Inc., 5500 Central Avenue, Boulder, Colorado 80301-2877, and in the United Kingdom by Westview Press, 36 Lonsdale Road, Summertown, Oxford OX2 7EW

Library of Congress Cataloging-in-Publication Data
Casamayou, Maureen Hogan.
  Bureaucracy in crisis : Three Mile Island, the shuttle Challenger,
and risk assessment / by Maureen Hogan Casamayou.
     p.   cm.
  Includes bibliographical references and index.
  ISBN 0-8133-1617-0
  1. Communication in organizations—United States—Case studies.
2. Risk communication—Case studies.   3. Bureaucracy—United States—
Case studies.   I. Title.
HD30.3.C36   1993
350'.007—dc20
                                                                        92-46920
                                                                        CIP

Printed and bound in the United States of America

The paper used in this publication meets the requirements
of the American National Standard for Permanence of Paper
for Printed Library Materials Z39.48-1984.

10   9   8   7   6   5   4   3   2   1

To Lou
My best friend and biking companion
for twenty-one years

Contents

Figures

Acknowledgments

I am deeply grateful to the many people who gave me their moral, substantive, and technical support along the way. This book would not have been completed without them. I wish to thank John T. Tierney for his patient guidance and thoughtful counsel when this work was first formulated and for encouraging me to apply for the Virginia Hartley Research Fellowship at The Brookings Institution. Without this, I doubt that the book would ever have been completed. Dennis Hale and Marc Landy also offered constructive criticism and strong support in the early stages of the project.

I also wish to give a very special thanks to Herbert Kaufman for his help throughout the project. He not only gave me the benefit of his fine intellect in shaping my arguments but also the gift of his indomitable spirit when my morale was low.

In the later stages of the work, I benefited greatly from the most generous encouragement and advice of Robert A. Katzmann and from the very valuable insights and commentaries offered by Kent Weaver and Bert Rockman. Philip A. Mundo and Joe White were also very helpful and constructive in their support of my work.

In addition, I am greatly indebted to the Governmental Studies Program of The Brookings Institution under the direction of Thomas E. Mann.

I am also very grateful to the Mount Vernon College faculty club for their moral support and helpful suggestions and to my friend and colleague James Burford, associate professor of fine arts, for designing the cover.

Carol Clark and James Dykes deserve special mention for their painstaking editing and proofreading as does Peggy Miller for her excellent preparation of the manuscript.

Last but not least, I wish to thank my husband, Lou, for his technical advice, his endless patience, and for his unwavering support, which has sustained me throughout the production of this book.

Maureen Hogan Casamayou

1

Introduction

During the years from the late 1970s to the late 1980s, two of the government's most technologically sophisticated agencies, the Nuclear Regulatory Commission (NRC) and the National Aeronautics and Space Administration (NASA), have been charged with serious organizational neglect in the wake of highly visible program failings. For the NRC, it was the near meltdown of the nuclear power plant at Three Mile Island (TMI) in March 1979; for NASA, it was the explosion of the space shuttle Challenger in January 1986. This book explores the reasons for these two organizational failures.

In the case of the NASA organization, which manages and promotes numerous space research and development programs, the cause of the accident was a leaking joint in one of the two solid rocket boosters that propel the shuttle into space. The accident was swift and catastrophic because a joint in the right Solid Rocket Booster (SRB) had failed to contain the hot gases from the burning solid fuel propellant. Just after liftoff, hot gases began to burn through the seal joint in the right SRB. Seconds later, the Challenger broke apart behind a ball of fire and a cloud of vapor in the sky. All seven crew members perished.[1]

With the NRC, a regulatory agency that oversees the nuclear power industry, the accident was slow moving, and the pivotal element was human rather than hardware failure. The plant operators in Metropolitan Edison's Unit–2 pressurized water reactor at TMI came very close to having a complete core meltdown. (A core meltdown occurs when the fuel is no longer cooled and begins to melt. The molten fuel ultimately melts through the reactor vessel and containment building floor and into the earth.) A small amount of radioactivity leaked into the atmosphere, but a core meltdown was averted. Had it not been prevented, the consequences would have been catastrophic. If large quantities of radioactive materials

1

had escaped into the atmosphere and seeped into the earth, there would have been untold damage to the environment and sickness and death to the public.

The accident at TMI began with a series of hardware failures during which a small valve that bounded the reactor core remained stuck open. The control-room operators were unaware of this leak, and the reading of a gauge compounded the problem because it led them to believe that there was actually too much water in the reactor core. (Poor control-room design increased the confusion of the operators.) While the existing water was draining from the reactor through this small leak, the operators turned off the emergency supply of water to the reactor. Although this was, technically speaking, an operator error, there were no available training and established procedures that prepared the operators for such a scenario.[2] In any case, two hours and twenty-two minutes later, after 32,000 gallons of water had drained from the reactor core, the leak was finally discovered.[3]

No lives were lost, and the amount of radioactivity released into the environment apparently was not enough to be a serious health hazard. The Kemeny Commission concluded that, "in spite of serious damage to the plant, most of the radiation was contained and the actual release will have a negligible effect on the physical health of individuals. The major health effect of the accident was found to be mental stress."[4] Another study, however, stated that no one could tell "how much radiation the people living near the plant were exposed to."[5] This study of thirteen residents living near TMI showed interviewees who exhibited fears and anxieties about the possible radiation effects of the accident. Some of them noted the alarming changes in the reproductive capabilities of their livestock and commented on the increased number of miscarriages in the area after the accident.[6]

For opponents of nuclear energy, the accident at TMI vindicated their claims about the inherent dangers of operating nuclear power and the insensitivity of the NRC toward plant safety.[7] Moreover, there was always the ominous question in the minds of the public of what might have happened had the leak not been detected in time to prevent a full-scale meltdown—the long-term effects of causing cancer and genetic disorders in future generations, not to mention "the immediate death of hundreds of thousands" and the "severe and irreparable environmental damage over a vast geographic area."[8] Surveys already indicated that the public exhibited an inordinate fear and dread of the potential for large-scale death and destruction from a silent and invisible enemy—radiation.

Actually, the public's perception of the dangers of nuclear power after the accident at TMI was examined by various social scientists.[9] One particular study found that there was no discernible shift in opinion about the overall safety of the technology. There was an increase of only 2 percent of respondents six months after the accident who believed that nuclear energy was unsafe. There were several reasons for this, most notably that an individual's "belief systems change slowly and resist contrary evidence."[10]

Initially, it might appear that these accidents were the painful, but inevitable, consequences of two complex state-of-the-art technologies. In other words, regardless of the level of designing and engineering competence used in the shuttle system and the nuclear power plant safety systems, sooner or later accidents were bound to happen because of unanticipated technical problems and errors in judgment by managers and operators of the system. Moreover, the interdependence of units, ranging from single component to actual subsystems, would seriously exacerbate the problem. For example, an unanticipated component failure or an error in judgment in one of these complex technological systems such as a space shuttle craft or a nuclear power plant could produce a series of chain reactions that could destroy the entire system.[11] Indeed, Charles Perrow argues that nuclear power plants are characterized by tightly coupled and complex technology so that the potential for unexpected and serious accidents is extremely high.[12]

Human failure, too, could set off a chain of reactions with a similar result. Investigations of the accidents, however, revealed that both NASA and the NRC were informed of the leaking seal joint and the operator error early enough for the agencies to have responded appropriately, which suggests that neither of these accidents was necessarily unanticipated or inevitable.[13] As early as 1977, an engineer at NASA alerted his superiors to the weaknesses in the seal joint and predicted that leakage (of the solid rocket fuel gases) would result in "catastrophic failure," because the seal joint was labeled by the NASA organization as a "criticality 1" item. Information about certain errors by nuclear plant operators surfaced at the NRC two years before TMI. An "event" involving a small leak in the reactor core—quite similar to the accident at TMI—was reported to the agency several years before TMI. The operator turned off the emergency pumps before the leak was found and by chance caught the leak before any serious damage was done. Indeed, a report warning of such a scenario made its way through the plant licensing bureau at agency headquarters. Thus, it would seem that, although the information was readily available for officials to reduce the uncertainty, they failed to act. Apparently, they took unnecessary risks.

These decisionmakers were not hampered by what Herbert Simon describes as their "bounded rationality"—that is, their lack of knowledge about all possible options (and criteria for judging them).[14] Nor were they motivated by their own self-interest, for this alone would have made them avoid such excessive risk.[15] Indeed, officials at these agencies found themselves "naked" before the American public as all facets of their inner workings were exposed in the quest for answers. Agency bureaucrats squirmed under the spotlight of public scrutiny; their integrity and credibility were questioned and their prestige was badly damaged. Finally, as public support and trust faltered, the agencies were faced with costly reorganizations and the specter of potential cuts in their program authorization or their annual appropriations, or both. It defies logic that NASA shuttle managers and NRC regulators would not take extraordinary measures to avoid such organizational jeopardy.

The compelling question here is: Why did these organizations take the inordinate risk of ignoring the early warnings—*inordinate* inasmuch as it was clear beforehand that such accidents would be devastating? Popular opinion may hold that these accidents were the unsurprising by-products of incompetent, lazy, and venal bureaucrats, but the evidence suggests that such interpretations are simplistic.[16] On the contrary, studies demonstrate that the complex mixture of variables operating both within an agency and throughout its external environment shape bureaucratic processes and outcomes.[17] For example, professional norms, organizational structure, resources, rules, and procedures can all have an impact on bureaucratic decisionmaking, although some may clearly be more important than others. Moreover, external forces from the Congress, the White House, and organized interests may also influence agency behavior.

Similarly, it would seem that these two case studies are characterized by some form of organizational pathology in which the agencies' response, or lack of response, to the information on the safety problems was affected in some way by internal and external factors. This study will examine various organizational and environmental factors that may have led to this excessive risk taking by NASA and the NRC. At least three explanations merit exploration: One is that various organizational, structural, and procedural blockages prevented warnings from reaching key people; another is that the warnings reached the officials but were misunderstood; the third is that the warnings were received and understood but deliberately ignored because of external pressures. Each of these will be examined in turn.

Hypothesis One:
Communication Blockage

The first and most obvious explanation of agency failures to heed early warnings is that these warnings simply did not reach key people in these organizations; therefore, appropriate action was not taken. Within organizations as complex as NASA and the NRC, breakdowns are possible in the formal communication channels.[18] According to Anthony Downs, a formal communication network transmits messages that are "explicitly recognized as 'official' by the bureau."[19] More specifically, as Herbert Simon points out, formal channels of communication would first transmit information—in this case, safety information—to critical decisionmakers whose responsibility it was to convey the decision to other parts of the organization.[20] In these two particular cases, even the first stage of information transmission may never have occurred because organizational structures and procedures blocked or hampered the upward flow of information.

It could be, for example, that the information on the flawed seal joint and the operator error never reached the top-level decisionmakers because of the winnowing process that is inevitable in hierarchical organizations.[21] When information travels up, it is sifted at the various organizational levels. Although this filtering process enables the upper level executives to handle the vast amounts of information emanating from the lower levels, it is at a cost—the information is condensed and subjected to the varying biases and motivations of the officials transmitting the information to the next level.[22] As a result, there is the tendency for a top-level official to "receive reports that tell him primarily what his subordinates believe he wants to hear."[23]

In his work *Organizational Intelligence*, Harold Wilensky examined the various causes of intelligence failures within organizations. He noted that when the shape of the organizational hierarchy is tall and "narrows sharply at the top," it tends to produce frustrated middle managers who see little prospect for promotion and will only pass along information that furthers their careers.[24] In any case, whatever the motivations of the subordinates, the information of the flawed seal joint and the operator error may have been so thoroughly winnowed down that the officials at headquarters were not made fully aware of the seriousness of the problem. A classic example of such a situation seems to have occurred on the eve of the Challenger launch, when the middle managers at the Marshall Space Flight Center declined to inform senior management of the Morton

Thiokol engineers' concerns about launching the Challenger in freezing temperatures.[25]

The organizational hierarchy can also distort or block information from reaching the top level when administrators sometimes reject as impertinent either counsel or demands by subordinates.[26] Such a situation can occur even when the subordinate is a staff officer with far more expertise than his superior.[27]

It is also possible that officials overlooked important clues to the safety problems that caused these accidents because of an absence of appropriate monitoring procedures. In the case of the NRC, so-called event reports on plant problems were submitted to various agency officials. The review of these problems was highly fragmented, however, and there was no coordinating procedure that highlighted serious deficiencies in plant operations.[28] As a result, reports about crucially important safety problems, such as those that caused the accident at TMI, may have been lost in bureaucratic paper shuffling, thereby failing to reach the attention of senior management. In the case of NASA, existing procedures for requesting budget expenditures to solve safety problems did not routinely pass through the offices of key agency officials. Consequently, the head of the entire shuttle program at the Johnson Space Center was totally unaware that there were problems in the booster joints and that funds were being expended to fix them.[29]

The lack of easy exchange of intelligence and information at the upper levels could also have been a result of the decentralized structure of these agencies. Both the NRC and NASA top management are in Washington, D.C., while their numerous field offices or space and research centers are located throughout the country.[30] The physical distance between the various units and subunits of the organization may create an isolation that encourages an unwillingness to pass along information. The Marshall Space Flight Center, in particular, was apparently well known for considering itself independent of headquarters, and its relatively remote geographical location in northern Alabama may have reinforced this outlook.[31]

At the NRC, this attitude may have been compounded in 1979 by the fact that even its headquarters was scattered around Washington, D.C., and the metropolitan area in at least eight separate organizational units. Furthermore, the extraordinary specialization of the various organizational subunits may have exacerbated whatever problems resulted from geographic dispersal and administrative decentralization. It may have produced a dysfunctional rivalry that impeded cooperation and prevented the sharing of important information about safety issues with the upper management levels. Indeed, Wilensky points out that, "as a source of information blockage and distortion, specialization may be more powerful than hierarchy."[32] He goes on to say that specialization in the armed forces and industry "encourages rivalry and restriction of information. Each service, each division, indeed every sub-unit, becomes a guardian of its own mission, standards, and skills; lines of organization become lines of loyalty and secrecy."[33]

Apparently, the failure of the American military to heed the early warnings of the Japanese invasion of Pearl Harbor in 1941 resulted from a combination of hierarchical distortions and interservice rivalries.[34] The signals of the pending attack on Pearl Harbor in 1941 lay scattered at a number of rival agencies; communication lines linked them, but essential messages never even flowed across the lines, much less to the top.

This may be especially true of NASA because the rivalries among the Kennedy, Johnson, and Marshall space centers have been well known within the agency from the earliest days of manned space flight. According to some observers, by the time of the Challenger accident, "the burgeoning rivalry between NASA's space centers [had] grown to overwhelm the larger mission of the agency."[35] Thus, Marshall may have withheld crucial information on the flawed joint from the upper levels of the shuttle organization at Johnson and headquarters because it would have appeared that "Marshall was not doing its job."[36] Indeed, as one Johnson official told an agency observer: "Everything coming out of that center had to have 'performance' writ large all over it."[37]

Communication problems may have been further exacerbated by the inherent difficulty each agency faced in maintaining coordination and communication with the private sector. The NRC monitors and regulates a huge nuclear power industry composed of numerous power companies, power plants, and private vendors. The important point for this study is whether there were adequate communication channels for any possible early warnings from the industry to penetrate the NRC organization.

Similarly, NASA maintains relationships with innumerable contractors and subcontractors that produce specific products or services for the agency. In this particular case study, the contractor that made the SRB was Morton Thiokol, and the question here is whether any problems associated with the SRB seal joint were conveyed properly by Morton Thiokol to the Marshall management. Therefore, communications failure is a plausible explanation for the disasters.

Hypothesis Two:
Misperception of the Received Communications

Had the communications advanced as they should have, however, it is possible that they would not have been properly understood. The early warnings may have reached the senior officials of both these organizations, but action might not have been forthcoming because they did not accurately perceive the safety problems for what they were. In other words, they misperceived the risks associated with the flawed seal joint and the operator error. As Herbert Simon has said: "Communication must make its impact upon the recipient. The communication has not really been 'communicated' when it reaches the desk of the recipient, but only when it reaches his mind. There is a potential gap 'twixt cup and lip."[38]

Thus, the NASA and NRC officials could have misperceived the risks by underestimating the dangers associated with the flawed seal joint and the operator error. Underestimating the risk could be explained by the theory of cognitive dissonance developed by Leon Festinger.[39] It states that individuals strive to achieve a consonance or consistency among their related cognitions (opinions, knowledge, or beliefs and so forth). They experience serious discomfort when two related cognitions are inconsistent or dissonant with each other.[40] When this happens, the individual will strive to "reduce the dissonance and achieve consonance."[41]

Festinger argues that the dissonance can be reduced first of all by recognizing reality and conforming to the information. So, for example, a cigarette smoker who is fully aware that smoking is harmful to her health may reduce the dissonance by changing her actions and not smoking.[42] Sometimes, people resist changing in this way either because it involves pain or loss, or because the present form of behavior may be "otherwise satisfying," or because making the change may be impossible.[43] Indeed, some individuals do not adapt to the reality but actually deny it through other forms of dissonance reduction. For example, a person could add new cognitive elements that support her case—that is, the smoker makes a point of finding out that the risk from smoking is far less than the risk from driving a car.[44] In addition, the smoker could resort to decreasing or downplaying one of the two related elements—smoking and its harmful health effect. So, for example, rather than give up smoking, the smoker will downplay the information on the cigarette packet that warns about the harmful health effects of the habit.[45]

Most important, in these efforts to reduce the dissonance the individual could very well seek the support within his or her environment—whether this be a small group or a large organization. If someone in the group disagrees with the person with the dissonant cognitions, he could be rejected or even derogated.[46] He may not even have to do much of this, however, if he is in a situation "where many people who associate with him all suffer from the identical dissonance."[47] Presumably, they all share with the individual the same belief or opinion that is threatened by the new information.[48] Indeed, Festinger elaborates as follows:

> Groups and organizations sometimes commit themselves to a certain course of action. At the time the action is taken, of course, most of the persons in the group or organization undoubtedly have cognitions which are mainly consonant with the action. Future developments, occurring either independently or as a consequence of the action, may then produce new cognitions which are dissonant with the knowledge that the action was taken and that it continues.[49]

A little later, Festinger comments upon the resistance of such a group to the reality of the facts, even "in the face of continual definite evidence to the contrary. Such instances may range all the way from rather inconsequential occurrences of short duration to phenomena which may almost be termed mass delusions."[50] Festinger's extension of his dissonance theory to the group or organizational setting has been supported by other scholars examining group decisionmaking.[51]

Thus, it could be that, because these officials at NASA and the NRC believed in the capabilities of the technology that they were managing and regulating, they experienced a dissonance from the new evidence that contradicted their initial perception. As a result, they were reducing the dissonance by downgrading the early warnings on the flawed seal joint and the operator error. They also may have reduced the dissonance by seeking new information that supported their original perception. In this way, the shuttle managers and the NRC regulators may have engaged in excessive risk-taking.[52] Especially in the case of NASA, the officials were drawn together in relatively small groups in the preflight briefings. The ensuing discussions for support on the flawed seal joint could very well have taken place among a group of managers strongly inclined to reduce the dissonance they were experiencing. Or, perhaps the group was so cohesive that it needed very little persuasion to agree with the dissonant reduction mechanisms of downgrading the joint and seek new evidence to support their initial expectations of the joint. Although it would be impossible to observe the actual group interaction about the seal joint, there are records that could indicate their reaction to the early warnings. Thus, if the records showed that the shuttle managers and the NRC regulators were downplaying the early warnings or seeking new information to support their original opinion that flying the shuttle was an acceptable risk, or both, then one could infer some kind of organizational or group dissonance. Thus, the NASA and NRC officials could have experienced a "gap 'twixt cup and lip" as they rationalized the bad news and sought new evidence to reinforce their position. In this way, they converted a high danger into an acceptable risk.

A misperception of communication could also mean that agency leaders may not even have recognized the risk associated with the operator error that was called to their attention. The professional antennae of these officials simply may not have been attuned to construe the information before them in this way. Such behavior could be explained by the presence of a dominant profession at the agency whose values and training may have predisposed the agency officials to view their central task in a biased manner. For example, at the Federal Trade Commission, the economists and lawyers approached the problem of attacking unfair trade practices in very different ways. Their criteria for case selection was strongly influenced by a professional bias that interpreted the data very differently.[53] The lawyers would choose cases that were likely to give them trial experience and that were easy to prosecute. The economists, however, would base their case selection criteria on economic theory. The question for them was not whether the case adhered to legal precedent, but whether it made sense in terms of microeconomic principles.[54] Similarly, the engineers at the NRC may have shaped a regulatory philosophy that viewed plant safety solely in terms of stringent design and engineering criteria while ignoring the importance of human factors. Consequently, when they received the early warnings of potential operator error, the critical safety information may not have registered in their minds.

Hypothesis Three:
External Pressures Overrode Warnings

Regardless of whether communications reached, and were understood by, agency officials, external forces—the White House, Congress, organized interests, and the media—may have induced NASA and the NRC to disregard the recognized risks.[55] Organizations do not operate in a vacuum, and public organizations are especially vulnerable to severe constraints because their very survival relies upon the political support from some, if not all, of these forces in their external environment. As a result, it is quite conceivable that forces in these agencies' external environment may have significantly affected these organizational failures.

For example, in the case of organized interests, it could be that certain forces pushed them toward a greater attention to safety matters (most conspicuously in the case of the NRC, with the Clamshell Alliance, Public Citizen, and other antinuclear citizens' groups). Moreover, especially in the case of NASA, it could also be that an agency lacked an organized interest in its external environment that represented interests whose top priority was to promote caution in the implementation of the agencies' program. Thus, other forces, arguably more powerful, worked in the opposite direction, diminishing the priority of such concerns.[56] Conceivably, therefore, the thrust from the NRC's and NASA's external environment was toward promotion—that is, production oriented—and output was valued far above any other consideration, including safety.

In addition, legislators may have been insufficiently vigorous and penetrating in their oversight of these agencies, which resulted in a failure to challenge either the nuclear regulators' neglect of operator procedures or the shuttle managers' sanguine assurances of flight safety. Moreover, continued belt tightening by a fiscally conservative Congress may have caused the NRC regulators and NASA managers to cut corners in various ways so that the regulatory focus virtually ignored the role of the human factors in plant operations while the shuttle hardware was merely good enough instead of optimal.[57] At NASA, this "satisficing" behavior may have been encouraged by the shortage of funds resulting from the shuttle program's gross mismanagement, which was a problem that also remained unchecked by congressional overseers.[58] How these pressures affected different parts of the organization, as well as their professionals—managers and engineers—is also worthy of study.

The media also may have unwittingly contributed to a diminished regard for safety concerns at the agencies. Possibly, tough investigative reporting by the media could have brought these safety problems into the public spotlight and perhaps averted these accidents. Media reports about safety concerns at the NRC were primarily a result of the agitation from antinuclear groups. At the local level, especially, the media received criticism for "flaccid" coverage of the TMI plant.[59] Conversely, NASA, long the darling of the media (especially of television), which lavished attention on the agency's programs, was under constant pressure to "perform."[60] In the immediate case at hand, repeated postponements of the

Challenger launch, combined with a succession of "put-downs" from the media, might only have added further pressure on program officials to drop their guard and get the shuttle launched.[61]

Other possible sources of pressure to discount concerns for safety include the private sector. With the NRC, this would include public utilities and vendor organizations such as reactor suppliers and architectural engineers. The long-standing closeness of nuclear energy regulators to the industry they are charged with regulating may have produced an organizational predisposition to meet the needs of the industry rather than to pursue the agency's own primary mission of securing safety.[62] In the case of NASA, one would examine agency relations with its payload customers and the White House. Most important, the agency's close associations with its contractor for the SRB, Morton Thiokol, may have meant that faulty monitoring of contracts produced shoddy workmanship and profligate waste that ultimately compromised safety standards.[63] Moreover, NASA's power to award, withhold, and cancel contracts may have made companies such as Thiokol less forthright in the difficult launch conditions of the shuttle Challenger.[64]

The Objective of This Book: Evaluating the Hypotheses

The evidence that follows explores the three explanations for these organizational failures to heed the early warnings of disaster—namely, that critical decisionmakers may not have received the warnings, or that they simply blocked the warnings from their minds, or that they were pressured into ignoring the warnings. These explanations, especially the last two, are not mutually exclusive. Conceivably, a combination of external forces and perceptual problems that blocked out the warnings could explain the TMI and Challenger disasters. The main goal of this study is to appraise the presumed causal factors.

I will also briefly describe and assess what these organizational crises meant to each agency. The obvious question here, of course, concerns the effect upon each agency when its operations and management were publicly challenged and scrutinized. Were internal procedures and organizational arrangements substantially altered? Was there a discernible change in these organizations' attentiveness toward safety concerns? What changes occurred in each agency's relations with Congress, with the White House, with the private sector, and with the media? The answers to these questions have important implications. First, they may mean that safety is strongly emphasized only after a disaster occurs—although the potential for disaster is clearly evident. Second, they may raise a more fundamental question of whether or not organizations like NASA and the NRC can prevent such accidents from reoccurring.

Whatever the solutions may be to this last question, they will have great relevance for other complex organizations that find themselves suddenly confronted with a crisis or an actual catastrophe because early warnings about safety problems were ignored over the years. If we conclude that there are no long-term remedies for minimizing or eliminating these kinds of organizational failures, then we are confronted with a broader question of whether the American public would be willing to accept such risks in exchange for the benefits of these technologies. During the process of reflecting on such questions, these two case studies may effectively illuminate our current understanding of risk taking by large-scale, complex, technological organizations.

My approach to this study has been that of a political scientist, rather than that of an investigative reporter, an economist, or a management analyst. The method of inquiry was eclectic; it involved many of the standard research techniques of a political scientist engaging in institutional analysis. It included reading histories and the pertinent secondary literature, scrutinizing statutes and administrative structures, examining agency testimony and internal memoranda, and perusing congressional committee hearings and reports. In the process of gathering evaluations and criticisms of organizational performance, I conducted eighty-seven personal interviews with individuals inside the NRC and NASA and on these agencies' oversight committees on Capitol Hill, others in the Executive Office of the President, and others with attentive organized interests. These interviews provided important background information that verified and, in some cases, complemented the findings in the primary and secondary literature. The interviewees wished to remain anonymous because of the public nature of this research.

The chapters that follow explore the major concerns outlined in this introduction. The case studies are dealt with separately. The findings and the implications of these case studies are assessed in the concluding chapter.

Notes

1. "Shuttle Destroyed, Killing Crew; Manned Space Flights Halted," *Aviation Week & Space Technology*, Feb. 3, 1986, pp. 18–19, 21. See also, William P. Rogers, *Report of the Presidential Commission on the Space Shuttle Challenger*, 5 vols. (Washington: GPO, 1986), 1:19–21. Two journalistic accounts of the accident and its political

causes are given by Joseph J. Trento, *Prescription for Disaster* (New York: Crown Publishers Inc., 1987); Malcolm McConnell, *Challenger, A Major Malfunction* (New York: Doubleday & Co., Inc., 1987).

2. See Cora Bagley Marrett, "The President's Commission; Its Analysis of the Human Equation"; Malcolm J. Brooks, "Human Factors in Design and Operation of Reactor Safety Systems"; and Charles Perrow, "The President's Commission and the Normal Accident," in *Accident at Three Mile Island; The Human Dimension*, ed. David L. Sills, C. P. Wolf, and Vivian B. Shelanski (Boulder, Colo.: Westview Press, Inc., 1982).

3. Descriptions of the sequence of events that comprised the accident are numerous. For example, John G. Kemeny, *Report of the President's Commission on the Accident at Three Mile Island: The Need for Change: The Legacy of TMI* (Washington: GPO, 1979), pp. 101–169; and Charles Perrow, *Normal Accidents: Living with High Risk Technologies* (New York: Basic Books Inc., 1984). For a journalistic account of the accident, see Mark Stephens, *Three Mile Island* (New York: Random House, 1980). A comprehensive listing of the literature dealing with the accident sequence and various other facets of the accident, such as its health effects, the impact on the nuclear power industry, and so forth, are contained in the work by M. Sandra Wood and Suzanne M. Shultz, *Three Mile Island* (New York: Greenwood Press, 1988).

4. Kemeny, *Report of the President's Commission on the Accident at Three Mile Island*, pp. 12–13.

5. Robert Leppzer, *Voices from Three Mile Island: The People Speak Out* (Trumansburg, N.Y.: The Crossing Press, 1980).

6. Ibid., pp. 23–50.

7. Daniel F. Ford and Steven J. Nadis, *Nuclear Power: The Aftermath of Three Mile Island* (Union of Concerned Scientists, Cambridge, Mass.: March 1980); Lee Stephenson and George R. Zachar, eds., *Accidents Will Happen: The Case against Nuclear Power* (Perennial Library, Harper & Row, 1979).

8. Baruch Fischhoff, Sarah Lichtenstein, and Paul Slovic, "Psychological Aspects of Risk Perception," in *Accident at Three Mile Island*, p. 12.

9. Ibid., pp. 1–93.

10. Robert Cameron Mitchell, "Public Response to a Failure in Technology," in *Accident at Three Mile Island*, pp. 30–35.

11. For a discussion of the notion of complexity see Herbert A. Simon, "The Architecture of Complexity," *General Systems Yearbook*, vol. 10 (1965), pp. 63–76; for a discussion of complexity (and its distinctive feature, interdependence) in social organizations, see Todd R. La Porte, "Complexity: Explication of a Concept," in *Organized Social Complexity*, ed. Todd R. La Porte (Princeton University Press, 1975), pp. 3–39.

12. Charles Perrow, *Complex Organizations: A Critical Essay,* 3d ed., New York: Random House, 1986), pp. 146–148; Perrow, *Normal Accidents,* pp. 15–61.

13. *Staff Report to the President's Commission on the Accident at Three Mile Island: The Nuclear Regulatory Commission* (Washington: GPO, 1979); U.S. Nuclear Regulatory Commission Special Inquiry Group, *Three Mile Island, A Report to the Commissioners and the Public* (Washington: GPO, 1980), vol. 2, p. 1; also, for a more journalistic account of the early warnings, see Mike Gray and Ira Rosen, *The Warning: Accident at Three Mile Island* (New York: W.W. Norton & Company, 1982).

14. Herbert A. Simon, *Administrative Behavior: A Study of Decision-Making Processes in Administrative Organizations,* 3d ed. (New York: Free Press, 1976), p. 154.

15. Here, I am alluding to the public-choice theory of decisionmaking. See, for example, Anthony Downs, *An Economic Theory of Democracy* (New York: Harper & Brothers, 1957); William A. Niskanen, Jr., *Bureaucracy and Representative Government* (Chicago: Aldine Press, 1971).

16. See Paul A. Volcker, chairman, *Leadership for America: Rebuilding the Public Service, Task Force Reports to the National Commission on the Public Service* (Washington: GPO, 1989), pp. 10–18.

17. For example, see James Q. Wilson, *Bureaucracy, What Government Agencies Do and Why They Do It* (New York: Basic Books, 1991); Herbert Kaufman, *The Administrative Behavior of Bureau Chiefs* (Washington, D.C.: The Brookings Institution, 1981), *The Forest Ranger: A Study in Administrative Behavior* (Washington, D.C.: Resources for the Future, 1967); John T. Tierney, *The U.S. Postal Service* (Dover, Mass.: Auburn House, 1988); Robert Katzmann, *Regulatory Bureaucracy* (Cambridge: MIT Press, 1980); Graham T. Allison, *Essence of Decision* (Glenview, Ill.: Scott, Foresman and Co., 1971).

18. There exist informal communication channels in most organizations, but this research focuses on the formal channels because the evidence that shows how the early warnings are communicated is more readily available and also, as Anthony Downs points out, "Formal messages make certain actions, decisions, or policies 'legal' within the framework of the bureau's power." See Anthony Downs, *Inside Bureaucracy* (Boston: Scott, Foresman and Co., 1967), p. 113.

19. Ibid.

20. Simon, *Administrative Behavior,* p. 154; also Herbert A. Simon, Donald W. Smithburg, and Victor Thompson, *Public Administration* (New York: Alfred A. Knopf, 1950), pp. 221–222.

21. Downs, *Inside Bureaucracy,* pp. 116–118.

22. There are various strategies that top level executives use to counter this tendency toward distortion. See Downs, *Inside Bureaucracy,* pp. 118–131. See also, Harold Wilensky, *Organizational Intelligence: Knowledge and Politics in Government and Industry* (New York: Basic Books, 1967), pp. 46–48.

23. Downs, *Inside Bureaucracy*, p. 118. For other sources that document this point, see Herbert Kaufman, *Administrative Feedback* (Washington, D.C.: The Brookings Institution, 1973), pp. 11–15; Herbert Kaufman, *The Forest Ranger: A Study in Administrative Behavior*, p. 69; Gordon Tullock, *The Politics of Bureaucracy* (Washington, D.C.: Public Affairs Press, 1965), pp. 137–141.

24. Wilensky, *Organizational Intelligence*, p. 45.

25. *Rogers Commission Report*, 1:85–111; Charles Peters, "From Ougadougou to Cape Canaveral: Why the Bad News Doesn't Travel Up," *Washington Monthly* (April 1986), pp. 27–31; "Top Aides at NASA Were Not Advised of Shuttle Clues," *The New York Times*, February 24, 1986, pp. A1, B6.

26. Ibid; Wilensky, *Organizational Intelligence*, p. 44; Peter M. Blau and W. Richard Scott, *Formal Organizations: A Comparative Approach* (San Francisco: Chandler Publishing Company, 1962), pp. 121–139.

27. Ibid., p. 123; Wilensky, *Organizational Intelligence*, p. 44.

28. Daniel Ford, "Three Mile Island: The Paper Trail," *New Yorker* (April 13, 1981), pp. 51–52.

29. *Roger's Commission Report*, 1:152–161.

30. Herbert Kaufman writes of the Forest Service in *The Forest Ranger*, p. 71, that despite "modern techniques of communication and transportation (that have shrunk) geographical distances," the "spatial distance" between headquarters and the field offices "reduces the frequency and length of contacts."

31. "Letter from the Space Center," *New Yorker* (November 10, 1986), p. 98.

32. Wilensky, *Organizational Intelligence*, p. 48.

33. Ibid.

34. Ibid.

35. "NASA Takes Hits from Scientists, Rogers Commission," *Christian Science Monitor*, June 4, 1986, pp. 1, 40.

36. Henry S. F. Cooper, "Letter from the Space Center," *New Yorker* (November 10, 1986), p. 98.

37. Ibid.

38. Simon, *Administrative Behavior*, p. 222.

39. Leon Festinger, *A Theory of Cognitive Dissonance*, 4th ed. (Stanford, Calif.: Stanford University Press, 1968).

40. Ibid., p. 9.

41. Ibid., p. 3. Moreover, if these elements are extremely important to them, the magnitude of the dissonance will be that much greater. Thus, the strength of the pressure to reduce the dissonance will be dependent upon the magnitude of the dissonance. See page 18.

42. Ibid., p. 6.

43. Ibid., p. 25.

44. They would also avoid new information that increases the dissonance. Ibid., pp. 21–22.

45. Festinger gives another example of the person who must choose between a concert and a dinner at a friend's. See pages 44–45.

46. Ibid., p. 182.

47. Ibid., p. 265.

48. Ibid., p. 194.

49. Ibid., pp. 194–195.

50. Ibid., p. 198.

51. Irving Janis, *Groupthink,* 2d ed. (New York: Houghton Mifflin Co., 1982). In Irving Janis' study of decisionmaking by various small policymaking groups in the White House, excessive risk taking is one of several symptoms of the groupthink behavior. See also, Mark E. Byrnes, "The Challenger Disaster: A Political Science Analysis," *Mid-American Journal of Politics,* Fall 1989, pp. 50–76. This author focuses on the actual eve of the Challenger launch, and his groupthink application is uneven, as the author admits, because of insufficient evidence (pp. 62–63). He concludes that it is Graham T. Allison's organizational process model that seems to be "the single most convincing theory" explaining the decision to launch (p. 61).

52. See Alexander L. George, *Presidential Decisionmaking in Foreign Policy: The Effective Use of Information and Advice* (Boulder, Colo.: Westview Press, 1980), who states that the diffusion of responsibility associated with group decisionmaking could also be an explanation for excessive risk taking. Yet, at the same time, he mentions that the evidence indicating that groups engage in greater risk-taking than the individual is inconclusive. A further study indicates that when such decisions are the result "of group interaction and achievement of consensus," there is more willingness to make more risky decisions than those made without such group interaction. See Michael A. Wallach, Nathan Kogan, and Daryl J. Bem, "Group Influence on Individual Risk Taking," in *Some Theories of Organization,* revised edition, ed. Albert H. Rubinstein and Chadwick J. Haberstroh (Homewood, Ill.: The Dorsey Press, 1966), p. 650.

53. See chapters 4 and 5, Katzmann, *Regulatory Bureaucracy.*

54. Ibid., p. 41.

55. There is an abundance of literature that discusses the impact of forces in the environment on organizational outcomes: J.D. Thompson, *Organizations in Action* (New York: McGraw-Hill, 1967); Jeffrey Pfeffer and Gerald R. Salancik, *The External Control of Organizations* (New York: Harper & Row, 1978); Philip Selznick, *TVA and the Grass Roots: A Study in the Sociology of Formal Organization* (Berkeley, Calif.: University of California Press, 1949); Donald P. Warwick, *A Theory of Public Bureaucracy: Politics, Personality, and Organization in the State Department* (Cambridge, Mass.: Harvard University Press, 1975); Wilson, *Bureaucracy.*

56. Richard M. Cyert and James G. March, *A Behavioral Theory of the Firm* (Englewood Cliffs, N.J.: Prentice-Hall, Inc., 1963), p. 35.

57. "Senator Says NASA Cut 70% of Staff Checking Quality: 15 Years of Reductions," *New York Times,* May 8, 1986, pp. 1, 7, B25; Simon, *Administrative Behaviour,* p. xxvii–xxix; James G. March and Herbert A. Simon, *Organizations* (New York: John Wiley and Sons Inc., 1978), p. 143.

58. "NASA Wasted Billions, Federal Audits Disclose," *New York Times,* April 23, 1986, pp. Al, A12.

59. Sharon M. Friedman, "Blueprint for Breakdown; Three Mile Island and the Media before the Accident," in *Journal of Communication,* vol. 31 (Spring 1981) pp.116–128.

60. "Maybe the Media Did Push NASA to Launch Challenger," *The Washington Post National Weekly Edition,* April 14, 1986, pp. 19–21.

61. Ibid.

62. Daniel Ford, *Cult of the Atom* (New York: Simon and Schuster, 1982), pp. 181–191.

63. "NASA Wasted Billions, Federal Audits Disclose," pp. Al, A12.

64. "GAO Investigates NASA Bias toward Morton Thiokol," *Aviation Week and Space Technology,* vol. 124 (June 2, 1986), p. 27.

CASE 1

The National Aeronautics and Space Administration

2

The Challenger Accident
and the Early Warnings

Let us begin with the NASA organization and explore the first possibility that the top-level officials were unaware of the safety problems that caused the Challenger accident. This chapter first describes the Challenger accident and indicates the pivotal role of the flawed seal joint in causing this disaster. Second, and most important, it demonstrates very clearly that early warnings of the flawed joint reached senior officials in the shuttle organization at NASA. There were instances where detailed information on the flawed seal joint did not reach the upper levels of the shuttle organization. By the summer of 1985, however, the dangers of flying the shuttle with a flawed seal joint were widely known within the organization and brought to the attention of senior officials. Let us first elaborate on the safety problem that caused the Challenger accident and about which NASA was forewarned.

The Challenger Accident

The Challenger accident began seconds after liftoff. A leak of combustion gas from the aft joint of the Solid Rocket Booster (SRB) appeared in the form of multiple puffs of smoke.[1] The escaping gases created a ring of flame around the joint seal, and the right SRB broke away from the vehicle, which ruptured the external fuel tank. Massive, "almost explosive" burning ensued, and the Space Shuttle Challenger, Mission 51–L, broke into several large segments and plummeted into the ocean.[2]

As Figure 2–1 shows, the circular joint design (in which the steel casing segments of the SRB are attached together by a tang and clevis joint, bands and 117 pins) is sealed by a process known as "pressure actuation"

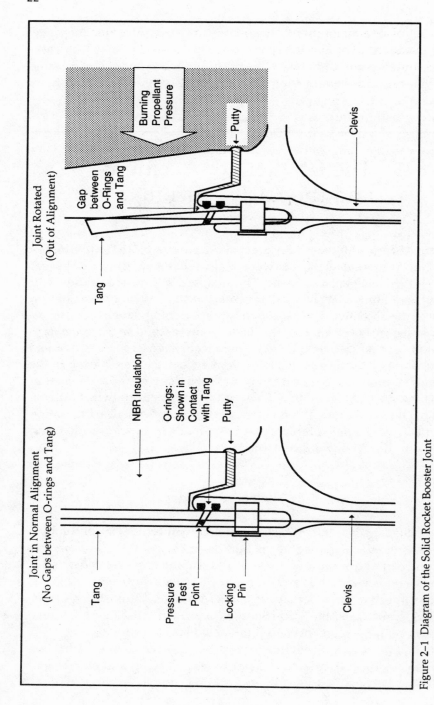

Figure 2–1 Diagram of the Solid Rocket Booster Joint

Source: U. S. Congress, House Committee on Science and Technology: *Investigation of the Challenger Accident*, H. Report 1016, 99th Cong., 2nd Sess., 1986, pp. 48–49.

that takes place after ignition.[3] The combustion gases force zinc chromate putty inside the joint into the space between the steel casing segments. This compresses the air between the putty and the primary seal causing the primary seal to expand, thereby sealing the gap between the tang and clevis.[4] If the first O-ring fails to seal, the second O-ring is designed as a backup to halt the flow of escaping gases. With the Challenger, both O-rings failed to seal the joint, which allowed the gases to escape through the gap between the tang and clevis and burned the rubber O-rings in the process.

The Early Warnings Alert NASA

Early warnings alerted the shuttle managers to a leaking seal joint in the SRB. The warnings revealed that the two O-rings sealing the joint were seriously hampered by the movement of the joint, by cold temperatures, and by erosion from escaping gases in the SRB. Let us elaborate briefly on the communication flows that conveyed the safety information on these problems with the seal joint to the top level of the shuttle organization. (A more complete description of the shuttle organization within NASA, as well as of the communication channels, is found in the Appendix.)

The NASA organization had well-defined channels for communicating early warnings. Figure 2–2 depicts the NASA organizational chart at the time of the Challenger disaster in January 1986. More important, Figure 2–3 indicates the four-level shuttle organization that was located within the Office of Space Flight at headquarters in Washington, D.C., and within its three space flight centers—Lyndon B. Johnson at Houston, Texas; John F. Kennedy at Cape Canaveral, Florida; and George C. Marshall at Huntsville, Alabama. Level 1 was at headquarters—the Office of the Associate Administrator of Space Flight—while Level 2 was at Johnson. Level 3 was also at Johnson as well as at Marshall and Kennedy. Finally, Level 4 consisted of all the contractors doing work on the shuttle. Levels 3 and 4 were responsible for the core elements of the shuttle while Levels 1 and 2 were strictly managerial and administrative.

The major formal communication channel of the shuttle organization was the Flight Readiness Review (FRR) process through which the shuttle managers, from each one of these levels, were briefed on the status of the upcoming shuttle mission. This process worked upward from the bottom—each lower level briefed the next level on the flight readiness of its particular program responsibility. Thus, by the time the mission team management

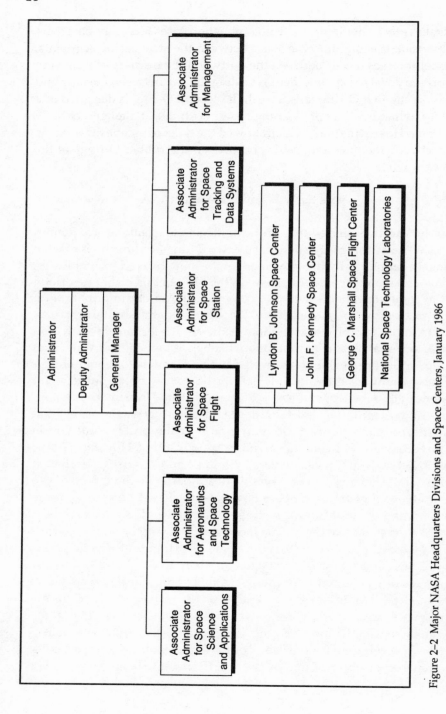

Figure 2–2 Major NASA Headquarters Divisions and Space Centers, January 1986

Source: William P. Rogers, *Report of the Presidential Commission on the Space Shuttle Challenger Accident*, 5 vols. (Washington, D.C.: GPO, 1986), 1:226.

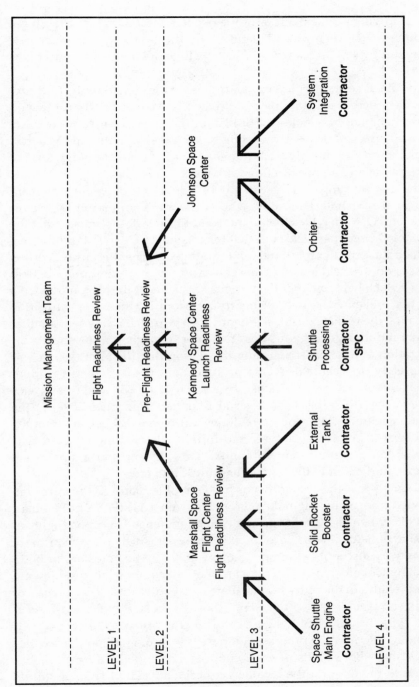

Figure 2–3 Flight Readiness Reviews in Shuttle Program Management Structure, January 1986
Source: *Report of the Presidential Commission on the Space Shuttle Challenger Accident*, 1:83.

was preparing for the final countdown, every facet of the shuttle's flight readiness had been reviewed. Figure 2–4 indicates the systematic review of the shuttle's flight readiness, which includes all hardware items of the shuttle.

The major source of the early warnings was from within the FRR process. They were first communicated to Level 3 at Marshall by the contractor, Morton Thiokol, who made the SRB. They then traveled upward to Level 1 at headquarters. The early warnings also traveled within the Marshall organization and directly from Marshall to headquarters, in the form of memoranda and ad hoc briefings at Level 1.

The first warning came as early as 1977 from one of NASA's own engineers at Marshall, Leon Ray, who wrote a memorandum telling his boss, John Q. Miller, the chief of the Solid Rocket Motor branch, that the primary O-ring might leak and that the secondary O-ring might not seal at all because of joint rotation.[5] Joint rotation occurred because of certain stresses on the field joints during the early stages of ignition. The field joints, which held together the various segments of the SRB, moved in a way that prevented the two O-rings from performing their proper function of sealing the rocket booster segments. Two years later, Ray sent another memorandum signed by his boss to senior managers in the shuttle organization at Marshall reiterating the reason that the joint design was completely unacceptable.[6] This problem was made known to upper management, at the very latest, by March 17, 1983, when Lawrence Mulloy, the SRB project manager at Marshall, informed Level 1 (the associate administrator for space flight) during an FRR briefing that the joint was officially no longer redundant (the secondary seal was unreliable because of joint rotation).[7] This "meant that a single seal failure could result in the loss of the shuttle and crew."[8]

Alarms about the second major problem of the joint, O-ring erosion, sounded from actual flight data. From November 11, 1981, until January 28, 1986, when the Challenger launched, evidence from postflight inspection of field and nozzle joints showed conclusively that the primary O-ring was susceptible to impingement or "blow-by" erosion, or both. Impingement erosion occurs when a jet of hot combustion gas, blowing through holes in the putty that insulates the joint, "strikes the surface of the ring and removes a portion of it."[9] Blow-by erosion, which surfaced in April 1984, occurs when hot gases blow by the primary O-ring before it seals, eroding it in the process and, possibly, impinging on the secondary O-ring.[10] Both kinds of erosion appeared on a significant number of shuttle flights until the Challenger accident.[11] The Marshall shuttle

Level	Date	Reviewing Office	Scope of Review
4	12/11/85	Thiokol Wasatch	Conducted by Thiokol Solid Rocket Motor Program managers in preparation for presentation to Marshall Space Flight Center (MSFC)
3	12/17/85	SRM Office	Conducted by Larry Ware, Mgr., of Solid Rocket Motor Program Office, MSFC. Material presented by Thiokol personnel.
3	1/3/86	SRB Project Office	Conducted by Larry Mulloy, Mgr., of the Solid Rocket Booster Project Office. This is a combined briefing on the SRM and the elements making up the booster assembly when integrated make up the Shuttle Solid Rocket Boosters.
3	1/9/86	Shuttle Projects	Conducted by Stanley Reinartz, Mgr., Space Shuttle Projects Office, MSFC. This review discusses all elements of the Shuttle managed by Marshall.
3	1/13/86	Center Board	Conducted by Dr. William Lucas, MSFC Director. Final discussion of Marshall hardware in preparation for review by the Space Transportation System Program Manager.
2	1/14/86	STS Program	Conducted by Arnold Aldrich, Space Transportation System Program Manager. First review dealing with the flight vehicle and associated ground support in its entirety.
1	1/15/86	Space Flight	Conducted by Jesse Moore, Associate Administrator for Space Flight. Remaining items that impact launch are discussed and assigned for disposition. Certificate of Flight Readiness is signed.
1	1/25/86	L–1 Review	Meeting of the Mission Management Team to receive reports on action items remaining from the Flight Readiness Review. All Action items should be closed by this time.

Figure 2–4 Challenger Flight Readiness Reviews

Source: U.S. Congress, House Committee on Science and Technology, *Report of the Committee on Science and Technology: Investigation of the Challenger Accident*, H. Report 1016, 99th Cong., 2nd Sess., 1986, p. 46.

managers were fully briefed by Thiokol specialists on the erosion before every upcoming shuttle flight in the FRR briefings.[12]

Furthermore, the upper-level shuttle managers also knew that there was a serious problem of joint rotation and O-ring erosion. They were briefed in detail at least twice during the FRR process in 1984.[13] In addition, during mid-July 1985, five months before the Challenger tragedy, Level 1 was given a detailed update on the sealing difficulties of the joint by Irving Davids from the Office of Space Flight at headquarters.[14] He, along with Roger D. Hamby, visited Marshall to discuss the O-ring erosion. Irving Davids then sent a memorandum (dated July 17, 1985) to Jesse Moore, the associate administrator for space flight.[15] Davids reviewed the history of the O-ring erosion on the nozzle and field joints, also noting that, if the primary O-ring is eroded and cannot seal, the secondary O-ring is not a reliable backup because of the joint rotation. He also pointed out that there had been twelve occurrences of primary O-ring erosion.[16]

Shortly after the Davids Memo was sent to Jesse Moore, another Memo was written by Richard C. Cook to his immediate superior, Michael B. Mann, in the Office of Comptroller at NASA headquarters.[17] The Memo described the "charring of seals between SRB segments" and noted, "there is little question, however, that flight safety has been and is still being compromised by potential failure of the seals, and it is acknowledged that failure during launch would certainly be catastrophic."[18]

Mann sent this letter to the Office of Space Flight at headquarters and then discussed it further with the officials, who had already been discussing the O-ring erosion with Richard Cook before the Memo had even been written.[19] Cook was monitoring the seal joint problem because his job was to assess its budgetary impact if additional funding were necessary to fix it. Apparently, management was considering a "capture" feature, which would still retain the old joint design, yet "get redundancy back into that joint without having to throw away half a million dollar SRB segments."[20] He received his information from the monthly assessments of the seal joint from "across the street," which was the propulsion division in the Office of Space Flight. This monthly assessment was formed through reports from the propulsion division to the administrator and from actually attending monthly briefings at the Office of Space Flight where the status of the O-ring problem was discussed as part of "a list of budget threats that was printed each month."[21] Cook was especially aware of the concern at head office about the charring, the joint rotation, and the unreliability of the secondary O-ring as a redundant feature.[22] The fact that Cook's information sources on the serious problems with the seal joint were from the propulsion division in the Office of Space Flight at headquarters indicates that senior management officials were extremely concerned and continually working on the problem.

Later, at a headquarters briefing on August 19, 1985, Level 1 shuttle managers were given a systematic analysis of the joint problem. Six of the people present at this meeting were from the Office of Space Flight, including Mr. L. Michael Weeks (the deputy associate administrator, technical); Mr. David Winterhalter, director of the Shuttle Propulsion Division; Mr. Harry Quong, director of Quality Assurance and Reliability and Maintainability; and Mr. Paul Wetzel, chief of the SRB Program; Lawrence Mulloy and another colleague came from Marshall, and Thiokol had six people attending, including Allan J. McDonald.[23] Thiokol and Marshall experts on the joint identified "all prior instances of field joint, nozzle joint and igniter O-ring erosion."[24] Moreover, the problem of joint rotation was seen as a serious inhibitor of secondary O-ring sealing capacity. Apparently, the headquarters officials were informed that only in the first 170 milliseconds at the ignition phase of liftoff (before the onset of joint rotation) was there a high probability that secondary O-ring would seal.[25] Thus, the timing of the sealing process was crucial—if the primary O-ring failed, the secondary O-ring had to respond quickly to seal the joint within the first 170 milliseconds.

Thiokol and Marshall, however, were aware that cold temperatures lessened the resiliency or elasticity of the O-ring material, which slowed the sealing process. Thiokol briefed Marshall on this problem during a Level 3 FRR on February 8, 1985.[26] The shuttle managers at Marshall were also aware of the resiliency bench test results done by Thiokol engineers in June 1985, which reinforced this finding.[27] Level 1 officials were also informed of the resiliency problem at the headquarters briefing on August 19, 1985, which was mentioned earlier. At this meeting, Thiokol made it plain that maintaining a resilient O-ring was of "the highest concern" in achieving a rapid sealing process in the joint.[28] Yet, there appeared to be a difference of opinion over how well Thiokol imparted the connection between temperature and resiliency. Mr. Weeks correctly claimed that the bench-test data indicating "that resiliency is a function of temperature," were not included in the briefing documents.[29] Yet, Allan J. Mcdonald, who gave the Thiokol presentation, found it puzzling that the members at the meeting missed the connection between temperature and resiliency. In an exchange with General Kutyna, a member of the Presidential Commission on the Space Shuttle Challenger (Rogers Commission) this point is explored at some length:

KUTYNA: Secondly, there has been some question that people understood that there was a temperature problem. I remember your conclusion chart, your file chart, and the very first bullet of that chart had the word 'resiliency' in it. Do you feel when you talked about resiliency at that meeting people got the connection between resiliency and temperature, that resiliency was a function of temperature, or was that lost?

MCDONALD: It may have gotten lost because we hadn't run a very long range of temperatures when we got the data.

KUTYNA: So it is possible that people at headquarters from that briefing did not understand temperature was a concern?

MCDONALD: I guess it is possible they could have.

KUTYNA: Is it probable?

MCDONALD: I don't know if it is probable, because we put it as the first bullet of why we thought that was our highest concern, and if that hadn't happened, we wouldn't have had that concern.[30] [All quoted material appears verbatim].

Mr. David C. Acheson, a member of the Rogers Commission, also commented on the fact that if "resiliency" was presented at the briefing, then it must have been presented in the context of temperature. He states:

You have the presentation at headquarters in August of 1985 that made it plain that resiliency was an important factor in the function of the O-ring. If you accept that concept, it is very hard for me to see why a lot of difference in temperature wouldn't be understood to make substantial difference in the functioning of the O-ring…. You are dealing with an elastomeric material which, certainly, you don't have to be an engineer to know is affected by temperature.[31]

Indeed, it is difficult to imagine that resiliency was not discussed in the context of temperature variation, because we already know that Thiokol and Marshall had made the connection between resiliency and temperature. Roger Boisjoly, the Thiokol expert on the seal joint, who had made at least one of the charts that McDonald used in his presentation, had secondary sealing capability and temperature in mind when he constructed the chart.[32] He states in his testimony before the Rogers Commission that he made the chart to show that the secondary O-ring was effective only in the first 170 milliseconds after ignition, "and I felt very comfortable with the fact that, if we were in that position of a launch that was above SRM–15 STS (51–C) that we were okay for that region."[33]

Finally, on the eve of the Challenger launch, Marshall shuttle managers balked at the recommendation of Thiokol managers to delay the launch because of the freezing temperatures, which presented a unique circumstance in the flight experience of the shuttle. Roger Boisjoly spelled out the reasons for delaying the Challenger launch until the temperature warmed. As will be detailed later, Boisjoly reiterated his grave doubt about the sealing capability of the secondary O-ring once the first 170 milliseconds at ignition had passed. He then presented in great detail the serious effects of cold temperatures on the timing function of both seals.[34] He used charts, the first of which was the original one that was used at the headquarters briefing the previous August. Initially, the Thiokol managers followed the counsel of their own engineers, which was to delay the launch, but after the unreceptive responses from the Marshall managers, they overrode their own experts and reversed the company's initial recommendation.[35] The Marshall managers believed that there was no reason to inform their superiors of what had occurred—especially because the Thiokol concerns had been "resolved" and there would be no launch delay.[36]

In sum, the evidence indicates that a very healthy flow of information concerning the serious flaws of the seal joint design penetrated the NASA organization. It is clear that Thiokol officials worked closely with Marshall officials in exchanging information about the ongoing seal joint problem. It is also clear that the headquarters officials were fully informed about the seal erosion problems. That headquarters received information on the joint through the FRRs, the Davids Memo, and evidence from Richard Cook's Memo to his boss, Michael Mann, indicates that the problem with the seal joint was widely known in the Office of Space Flight. Finally, the August briefing at headquarters involved "top technical managers" who received a thorough presentation of the status of the seal joint. The Committee on Science and Technology of the House of Representatives (the US House Committee) investigating the Challenger accident concurred with the Rogers Commission that:

> The O-ring erosion history presented to Level I at NASA headquarters in August 1985 was sufficiently detailed to require corrective action prior to the next flight....

Despite the clarity of the Commission's conclusions, none of the participants at this meeting (all with technical backgrounds)—NASA or Thiokol—recommended that the Shuttle be grounded until the problem with the seals was solved.[37]

This is not to say, however, that the communication of these early warnings proceeded smoothly in all instances.

Level 3 Blocks Some Early Warnings

The eve of the Challenger launch could be construed to be an occasion when the Level 3 managers withheld from Level 1 and Level 2 the vital concerns of the Thiokol experts about launching in freezing temperatures. The Marshall managers challenged the initial recommendation of the Thiokol group of engineers and managers during the first teleconference. Later, after the Thiokol group had caucused, the managers resumed communication with Marshall and recommended that the launch proceed. Technically, therefore, there was no reason to contact Level 2 or Level 1 because there was no delay. Considering that the company had already recommended proceeding with the launch, even if Marshall had passed along the initial reservations of Thiokol, it is highly doubtful that informing the top-level managers would have changed anything. After all, the top level had been fully informed of the complexity of the seal joint problem the previous August and had not done anything to stop, or even slow down, the shuttle launches. The US House Committee investigating the Challenger accident drew a similar conclusion:

> The Committee finds that Marshall management used poor judgement in not informing the NSTS Program Manager (at Level 2) or the Level 1 Manager of the events that took place the night before the launch, specifically the stated concerns of the Thiokol engineers. However, the Committee finds no evidence to support a suggestion that the outcome would have been any different had they been told.[38]

The seriousness of the seal joint problem, however, could have been conveyed more frequently from the lower-level shuttle managers at Marshall to their superiors through the FRR process. This fact was of particular concern to the Rogers Commission, as its executive director, Dr. Alton Keel, states:

I think what's troubling us is not that there was erosion—everyone knew that—but the severity of it. And, for example, going back to the 51E Flight Readiness Review that was done at the Project level, the Level III level, was an extensive briefing on the whole O-ring history. When it got up to Level I, and plus they drew the conclusion that temperature made it worse.

When it got up to Level I it basically was, in fact, winnowed down to one bullet entry that said evidence of hot gas primary O-rings on two case joints: Concern: mission safety. Resolution: acceptable risk because of limited exposure and redundancy.[39]

The geographic dispersion and decentralization of the NASA organization produced an intercenter rivalry that probably encouraged the Marshall shuttle managers to try to minimize the problem and contain it as far as possible within the space center. For example, there was an evident intercenter rivalry among the three manned space flight centers—Marshall, Johnson, and Kennedy. They constituted the bulk of the shuttle program, including resources such as money and technical expertise, which left a relatively trim shuttle headquarters organization at the Office of Space Flight. This fact, together with their divided responsibilities in the shuttle program, produced three "fiefdoms" that sought to expand their jealously guarded turf at every opportunity. One researcher on NASA management policies described a "built-in rivalry" that extended among all nine field centers. His observations are especially relevant to Marshall, Kennedy, and Johnson: "Each center nourishes a conviction that it is the best of the lot. Each center is hard at work to make its own place strong and secure in whatever lies ahead for NASA. No center is willing to reveal its entire hand to other centers or for that matter, to Headquarters."[40] What further exacerbated this problem was the decision to place the location of Level 2 management, which was responsible for running the shuttle program, at Johnson. Although the Level 2 organization at Johnson was separate from the Level 1 organization, its very location gave Johnson a preeminence that probably heightened intercenter jealousies and suspicions. One observer wrote that "All centers are equal, but Johnson is more equal, according to many NASA veterans and retirees. Johnson gets most of the television time, and the astronauts radio their reports to 'Houston.'"[41] Because of this, the Marshall people were probably reluctant to impart the full extent of the joint problem to the upper levels during the FRRs, especially because "it had its eye on a large piece of the space station."[42] Such a goal would not be furthered by bearing bad news and being blamed for program problems in full view of its archrival in Texas.[43] In addition, such openness might adversely affect the shuttle managers' careers.[44]

Thus, in 1985, when the condition of the seal joint was extremely serious, the full extent of the joint problem was conveyed directly to the top level of the shuttle organization outside the routine FRRs. This information was conveyed directly from Marshall to headquarters, bypassing Level 2 at Johnson. Headquarters personnel went down to Marshall to investigate the O-ring erosion problem after the unsettling finding that the primary O-ring had failed on flight STS 51–B. Subsequently, the full extent of the joint problem was aired at the headquarters on August 19. It was strange that Level 2 was not invited to this crucially important briefing, because it was this level that was supposed to run the overall shuttle program. Yet, the actions of Level 2 itself weakened its oversight on operations at Marshall. In 1983, the Safety Reliability and Quality Assurance Director at Johnson decided that the Marshall monthly problem reports need not be reported to Level 2 after 1983, because by then the shuttle had become "operational."[45]

In any event, Level 2 management was by no means ignorant of the O-ring problems. Although this level was an apparently weak link in the communication flow, there were enough key people in the top management of the shuttle program who knew that the joint design was seriously flawed—and that its failure would cause total destruction of the space shuttle and its crew.[46]

Thus, despite these problems in the communication of the early warnings, enough of the early warnings did reach the upper levels of the shuttle organization. Level 1 knew of the detailed weaknesses of the seal joint by the summer of 1985. The shuttle managers knew the joint was failing, that it was a critical component, and that, therefore, it was just a matter of time before there would be a tragedy. Why, when the shuttle managers were alerted so frequently to the seriousness of the joint problem, did they not slow down the launches and spend time trying to understand the joint problem and reassess it? It could be that the shuttle managers did not believe that the seal joint was a serious risk—despite information to the contrary. Perhaps there was a gap "'twixt cup and lip" in which the early warnings reached only the desks of the shuttle managers, but not their minds. In other words, when the shuttle managers received the early warnings, they misperceived them so that the serious risk associated with the seal joint problem was either underestimated or unrecognized. The following chapter elaborates further on the validity of this explanation by examining how the shuttle managers responded to the information on the flawed seal joint.

Notes

1. William P. Rogers, *Report of the Presidential Commission on the Space Shuttle Challenger*, 5 vols. (Washington: GPO, 1986), 1:71–72.
2. "Shuttle Destroyed, Killing Crew; Manned Space Flights Halted," *Aviation Week & Space Technology* (February 3, 1986): 18–19, 21.
3. *Rogers Commission Report*, 1:57–58.
4. Ibid.
5. Ibid., 1:123–124.
6. Ibid.
7. Ibid., 2:H–1.
8. U.S. Congress, House Committee on Science and Technology, *Report of the Committee on Science and Technology: Investigation of the Challenger Accident*, H. Report 1016, 99th Cong., 2nd sess., October 29, 1986, p. 53.
9. *Rogers Commission Report*, 1:135.
10. Ibid., 1:130.
11. Ibid., 1:129–131.
12. Ibid., 2:H–1 to H–3.
13. Ibid., 2:H–1, H–2.
14. Ibid., 1:139, 248; 2:H–1.
15. Ibid., Memo written by Irving Davids to Associate Administrator for Space Flight, "Case to Case and Nozzle to Case 'O' Ring Seal Erosion Problems."
16. *Investigation of the Challenger Accident*, pp. 195, 376–377.
17. Memo written by Richard C. Cook to Michael Mann, "Problem with SRB Seals," July 23, 1985, *Rogers Commission Report*, 4:391.
18. Ibid.
19. Ibid., 4:397, sec. 720; 4:378, sec. 682–683.
20. Ibid., 4:379, sec. 685.
21. Ibid., 4:378, sec. 684.
22. Ibid., 4:379, sec. 685–687.
23. Ibid., 5:1051–1052, sec. 1911; 4: 786, sec. 1400.
24. Ibid., 1:139–140; 2:H–1 to H–2.
25. Ibid., 1: 140; 4: 786, sec. 1400.
26. Ibid., 1:136.
27. Ibid., 1:136–137.
28. *Investigation of the Challenger Accident*, p. 158.
29. Ibid.

30. Ibid.

31. *Rogers Commission Report,* 5:1536, sec. 2663.

32. Ibid., 1:89.

33. Ibid., 4:678, sec. 1208.

34. Ibid., 1:88–89

35. For a chronological account of the events related to temperature concerns and the O-rings twenty-four hours before the Challenger launch, see the *Rogers Commission Report,* 1:85–103.

36. Stanley R. Reinartz, manager of the Shuttle Projects Office, was the person in the chain of command who would have informed Level 2. The testimony given to the *Rogers Commission Report* shows he decided against it and was not urged to report the initial concerns of Thiokol. See volume 5:916–917, sec. 1678–1682.

37. *Investigation of the Challenger Accident,* p. 159.

38. Ibid., p. 27.

39. *Rogers Commission Report,* 5:1668, sec. 2869.

40. Erasmus H. Kloman, "NASA: The Vision and the Reality," *Report of the National Academy of Public Administration,* Washington, D.C. (April 1986), p. 42.

41. "Building the Shuttle," *Washington Post,* April 6, 1986, pp. Al, A12.

42. Henry S.F. Cooper, Jr., "Letter from the Space Center," *New Yorker* (November 10, 1986), p. 98.

43. James Clay Thompson, *Rolling Thunder* (Chapel Hill: University of North Carolina Press, 1980), p. 99. "Building the Shuttle," *Washington Post,* April 6, 1986, pp. Al, A12.

44. Harold L. Wilensky, *Organizational Intelligence: Knowledge and Politics in Government and Industry* (New York: Basic Books, 1967), p. 45.

45. *Rogers Commission Report,* 1:154.

46. *Investigation of the Challenger Accident,* p. 208.

3

Explaining the Accident: Misperception of Received Communications

Because the early warnings reached key people in the shuttle organization, it is necessary to examine the shuttle managers' response to the information on the seal joint problems. Perhaps the shuttle managers failed to consider the flawed seal joint problem sufficiently seriously. In other words, they misperceived the risk by underestimating the dangers of flying the shuttle with a seriously flawed seal joint. This chapter briefly elaborates upon the shared belief among the shuttle managers that the risk from the deteriorating seal joint was acceptable. It then shows how the shuttle managers justified this risk-taking with each shuttle mission by downgrading the various problems associated with the seal joint.

NASA's Confidence in the Seal Joint

One of the remarkable aspects of this organizational failure was the degree of unanimity among the shuttle managers on the safety of the seal joint. The testimony given to the Presidential Commission on the Space Shuttle Challenger (Rogers Commission) by Lawrence Mulloy, the Solid Rocket Booster (SRB) program manager at Marshall, is most illuminating in this regard. His statements include the reassurance that the whole of the shuttle management had "accepted" the seal erosion as no threat to the safety of the shuttle:

We had been flying since STS–2 (launched November 11, 1981) with a known condition in the joint that was duly considered and accepted by Thiokol, it was accepted by me, and it was accepted by all levels of NASA management through the flight readiness review process, through special presentations that we had put together and provided up here to the headquarters people.[1]

In testimony before the Rogers Commission, other shuttle managers also expressed a similar confidence in the joint. No one among them expressed doubts about the soundness of the joint and "rippled the waters" by charging that NASA was flying an unsafe shuttle. If anyone had expressed doubts before each flight and been overruled or ignored, he would presumably have sought to point out the objection to the Rogers Commission to avoid personal culpability. It seems surprising that there was such a "united front" on this question for over five or six years, and in the face of an ever worsening situation with the joint. They journeyed down a road that led them consistently to underestimate the risk of the flawed seal joint. Larry Mulloy, the SRB manager at Marshall, made the following remarks during his testimony at the Rogers Commission hearings:

> You ask why wasn't more done. You know, in the six years previous. And I have had the question posed to me many times in the last four months, and I have asked it of myself many times since the tragic accident. And my answer has been in hindsight, obviously, more should have been done.
> The turning, I think we started down a road where we had a design deficiency. When we recognized that it had design deficiency we did not fix it. Then we continued to fly with it, and rationalized why it was safe, and eventually concluded and convinced ourselves that it was an acceptable risk.
> That was—when we started down the road, we started down the road to eventually having the inevitable accident. I believe that.[2]

The report of the House Committee on Science and Technology dubbed this passage from Mulloy's testimony as an indication of a "collective rationalization" that basically downgraded the risk of flying the shuttle with a flawed seal joint.[3] These rationales were laid out in the briefing slides of the FRRs and were approved by the upper levels of the shuttle management.[4] Indeed, the serious problem with the seal joint was known and accepted by the Office of Space Flight at headquarters. When Michael Mann in the Controller's Office at headquarters responded to Richard Cook's memo by making enquiries with the people across the road (the Office of Space Flight), he "got the feeling [from his discussion with the engineers] that maybe the memo overstated the concerns."[5] After all, he was told that "there were quite a few actions being taken within the program office to resolve the issue, that there were extensive reviews going on."[6] Even at the August meeting at headquarters, when the serious problems with the seal joint were systematically laid out: "there was plainly a failure of NASA technical managers, and for that matter those at Thiokol, to grasp the seriousness of the problem."[7] More specifically, "none of the participants at this meeting (all with technical backgrounds)—NASA and Thiokol—recommended that the Shuttle be grounded until the problem with the seals was solved."[8] They accepted the rationalizations that had been developed by the shuttle organization at Marshall since the problems had begun to develop. Not one among the shuttle managers challenged the soundness of these rationales that led to the extraordinary risk taking that brought the agency to its knees.

Let us elaborate further on the shuttle managers' attitude toward the gravity of the flawed seal joint by showing how they downgraded the early warnings on its condition.

Downgrading the Seal Joint Problems

The joint was riddled with several serious shortcomings, any one of which could have played a role in preventing the joint from sealing, with catastrophic consequences. First, the joint moved or "rotated" as a result of the sheer force of the combustion gas pressure in the early ignition stage. This diminished the sealing capability of the primary and secondary O-rings. Second, the putty material, which was supposed to act as a thermal barrier, instead allowed the propellant gas to pass through it and to impinge on the primary O-ring. In some cases the hot gas would erode the primary O-ring as it passed by and impinge on the secondary seal. This was known as "blow-by" erosion, and it tended to occur when the timing mechanism of the O-rings was too slow, probably a result of joint rotation or cold temperatures.[9] Clearly, the joint should have been scrapped, the shuttle grounded, and a redesign expedited; yet, the shuttle managers acted as though the joint were safe. The following evidence shows how the shuttle managers responded to the early warnings on the various design flaws by "quick fixes," spurious rationalizations of the O-ring erosion, and a very narrow definition of O-ring redundancy. All these were efforts to downgrade the gravity of the early warnings and to upgrade their assumption that the joint was an acceptable risk.

"Quick Fixes" and Spurious Rationales for the O-Rings

The first warning came as early as 1977 during the testing phase of the joint design. Certain NASA engineers—Leon Ray and John Q. Miller—advocated a total redesign of the joint because of an unanticipated amount of joint movement during the ignition phase before liftoff. They told their superiors at Marshall that this joint rotation greatly weakened the capability of the primary O-ring to seal while it rendered the secondary or backup O-ring totally ineffective.[10] Thus, the design was totally unacceptable because it allowed the hot gas to leak from the joint. Furthermore, the officials of the Parker Seal Company that manufactured the seals agreed with Ray and Miller, stating that the "O-ring was being asked to perform beyond its intended design and that a different type of seal should be considered."[11]

The Marshall management, however, seemed satisfied with the conclusions of contractor Morton Thiokol that, although joint rotation would reduce the compression on the primary O-ring and thus affect its ability to seal, this would not cause any "significant problems."[12] In this way, the fundamental problem of resolving joint rotation by a redesign was never actually addressed by the shuttle managers. Instead, Marshall took the route of makeshift "quick-fixes" as larger O-rings and metal shims were used to resolve the reduced compression problem of the primary O-ring.[13] (Outside observers have argued that this did not produce adequate O-ring squeeze at all, but actually widened the gap because the heavier shim simply bent the joint farther outward.)[14]

A second major problem with the joint surfaced from actual flight experience when the hot propellant gases penetrated the putty and eroded the O-rings. This happened on well over half of the shuttle missions until the Challenger accident.[15] The shuttle managers responded by developing spurious rationales for blocking out the reality of the hard facts confronting them.

A Safe Margin of Erosion

The first rationale for downgrading the gravity of the O-ring erosion was developed after the third instance of primary impingement erosion on flight STS 41–B, which was launched in February 1984. Thiokol, which had found erosion on two earlier flights, developed the rationale of a safe margin of erosion in a report submitted to Marshall in early March

1984. This rationale was subsequently adopted by the Marshall shuttle managers and appeared for the first time in the FRRs for the upcoming mission, STS 41–C. Basically, it was decided that this impingement-erosion was an acceptable risk because it fell within a margin of "safe erosion" (0.092 inches on the field joint and 0.072 inches on the nozzle joint).[16] Actually, these technically astute shuttle managers had devised a safety factor from a margin of erosion, when the joint was not designed to erode in the first place.[17] In normal engineering language the

> "Safety factor" is to allow for uncertain excesses of load, or unknown extra loads, or weaknesses in the material that might have unexpected flaws, etc. If now the expected load comes on to the new bridge and a crack appears in a beam, this is the failure of the design. There was no safety factor at all; even though the bridge did not actually collapse because the crack only went one third of the way through the beam. The O-rings of the Solid Rocket Boosters were not designed to erode. Erosion was a clue that something was wrong. Erosion was not something from which safety could be inferred.[18]

Moreover, this margin was derived from a mathematical model whose validity was challenged by several scientists who were members of the Rogers Commission investigating the Challenger accident.[19] Even more astonishing is that NASA believed it could so confidently make predictions about a flight anomaly it barely understood. NASA officials did not know the reason that erosion would occur on several consecutive flights and then suddenly appear on different joints and in different places with varying degrees of seriousness. It is true that Marshall had notions about the possible causes of seal erosion that were gleaned from each postflight inspection. Thus, in a way, its true laboratory was actually the shuttle launches themselves with full payload and crew aboard!

NASA was not even close to achieving control of the problem, however, and simply because one flight made it through liftoff with an "acceptable [amount of] erosion" was no guarantee that future flights would escape harm. As a member of the Rogers Commission pointed out, "...I don't understand how the logic works, that because something just made it, that the next time it wouldn't be a bigger variation."[20] Or, as another member of the Commission stated:

> The fact that this danger did not lead to a catastrophe before is no guarantee that it will not the next time, unless it is completely understood. When playing Russian roulette the fact that the first shot got off safely is little

comfort for the next. The origin and consequences of the erosion and blow-by were not understood. They did not occur equally on all flights and on all joints; sometimes more, sometimes less....In spite of these variations, from case to case, officials behaved as if they understood it, giving apparently logical arguments to each other depending on the 'success' of previous flights.[21]

Thus, those missions that were later found to have experienced seal erosion only increased the confidence of the shuttle managers because they had launched just as successfully as those exhibiting no erosion. For example, two more flights after STS 41–B, in 1984, also experienced impingement erosion.[22] Once again this was found to be within the acceptable limits of the worst possible case and there was no apparent alarm. Each successful flight became another justification for the next flight because each safe return apparently indicated to the shuttle managers that the joint was an acceptable risk. In this way, the successful launches themselves became an additional rationale for justifying the upcoming flight. For example, Thiokol's summary of the erosion from flight 41–C at a Level 3 briefing for flight STS 41–D was:

> All primary seals performed well.
> No compromise to STS 13 (flight 41–C).
> Similar O-ring erosion seen on previous motors, i.e.
> QM–4, STS–2, and STS–11 [STS 41–C].[23]

The irony, of course, is that, instead of becoming more alarmed as more flights showed evidence of erosion, the agency became more confident than ever that its predictions were sound, because the erosion data vindicated its mathematical model and laboratory test data. In addition, from the subsequent widening erosion data base, the agency could usually compare the most recent erosion data with a more serious case from the past to downplay the gravity of the situation.

When a new kind of erosion—blow-by erosion—surfaced alongside the old problem of impingement erosion, NASA management still did not appear to be shaken from its complacency. "Blow-by" erosion resulted from the hot gas that was now blowing by the primary O-ring before it sealed. The first occasion was in August 1984 on flight STS 41–D. The blow-by erosion was more pronounced on flight STS 51–C in January 1985. This flight not only showed impingement erosion on two field joints, but also showed that the hot gas was passing by the primary O-ring and attacking the secondary O-ring. In the process, it was eroding the primary O-ring and heating the secondary O-ring.[24] Thus, before the primary O-ring finally sealed, the hot gas was penetrating farther down the seal joint toward the outside of the rocket booster.

Once again, NASA reacted by maintaining that the joint was not in jeopardy because this new form of erosion was acceptable and, therefore, safe. Just as the shuttle managers developed a margin of safe erosion for impingement, they also developed a similar safety margin for "blow-by." Furthermore, when the "blow-by" erosion became more pronounced on later flights, the shuttle managers reasoned that the erosion was still acceptable because it had previously occurred with no serious consequences.[25]

The Leak Check Test

An additional rationale was developed after the worst damage ever inflicted on the O-rings prior to the Challenger launch. It was flight STS 51–B, launched in April 1985, in which the primary O-ring had failed completely because of erosion. Although the secondary O-ring had apparently sealed, it was also damaged by erosion.

The failure of the primary O-ring meant that there was no such thing as a safe margin of erosion—a limit beyond which the hot gas would not penetrate. The shuttle managers at Marshall, however, contended that this development did not actually compromise their rationale of a safe margin of erosion because the rationale was only geared to predict impingement erosion but not when it was combined with "blow-by" erosion. Nevertheless, the shuttle managers waived a briefly imposed launch constraint by using another rationale, which involved increasing the pressure on the routine preflight leak-check test to "resolve" the problem. This test inserted pressure into the joint to determine whether the O-rings would seal. When the seal held, the shuttle managers reasoned that the joint was working properly. The problem was that the pressure came from an outside vent and entered the joint between the locations of the primary and secondary O-rings. As a result, the pressure was hitting the primary O-ring in an upward direction—the opposite from which the hot gas would be flowing.[26]

Consequently, the leak-check test actually weakened the primary O-ring and increased the number of holes in the putty for the hot gas to pass through. This, in turn, only increased the severity of the impingement erosion. The shuttle managers were fully aware of this fact. Larry

Mulloy, the SRB project manager at Marshall, acknowledged this paradox during his testimony at the Rogers Commission hearings:

> WALKER: Do you agree that the primary cause of the erosion is the blow holes in the putty?
>
> MULLOY: I believe it is. Yes.
>
> WALKER: And so your leak check procedure created blow holes in the putty.
>
> MULLOY: That is one cause of blow holes in the putty.
>
> WALKER: But in other words, your leak check procedure could indeed cause what was your primary problem. Didn't that concern you?
>
> MULLOY: Yes, sir.[27]

Thus, although the shuttle managers were aware of these drawbacks, they must have reasoned that because the seal held during the test, it would also hold during the actual launch.

In reality, nothing was done to resolve the critical condition of the joint. It was business as usual as Chairman Rogers inferred from his exchange with Larry Mulloy, the SRB program manager at Marshall:

> ROGERS: And so each time one of these flights took off that you knew there was a constraint on...you had to make a decision to waive it, what went through your mind?
>
> MULLOY: Okay, what went through my mind is, we looked at the most recent observation of recovered hardware. We compared what we were seeing to our previous successful experience with the joint, realizing that we were having some O-ring erosion, looking if we were seeing anything that changed the previous rationale. That is what led to opening the problem report, when we saw that we violated the primary O-ring. That was something that was different and therefore required additional analysis and test until that was done.
>
> ROGERS: But what did you do about it, though? It seems to me in that case, when you said that you addressed it, no change was made in it. All you did

on these waivers was to waive it. You just apparently—there is no indication. What did you do? There is no nothing in this chart that suggests that
you corrected the joint. Each time there was further experience, further
erosion, and we don't see any examples of correction or effective action
taken or anything of that kind.[28]

Indeed, how could the problem be resolved, when nothing was done
to improve the performance of the joint? One could argue that the shuttle
managers still could rely on the redundancy of the seal joint. In other
words, they could count on the secondary O-ring, if the primary O-ring
failed because of erosion. After all, this had already happened in April
1985, during mission STS 51–B, and the secondary O-ring held.
Actually, the shuttle managers were including redundancy in the briefing
slides of the FRRs as a measure of overall flight readiness from the very
beginning of the shuttle flights. Moreover, once the primary O-ring failed,
redundancy, as a rationale, obviously assumed a greater significance. The
presence of this rationale is especially curious because, in December 1982,
the NASA organization officially declared that the joint was no longer
redundant. The secondary O-ring was found to be unreliable in tests because of joint rotation.

Other Serious Problems:
Redundancy and Cold Temperatures

Yet, the shuttle managers evidently refused to accept the official
NASA declaration in December 1982 that the joint was no longer redun-
dant. The redundancy of the joint was officially rescinded in the Critical
Items List, as follows:

This gap may, however, in some cases, increase sufficiently to cause the
unenergized secondary O-ring to lose compression, raising question [sic] as to
its ability to energize and seal if called upon to do so by primary seal failure.
Since, under this latter condition only the single O-ring is sealing, a rationale
for retention is provided for the simplex mode where only one O-ring is acting.[29]

The change in criticality status was a blanket change; it applied to
every part of the joint and throughout the whole process of liftoff. In
other words, it was made with no qualifications or exceptions. The joint
was no longer redundant because the secondary O-ring might not seal

during joint rotation. Therefore, although physically it was still part of the joint, it should really have been mentally discarded as the joint became reclassified as a "single point failure."[30] This point is well illustrated in an exchange between Dr. William Lucas, the director of Science and Engineering at Marshall, and Chairman Rogers during the Commission hearings:

ROGERS: Well let's go back. What was the condition before this change? What was it called, Criticality 1R? And now, what did that mean?

LUCAS: That meant that one had a redundant seal throughout the whole period of flight.

ROGERS: Now when you take off the "R" as they did here, what does that mean to you?

LUCAS: Well, if you only looked at 1 versus the 1R, it would mean it's Criticality 1. But if you read —

ROGERS: Well let's just stick to that. That is the change, as I understand it, that was made, and I think that it was construed to mean that there was no redundant seal after this change was made.[31]

Apparently, the shuttle managers at Marshall, including Dr. Lucas, Lawrence Mulloy, and George Hardy, had developed their own interpretation. They interpreted redundancy to mean partially redundant.[32] They argued that in the early ignition phase of liftoff, the secondary seal is redundant. Thus, it was reasoned that if the primary O-ring failed, there was still time for the secondary O-ring to seal before the onset of joint rotation.[33] This interpretation was also shared by the Associate Deputy Administrator for Technical Concerns Lawrence Weeks, who granted a waiver on the criticality status of the O-ring in March 1983 because he believed that the secondary O-ring still had some capability—it was, to a degree, redundant: "It doesn't say that, but everybody knows you have a dual O-ring."[34] In this way, the shuttle managers interpreted this section to mean that the primary O-ring was a single failure point only during joint rotation when the secondary O-ring might not seal.[35] Thus, the shuttle managers still continued to include redundancy as an indication of flight readiness in the FRR briefings.

It is reasonable to assume, however, that this qualified meaning of redundancy would have been spelled out in the official declaration of the criticality change from one of redundancy to a single point failure. In any case, the actual time to which they were alluding was only 160 to 170 milliseconds. As Dr. Sally Ride (a member of the Rogers Commission) remarked: "It is not clear to me that you've got the data to say that, to discriminate at the level of milliseconds, which is what you are really doing."[36] In other words, Marshall was risking the safety of the shuttle, crew, and its valuable payload, on a so-called redundancy that lasted for less than two-tenths of a second.

Moreover, there was still the question of whether the secondary O-ring was able to hold its seal, not only during joint rotation but also through the rest of the launch. Indeed, it would seem fruitless to argue that the joint was redundant at early ignition, if the secondary O-ring simply failed immediately after. The shuttle managers did maintain that the secondary O-ring would hold. As George Hardy (the deputy director of science and engineering at Marshall) explained to a skeptical Dr. Ride:

HARDY: I can't have blow-by the primary unless I am trying to pressurize the secondary seal. So it is not a situation where for some number of milli-seconds I've got blow-by the primary and then later I call on the secondary seal. I am calling on the secondary seal to function the instant I get blow-by the primary seal.

RIDE: I think that Mr. Boisjoly [the Thiokol engineer who urged a delay in launching the Challenger] described it very well when he said that it is kind of a race. Although you've got blow-by past the primary and the secondary is presumably holding at that point, the race is between the erosion that is occurring on the primary and its attempt to seal. So it is whether it seals first or erodes first.

HARDY: Which erodes first, Dr. Ride?

RIDE: The primary.

HARDY: Well, if I have initiated—early in the ignition transient phase, if I have initiated a sealing of the secondary seal, subsequent erosion on the primary seal is not of interest.

RIDE: Well, it is if the primary erodes to the point that when joint rotation occurs then you no longer have the secondary.[37]

Even if we allow NASA this point—that redundancy does operate during the crucial ignition phase of liftoff—this means that the timing function of the secondary O-ring is most crucial for its effectiveness. If the primary O-ring fails, then the secondary O-ring must perform at lightning speed to seal the joint. One would expect, therefore, that the shuttle managers would be highly sensitive and extremely alert to any factors, such as cold temperature, that would even remotely retard the sealing process of both the primary and secondary O-rings. With the secondary O-ring, especially, great reliance is placed on its ability not only to seal (in less than two-tenths of a second during early ignition phase) but also to maintain that seal during joint rotation. This was pointed out by a commission member, Dr. Arthur B. C. Walker, Jr., during the Rogers Commission hearings:

> But if you have a situation where the rotation begins to occur even after the seals have been made, is this not where temperature is truly critical and where, the tests carried out at Morton-Thiokol measuring the response of the seals as a function of temperature should have been very critically considered, because now at lower temperature the seal is going to have a harder time following the movements of the metal parts?[38]

It is true that NASA routinely checked the O-ring "squeeze" (enough compression for the O-ring to function) with this in mind, but it was amazingly complacent about the postflight erosion data that indicated a link between cold temperatures and the slowness of the O-rings in sealing the joint. Even when they were warned on the eve of the Challenger launch of the dangers of going beyond their data base and flying in freezing temperatures, they let the shuttle fly regardless of the cold temperature.

At a preliminary meeting in the early afternoon on January 27, the implications of the cold weather from the past few days was discussed. According to the testimony of Roger Boisjoly, he was especially concerned about launching the Challenger in cold temperatures because, in contrast to the STS–C launch in January 1985, the severe cold at the Cape had been continuous for the past few days:

> When I got off the plane a year ago last January for the SRM–15 (STS–C) launch, it was very cold, like 17 or 18 degrees when I got off the plane at Orlando. The next few days, although it remained cold, it got warmer, and by launch time, like I said, it was probably in the 60s, but it did get warmer.

Now what was concerning me about this piece of information was it was the reverse, it had been cold for several days and was getting colder. And that is why I noted that because that just turned the gain up on my concern because it was away from goodness again. SRM–15 that I am referring to was the coldest launch up to that point in time.[39]

The outcome of the meeting was a general consensus that the Challenger launch should be delayed until temperatures warmed. Moreover, Boisjoly played a leading role in the discussions: "Okay, I felt we were very successful in convincing engineering and management of the problem....By now we heard that the overnight low was predicted to be 18 degrees Fahrenheit, and again my concern deepened of what I just spoke, it was going the wrong direction from the past experience base."[40]

Boisjoly points out that during this meeting "there was never a pro-launch statement ever made by anybody."[41] If anything, he states, the Thiokol group was "very comfortable" with its conclusion that Thiokol should "not fly outside of our data base."[42]

When Roger Boisjoly presented his argument later that evening at 8:45 during the teleconference with key personnel from Marshall, Kennedy, and Morton Thiokol, however, this conclusion was unenthusiastically received by the Marshall people. The Marshall line managers challenged Boisjoly on the grounds that his conclusions were not based on quantifiable data. Boisjoly recounts his conversation during the teleconference with Lawrence Mulloy on the eve of the Challenger launch. He "expressed deep concern about launching in cold temperature" and presented his first chart that had been used in the Washington presentation.[43] This showed that there was only a high probability of the secondary O-ring's sealing in the first 170 milliseconds at ignition. His next chart elaborated much more on the critical role that temperature played in the timing function of the O-rings.

> I started off talking about a lower temperature than current data base results in changing the primary O-ring sealing timing function, and I discussed the SRM–15 [Flight 51–C, January, 1985] observations, namely, the 15A [Left SRM, Flight 51–C] motor had 80 degrees arc black grease between the O-rings, and make no mistake about it, when I say black, I mean black just like coal. It was jet black. And SRM–15B [Right SRM, Flight 51–C] had a 110 degree of black grease between the O-rings. We would have low O-ring squeeze due to low temperature which I calculated earlier in the day. We should have higher O-ring shore hardness....

Now, that would be harder. And what that really means basically is that the harder the material is, it would be likened to trying to shove a brick into a crack versus a sponge. That is a good analogy for purposes of this discussion. I also mentioned that thicker grease, as a result of lower temperatures, would have a higher viscosity. It wouldn't be as slick and slippery as it would be at room temperature. And so it would be a little bit more difficult to move across it.[44]

A seemingly exasperated Mulloy responded to Boisjoly's presentation by accusing Thiokol of generating new Launch Commit Criteria and asking whether they wanted the shuttle to launch the following April. Mulloy explained this reaction to Boisjoly's presentation during his testimony at the Rogers Commission on the Challenger accident. He said these comments were governed by a "single thought," that Thiokol was:

Proposing to…generate a new launch criteria on the eve of the launch, after we have successfully flown the existing Launch Commit Criteria 24 previous times. With this LCC, i.e., do not launch with a temperature greater [sic] than 53 degrees, we may not be able to launch until next April. We need to consider this carefully before we jump to any conclusions.[45]

Later in his testimony, Mulloy further justified his actions by first explaining the reason that he refused to accept that "blow-by" was related to temperature and then by using a whole series of rationalizations that have already been proven spurious. He marshaled his argument as follows:

This is a condition that we have had since STS–2, that has been accepted; that blow-by of the O-rings cannot be correlated to the temperature by these data. STS–61 had blow-by at 75 degrees. Soot blow-by of the primary O-rings has occurred on more than one occasion, independent of temperature. This is the nature of challenges. Think about this, think about your data.

Primary erosion occurs due to concentrated hot gas passed through the putty. I just wrote that down to say we know why we get erosion. We have done tests, we have done analyses, we understand the limits that the erosion can be, and we understand by tests how much we can withstand.

…The secondary seal is in a position to seat. It is in a position to seat and seal by the 200 psi and 50 psi pressurization at leak check. The primary may not seal due to reduced resiliency and increased durometer, may not seal, the worst condition, if the worst thing happens.

Plot of flights with incidents of O-ring thermal distress

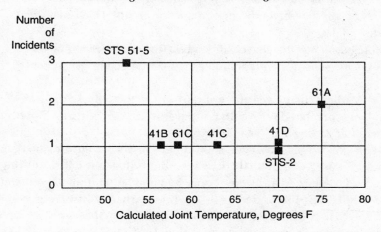

Plot of flights with and without incidents of O-ring thermal distress

Figure 3–1 Plot of Flights with and without Incidents of O-ring Thermal Distress

Note: Thermal distress defined as O-ring erosion, blow-by, or excessive heating.
Source: Report of the Presidential Commission on the Space Shuttle Challenger, 1:146.

However, during the period of flow past the primary the secondary will be seated and seal before significant joint rotation occurs, which is less than 170 milliseconds.

My conclusion was that that condition has been recognized by all levels of NASA management and is applicable to 51–L [the Challenger launch].[46]

Clearly, Mulloy dismisses the contention of the Thiokol engineers that blow-by is correlated with cold temperatures, asserting that blow-by also occurred at 75 degrees (see Figure 3–1).

He and his colleagues, however, should have analyzed the erosion data more closely. Figure 3–1 shows that of twenty flights that flew with an O-ring temperature of 66 degrees and above, only two had both impingement and blow-by erosion (STS 61–A and STS 41–D) while one had only impingement erosion, (STS–2). In contrast, three of a total of four flights that flew below 66 degrees evidenced both impingement and blow-by (STS 51–C, STS 61–C, STS 41–C), with the fourth suffering only from impingement erosion (STS 41–B).[47] Following Mulloy's own dictum of challenging and thinking about the data, one arrives at a totally different conclusion from his—that the probability of O-ring blow-by (not to mention impingement erosion) "is increased to almost a certainty if the temperature of the joint is less than 65 degrees."[48]

In any case, after this very cold reception by the Marshall managers, Thiokol left the teleconference for further discussion among its managers. Meanwhile, Allan J. McDonald, the Thiokol director of the Solid Rocket Booster Project who was at Kennedy, took issue with Mulloy about launching the Challenger below freezing. McDonald argued that the launch-commit criteria for the motor was only between 40 and 90 degrees. Mulloy countered this by saying that the propellant temperature was actually 55 degrees:

> And that the other elements can be below that; that as long as we don't fall out of the propellant mean bulk temperature. I told him I thought that was asinine because you could expose that large solid rocket motor to extremely low temperatures—I don't care if it's 100 below zero for several hours—with that massive amount of propellant, which is a great insulator, and not change that propellant mean bulk temperature but only a few degrees, and I don't think the spec really meant that.[49]

Meanwhile, the Thiokol meeting was taking place and things were not going well for Roger Boisjoly and Arnold Thompson. Both began an impassioned plea to remain with their initial recommendation:

Arnie actually got up from his position which was down the table, and walked up the table and put a quad pad down in front of the table, in front of the management folks, and tried to sketch out once again what his concern was with the joint, and when he realized he wasn't getting through, he just stopped.

I tried one more time with the photos. I grabbed the photos, and I went up and discussed the photos once again and tried to make the point that it was my opinion from actual observations that temperature was indeed a discriminator and we should not ignore the physical evidence that we had observed.[50]

All of this was to no avail, and Thiokol faxed its recommendation to Marshall for launching the Challenger at the scheduled time the following morning at 11:45, January 27, 1986.

In sum, the evidence so far indicates that there was a gap "'twixt cup and lip" when the shuttle managers received the early warnings on the seal joint. Despite the critical problem of the seal joint, the shuttle managers were disinclined to accept the reality of the early warnings. They resorted to "quick fixes" and then later developed "rational" justifications for launching the shuttle (which, on closer examination, proved to be less than sound). In this way, they believed that the joint was an acceptable risk, given the thicker shims, the safe margin of erosion, the redundant seal, and, most important, the safe return of the shuttle. Indeed, the new erosion data from the increasing number of returned flights proved that the margin of erosion was safe. Yet, we still have to explore the possible role that external forces may have played in contributing to this excessive risk-taking. NASA, like all public organizations, does not operate within a vacuum and certain conditions in NASA's external environment could have inadvertently encouraged the agency to take excessive risks with the shuttle. The following chapter examines the evidence of launch pressures within NASA, particularly as they relate to the external forces in the agency's environment.

Notes

1. William P. Rogers, *Report of the Presidential Commission on the Space Shuttle Challenger,* 5 vols. (Washington: GPO, June 6, 1986), 5:841, sec. 1533–1534.
2. U.S. Congress, House Committee on Science and Technology, *Report of the Committee on Science and Technology: Investigation of the Challenger Accident,* H. Report 1016, 99th Cong., 2nd sess., October 29, 1986, p. 161.

3. *Investigation of the Challenger Accident,* p. 161.

4. *Rogers Commission Report,* 2:H–1, H–10 to H–12.

5. Ibid., 4:397, sec. 720.

6. Ibid.

7. *Investigation of the Challenger Accident,* p. 160.

8. Ibid., p. 159.

9. *Rogers Commission Report,* 1:60–66; *Investigation of the Challenger Accident,* pp. 63–64.

10. *Rogers Commission Report,* 1:123.

11. Ibid., 1:124.

12. Ibid., 1:123.

13. Ibid., 1:125.

14. "The Challenger Disaster," *Defense Science,* May 1988, p. 14.

15. *Rogers Commission Report,* 1:129–131.

16. Ibid., 2: H–12.

17. Ibid., 1:H–18.

18. Ibid., 2:F–2.

19. Ibid., 5:1590, sec. 2736–2737; 5:1514, sec. 2604–2605.

20. Ibid., 5:1519, sec. 2617.

21. Ibid., 2:F–1.

22. Ibid., 2:H–1 to H–2.

23. Ibid., 2:H–16.

24. Ibid., 2:H–2.

25. Ibid., 2:H–41.

26. *Investigation of the Challenger Accident,* pp. 184–185.

27. *Rogers Commission Report,* 1:134.

28. Ibid., 5:1513, sec. 2600–2601.

29. Ibid., 5:898.

30. Ibid., 5:835, sec. 1517.

31. Ibid., 5:1037, sec. 1872.

32. Ibid., 5:833, sec. 1511; 5:836, sec. 1519–1520.

33. Ibid., 5:833–835, sec. 1513–1518.

34. Ibid., 5:1664, sec. 2856.

35. Ibid., 5:837, sec. 1524

36. Ibid., 5:836, sec. 1520.

37. Ibid., 5:836–837, sec. 1520–1521.

38. Ibid., 5:837, sec. 1522.

39. Ibid., 4:789, sec. 1409–1410.

40. Ibid., 4:789, sec. 1410.

41. Ibid., 4:792, sec. 1417.

42. Ibid., 4:791, sec. 1416.

43. Ibid., 1:88–89.

44. Ibid., 4: 790–791, sec. 1413–1414.

45. Ibid., 1:96.

46. Ibid., 5:841, sec. 1534, 1536

47. Ibid., 1:146.

48. Ibid., 1: 145

49. Ibid., 4:702, sec. 1234.

50. Ibid., 4:793, sec. 1419.

4

Explaining the Accident: External Forces

As is true of all federal agencies, NASA relies on the political support of Congress, the White House, the media, and its client group—the aerospace companies. As a result, it is very susceptible to influence by these outside forces. This chapter indicates that there was a strong link between the agency's failure to respond to the early warnings and its relationship with external forces. For example, promotional forces (those forces oriented toward the production aspects of a program) in the agency's external environment played a significant role in creating and exacerbating the launch pressures that were identified as a major contributor to the Challenger tragedy. The Report of the Presidential Commission on the Space Shuttle Challenger (Rogers Commission Report) devotes an entire chapter in its summary report to the "pressures on the system," repeatedly stating the immense discrepancy between the organizational resources and the overambitious launch rate.[1] A congressional investigation of the Challenger accident gave a much more forthright appraisal of the connection between the launch rate and agency behavior. The report of the House Committee on Science and Technology unequivocally stated that:

> There is no doubt that operating pressures created an atmosphere which allowed the accident on 51-L to happen. Without operating pressures the program might have been stopped months before the accident to redesign or at least understand the SRB joint. Without operating pressures the flight could have been stopped the night of January 27.[2]

In other words, the tight launch schedule caused the shuttle managers to ignore the serious problems with the seal joint because it interfered with achieving the agency's ambitious launch rate. Most important, external forces could have reined in these shuttle managers, but they failed to do so. On the contrary, the White House, Congress, and the media played an important role in creating the launch pressures and later succeeded in intensifying them. Let us first elaborate on the failed potential of external forces for containing the promotional drive of the shuttle managers and then explain the reasons for this.

The Potential for Reining in the Shuttle Managers

After the accident, there was considerable hand-wringing among NASA's supporters—especially among the media and within Congress—over their own lack of diligence in ensuring that NASA paid attention to flight safety. One journalist stated that "many reporters and editors have expressed regret at not digging deeper in the past."[3] Unlike the safety problems associated with the orbiter's main engine and the thermal tiles, the Solid Rocket Booster (SRB) joint was not a conspicuous problem. Indeed, just three days before the Challenger accident, the House and Senate authorization subcommittee staff held three days of meetings and reviews of technical items at Marshall, and the problem with the O-ring was not mentioned.[4] Similarly, only one day before the accident, the Senate and House oversight committees held an all-day session at the NASA Headquarters with the associate deputy administrator and as many as thirty project directors, but nothing was said about the O-ring problem and its current status in the program.[5]

Yet, both the media and the Congress had considerable resources for exposing the agency's difficulties with the flawed seal joint and for reining in the shuttle managers. The media, for example, have always prided themselves on their investigative powers, geared to "exposing the misdeeds of public officials."[6] Their critical investigative approach toward the Justice Department and the Environmental Protection Agency in recent years could as easily have been applied to NASA. Perhaps with sufficient digging, the media would have unearthed the flawed seal joint and then blasted the agency for its reckless attitude toward shuttle flight safety. NASA has always been extremely concerned with maintaining friendly relations with the press. It is vital to maintain favorable public relations because NASA lacks an organized broad base of political support to fall back on in troublesome times.[7] Other agencies, such as the Veterans Administration, can rely on myriad veterans organizations throughout the land to flex their muscle in Congress for the agency; NASA lacks such resources.[8] So, tough investigative reporting of the agency record on flight safety would have exerted a sobering influence on the shuttle managers as they scrambled to reassure the public of their commitment to safety. This kind of reporting may very well have discovered the agency's chronic neglect of the flawed seal joint, in which case effective action undoubtedly would have resulted.

Imagine, for example, that it is the summer of 1985, shortly after the crucial August 19 briefing of senior shuttle managers on the seriousness of the seal joint. It is also the time when NASA had already launched a nationwide public relations campaign for selecting a teacher to send into space. One morning, stunned shuttle managers see national headlines screaming, "Rocket Booster Joint Unsafe, Yet Shuttle Not Grounded," or "NASA Sending First Teacher to Space in Unsafe Shuttle." Then, in the evening, these shuttle managers listen in horror and dismay as Dan Rather begins the CBS Evening News with the following top story:

> It seems that for three years now NASA has ignored persistent warnings about an unreliable seal in the Solid Rocket Boosters that power the shuttle into space. Unidentified sources claim that these seals could fail at any time—it just needs one to malfunction for the mission to end in catastrophic failure.

Congress also had considerable potential for discovering the O-ring problem. Congress has its own resource or support agencies that report on agency activities and complicated technical issues.[9] These are the Office of Technology Assessment, the General Accounting Office (GAO), the Congressional Budget Office, and the Congressional Research Service. Congress also has its own independent oversight and investigative committees (the government operations committees in the Senate and the House) whose broad powers reach to "governmental activities at all levels."[10] Furthermore, a recent study on congressional oversight by Joel D. Aberbach revealed that congressional members and their staffs characteristically build and actively use information networks that will yield not only general information about "programs or agencies" under their jurisdiction, but also complaints and criticisms.[11] The committee's information network or intelligence system described by Aberbach features a very healthy rapport between the congressional staffers and agency personnel. While one-third of senior Senate committee staffers and over one-fourth of the House staffers, for example, engaged in fairly frequent informal contact with political appointees, a majority of the senior committee staffers in both chambers held "at least weekly informal discussions with top civil servants."[12] In addition, more than one-third of these people had extensive contacts below the supergrade category "at lower levels within the agencies who provide...useful information for oversight."[13] Other sources of information are derived from the committee's own hearings, from state and local officials, "from newspapers and magazines, watching television, checking the specialized media, and reading government-produced reports and notices."[14] Finally, individuals and interest groups are important sources of information (most notably in the form of criticisms and complaints) about programs and agencies.[15]

Most important, Morton Thiokol, the company that actually manufactured the SRB, knew about the flawed joint. It clearly possessed a detailed awareness of the flawed seal joint because its own engineers were the experts. Why, if the shuttle managers would not halt the launches to redesign the joint, did the company not leak this information to either Congress or the media? It had the financial incentive to apply the brakes on the program. The company was liable to a fine of $10 million from any accident attributable to a flawed booster rocket. There was also the argument that the risk of agency retaliation for publicly acknowledging inadequacies was not that serious because there were no companies with the same level of experience that could quickly gear up with the same level of expertise. The subsequent delays and additional costs of changing contractors would cause indescribable problems for a program that was already behind schedule.

If the problem of the flawed seal joint were to have surfaced, Congress could have used its formidable array of oversight powers to stop the launches and expedite the redesign of the joint.[16] For example, the authorization committee has statutory controls over policy, program duration, the amount of money authorized, the agency personnel, the administration of the organization, and the procedures for implementing programs. The appropriations committee specifies the purposes for which the money is appropriated, sets the funding levels, and can affect matters of policy or administrative performance.[17]

Any number of these powers could have been used as leverage over NASA; in fact, they had been used previously. Senator Jake Garn (R-Utah), a member of NASA's appropriations committee in the Senate (Subcommittee on Housing and Urban Development-Independent Agencies) and an ardent supporter of NASA, warned NASA Administrator James Beggs to be more responsive in providing information about the agency's long-term plans for the space station or else "money will be cut off again, as it was in this particular fiscal year, to get more of the answers. That always is an effective tool. If you take their money away from them you get answers."[18] A similar demonstration about flight safety and the flawed seal joint could have sufficiently ruffled the agency's feathers for the shuttle managers to have expedited the redesign efforts and at least thought twice about launching the shuttle as the O-ring erosion reached a critical condition by the summer of 1985.

Furthermore, the White House had important ways of influencing the agency. President Reagan could have threatened to fire Beggs, barring an expeditious resolution of the problem. Moreover, there was financial leverage available to the Office and Management and Budget (OMB), which could have threatened to withhold any additional funding from the agency until concrete progress had been made on the problem.

The Absence of Counterpressures on NASA

Why, therefore, did none of these kinds of things happen? Why did these external forces—especially Congress, the White House and the media—fail to exercise their responsibilities in calling this executive agency to account for its laxness toward the flawed seal joint? External forces failed to exert their potential for reining in the shuttle managers because they simply assumed that the agency was attending to safety concerns. After all, as yet, there had been no serious accidents. Also, at certain times, NASA did, indeed, demonstrate its attentiveness toward flight safety. It frequently delayed the shuttle launches—sometimes within minutes before liftoff—because of hardware or computer failures, or because of unfavorable weather conditions, which undoubtedly imparted an image of safety consciousness among the agency's overseers.

Yet, there is a deeper reason that encouraged such complacency among NASA's external forces. Such an attitude can be partly understood in terms of the costs and benefits that various groups and individuals assign to a particular course of action.[19] In this way, one can argue that the space shuttle program only galvanized those interests in the White House, Congress, the private sector, and the media that supported the program because of the benefits (for example, political or economic) derived from the space shuttle program. In such a promotional context, safety and caution appear to threaten short-term gains; thus, although there is every incentive to think in the short term of maintaining, and even expanding, their gains, there is very little incentive to consider safety and caution as serious concerns.[20]

Those interests opposed to the space shuttle program might be predisposed to the role of safety watchdog by using the issue of safety laxity as

62

a way of discrediting the agency. There were few groups, however, that opposed the space shuttle program. The U.S. manned space program is very popular, partly owing to the glamour, but also because the monetary costs of the program are so widely distributed among the taxpaying public that there is little likelihood of disgruntled citizens organizing against space program funding. Moreover, the cost of catastrophic failure would have a minimal impact on the general public: the risk of fatality is borne only by the crew and not by members of the public. As we shall see later, legislators such as Walter Mondale and certain segments of the scientific community that did oppose the funding for this new manned space program concentrated on the costliness and scientific nonproductiveness of the program at a time of nationwide economic retrenchment, but they were unsuccessful. Once the shuttle was in operation, there apparently were no motivated individuals digging around at the agency and alerting Congress and the media about an issue, such as the neglect of safety concerns, that would discredit the agency. As a result, the space policy arena was monopolized by a small group of beneficiaries who were unconstrained in encouraging the agency at the expense of caution and safety.

Congress

Consider, for example, Congress—NASA's principal overseer. One could argue that there were no incentives for committee members to rock the boat by raising awkward questions about safety concerns because they were much more concerned with protecting their gains from the space program in their own constituencies. Joel D. Aberbach, in his book, *Keeping a Watchful Eye*, makes the argument of the constituency connection to explain the reason that congressional oversight occurs in an "advocacy context—an environment of support for the basic goals of programs and agencies."[21] After all, by keeping their constituencies happy with the continued funding of NASA installations and contractors in their state or district, they were nurturing the electoral connection.[22] The glamour of space exploration and the successful moon landing by the agency may also have helped to encourage a less than attentive attitude toward safety concerns in its oversight activities, as one staffer observed:

> The space program has rarely seen tough oversight because it is an enormously attractive political tool. Patriotic endeavor embodies a pioneering spirit [and so] committeemen like to associate themselves with an agency that has achieved so much. [They were] very much cheerleaders.[23]

One staffer did observe that institutional reasons might have influenced the oversight of NASA: "Congress is an institution that is so overworked and strained that if something is going well, there is not much oversight."[24] Another staffer concluded, there was "no one against space [so that] Congress did not find it attractive or easy to do a proper overseeing job."[25]

In any case, committee hearings of the agency's appropriations committee (Subcommittee on HUD-Independent Agencies) and authorization committee (House Committee on Science, Space, and Technology and Senate Committee on Commerce, Science, and Transportation) were focused (and correctly so) on the management, planning, cost, and performance of the space shuttle program. During the development of the shuttle, however, and from 1982 when President Reagan confidently announced that the shuttle was "operational," issues of flight safety were raised in the agency's congressional hearings of its oversight committees. In 1978, for example, a Senate subcommittee hearing was specifically devoted to a review of the shuttle main engine development.[26] As one source describes it, "the years 1978 and 1979 were the season of engine fires."[27] In addition, in the Senate during 1979, the agency appropriations subcommittee held a special hearing on the space shuttle and Galileo programs where concerns were raised about the agency's alleged deferral of a thermal tile test.[28] Moreover, an in-depth analysis of the thermal tiles and main engine problems was aired in the hearings before an appropriations subcommittee of the Armed Services in 1980.[29] Beyond this, the safety problems associated with the thermal tiles, the main engines, and the solid rocket nozzles were raised in both the authorization and appropriations committee hearings.[30] In addition, the authorization committees received reports from the agency's safety panel—the Aerospace Safety Advisory Panel (ASAP)—in which safety problems were described in some detail regarding the thermal tiles, main engines, landing gear, and shuttle brakes.[31]

Thus, it would appear that the agency's committees were neither ignorant nor unconcerned about the safety aspects of the shuttle program. Perhaps a more accurate assessment of the shuttle program oversight would be that the committees were not sufficiently concerned to engage in an active monitoring style—including self-starting action that consistently worked through the information networks for developments on new safety problems and, most important, responded to the information by rigorous review.[32] The safety problems just cited were ones that surfaced early in the program and continued to be considered by the committees more or less rigorously. When the erosion problem really began to become serious in 1984 and 1985, however, a true test of effective oversight would have been for the committees to have unearthed, through their own initiative, the erosion problems with the seal joint. The special committee debriefings of each flight would have provided an excellent opportunity to broach the issue of flight safety, particularly the seal joint erosion. These were depicted by one staffer, however, as "largely PR stuff" and "candy covered."[33] (These debriefings usually were conducted by the returning crew members with a narration from film and slides.) No one thought of asking whether there were any serious problems with the flight; "We should have asked those questions," stated the same staffer, "like 'are you having any problems with the shuttle? If it's so great then why aren't you flying more often?'"[34] If they had asked these questions, then "one way or another, they [the committee members] would have found out [about the seal joint problem]. If word gets out that you are being tough—we'll get the answer. If they [the agency officials] think you're in the cheerleader role, they know that you don't give a damn and officials will not go to you about problems."[35]

Actually, information on the seal joint problem did reach at least one senior member of the House authorization committee and the agency's own watchdog panel that reported to Congress, but there was no subsequent thorough investigation to ascertain the seriousness of the problem and take appropriate action. The O-ring erosion in the seal joint was made known to House Representative Don Fuqua, the retired chairman of the House authorization committee, who stated that he knew about the problems with the O-rings: "I talked with [officials] and thought they had solved it. I don't get into internal management of NASA. That's not my job."[36] Yet, it would seem that when a member insists on an accounting of just how the problem is being handled, it demonstrates a genuine concern for safety standards rather than an obsessive desire for the type of micromanagement to which Fuqua alludes.[37]

Similarly, the agency's own safety watchdog panel, the ASAP, which presents an annual report to the authorization committee, was also aware of the seal joint problem, but according to Seymour C. Himmel, a member of ASAP, "This was considered to be one (problem) well in hand [by the panel] and attended to."[38] As a result, the seal joint problem "was never made a part of the safety panel's formal reports."[39] Thus, in both cases, instead of engaging in rigorous follow-through, the parties concerned were willing to take the agency on faith and accept its confident assurances that the problem was under control.

Other Beneficiaries of the Space Shuttle

The media also found it very profitable to ignore flight safety and concentrate on activity that brought them positive gains. The glamour of the shuttle coverage is what boosts the viewing audience and readership—not disconcerting investigative reports of news that people do not really want to know. Besides, reporting on such things as Senator Garn's enthusiastic send-off by his senate colleagues before his space shuttle ride, or the excitement surrounding the space flights of the first female and black astronauts was easy, simple, and fun.[40] As one *Washington Post* reporter remarked, "It was almost like writing about entertainment or something."[41] Indeed, the media especially delighted in highlighting the gimmickry in which NASA's public relations office excelled, such as the French astronaut whose space fare was billed "Extraterrestrial Edibles" (jugged hare, crab mousse, cantel cheese, and pâté, to say nothing of the champagne that was smuggled aboard).[42] There was also the Saudi Arabian prince whose shuttle flight was followed by an extravagant reception for 200 guests from the Saudi and American Aerospace communities, Arab-world embassies, U.S. Congress, and the media.[43]

Similarly, the White House seemed to think only in terms of the rewards of the shuttle program. The space shuttle, nearing the end of its development phase, was exploited as a typical Reaganesque combination of government economy and private enterprise: it was a quasi-commercial space shuttle that would pay for itself. President Reagan declared in 1983:

> Private companies are already beginning to look to space. In this regard the space shuttle program could well be compared to the first transcontinental railroad. And when profit motive starts to pay, hold onto your hats, the world is going to see what entrepreneurial genius is all about and what it means to see America get going.[44]

Furthermore, a fiscally conservative administration was eager to see NASA's latest publicity gimmick—the Teacher-In-Space Program—come to fruition as the White House was well aware of the great political gains from exploiting the popularity of a "cheap" form of manned space flight. The shuttle program was even used by President Reagan to garner support in his 1984 presidential reelection campaign. Reagan slammed his opponent, Senator Walter Mondale, who had been a staunch opponent of the space shuttle in 1972. He declared, "We support high tech, not high taxes, [with Mondale's kind of pessimism] America could have never gotten off the ground. With your space shuttle, we have again and again."[45]

Finally, Morton Thiokol was equally beholden to the tight launch schedule. As one commentator pointed out, Thiokol's SRB contract had become extremely lucrative because:

> the rapidly expanding flight schedule meant a sharply increasing demand for boosters.... Morton Thiokol's fiscal 1985 profits reached a record of almost $198 million on sales of just under two billion dollars. The company's aerospace division accounted for almost half these record profits and sales, with the bulk coming from the shuttle booster contract.[46]

Thus, one could argue that although the $10 million fine mentioned earlier was an incentive for safety and caution, protecting the company's "overall corporate health" provided an even greater disincentive for such behavior.[47] In other words, the incentive was much stronger not to upset the launch schedule by slowing down the launches or even halting the program for safety considerations. The penalty for such behavior could hurt the company's huge profit margin and, even worse, possibly jeopardize the company's inherent contractual advantage in the negotiations for the second phase SRB contract "that would cover the next sixty sets of boosters, a procurement award worth a billion dollars."[48] Indeed, Thiokol's competitors were vigorously lobbying Congress to break the company's monopoly on manufacturing the SRBs.[49] Now, although Thiokol was the only one among NASA's external forces that made any attempt to rein in the agency, this was at "the eleventh hour" and proved unsuccessful; the Thiokol managers reconsidered their recommendation to delay the launch after the less than enthusiastic response from the Marshall managers.

In sum, in NASA's space policy arena, external forces that were attentive to the welfare of the shuttle program were least likely to be oriented to safety concerns. Their self-interests encouraged them to focus on the promotional aspects of the program. The fact that there had been no previous accidents may have reinforced the notion that safety problems were being addressed.

Although there was relatively little interest in safety problems, external forces played an important role in both creating and exacerbating the launch pressures that weighed on the shuttle managers. It is first necessary to demonstrate how external forces played an indirect role in creating the launch pressures that they later more directly intensified. Cost-conscious officials in both the White House and Congress induced NASA to promote the shuttle program on the basis of its cost effectiveness. Meanwhile, both the White House and Congress accepted the unre-

alistic launch rate that supported the cost-effectiveness argument. This
course of action had most serious consequences because it produced both
stressful operating pressures in an organization forever playing catch-up
with the launch rate and critical supporters who only increased the pressures to achieve such an ambitious launch goal.

The Creation of the Launch Pressures

The launch pressures originated during the late 1960s and early 1970s
when NASA was desperately seeking the acceptance from the White House
and Congress of a new manned space program—the space shuttle. After
the moon landing in 1969, the agency faced an uncertain future with no
clear direction from either Congress or the White House. NASA realized
that a new manned space program was crucial for agency survival. Without a manned space program, "NASA could lose a lot of its leverage."[50]

Yet, it found that its political and financial support was dwindling. The
agency was faced with waning public interest in space exploration and a new
budget-conscious administration and Congress. The American public saw
little justification for pouring money into another manned space program
when they were preoccupied with more pressing problems such as inflation,
crime in the streets, and the Vietnam War. Thomas O. Paine, NASA's administrator, made this point about the mood of the nation in the late 1960s:

> Kennedy being assassinated. The Vietnam War. The rebellion in the schools.
> And so the decision not to fly for a long period of time was one that didn't
> turn a hair on the American people. They didn't give a damn. By then, hell,
> we had been to the moon. What do you care if we fly another orbital flight
> or not. We know we can do it.[51]

Yet, as is true of all organizations, NASA had extremely strong survival instincts. As Herbert Kaufman states, "Generally, organizations tend
to resist termination—they struggle to survive—even if they complete
their assigned missions and even when many outside observers are of
the opinion that their demise would be a blessing to everyone."[52]

Therefore, after considering other possibilities such as the space station
and the Big Gemini, the new NASA administrator, James C. Fletcher,
deemed them politically infeasible and decided that "the only way to go
was some sort of shuttle."[53] Instead of selling the space shuttle as a research and development program that was akin to pouring money into a

bottomless pit, NASA adopted a new strategy for the changed political climate and justified it in terms of its economy. Although a Rand Corporation study concluded that the shuttle program "was not easy to justify," and that "criteria other than cost should be used to justify its desirability," the economic argument was a fundamental pillar in the agency's strategy for selling the shuttle program.[54]

In this way, Fletcher proposed the novel idea of a reusable space shuttle, a new economical form of manned space flight in which the craft would be cheaper than expendable launch vehicles (ELVs). Its operation would be similar to a routine airline flight whose costs would be absorbed primarily by the customers.[55] Conservative estimates from economic analysis quoted roughly thirty flights a year as the crossover point where the shuttle would be more cost effective than ELVs. Fletcher was not satisfied with this since the long-term savings were the chief selling point with OMB and Congress. He went further, and using the highly optimistic findings of a 1971 Mathematica, Inc., report (sponsored by NASA), he set the projected annual flight rate at sixty, declaring that payloads would cost as little as $100 a pound.[56] (Shortly after, this figure was reduced to fewer than fifty flights a year.) Fletcher, according to one source, "made his subordinates join in the myth of the economic shuttle."[57] One of these subordinates, Dr. John Naugle, commented that:

> We had to argue that it [the shuttle] was cheaper. It would be cheaper than the expendable launch vehicles. It would be better than all the expendable launch vehicles....Well there was a feeling that we were on the razor's edge. That if we said a wrong thing, or anything like that, the shuttle would be killed.[58]

The recollections of Senator William Proxmire, a long-standing member of NASA's Senate appropriations committee and early opponent of the space shuttle program, portray an agency exuding confidence—bent on the hard sell of a program and stretching the truth to the point of incredulity. During the Senate hearings before the committee on appropriations in April 1987, Proxmire made this statement to Fletcher, who returned to the agency after the Challenger accident:

> As you know only too well Dr. Fletcher, I presided over many hearings in the formative days of the shuttle and was told over and over again that the shuttle was the greatest thing since sliced bread. [In 1976]...you told the subcommittee, "The fact is that we can go ahead with the space shuttle and can launch all of the known payloads in the future. We think it is quite

reasonable to assume that the flight rate would go up by 60 a year." I might add that in 1983, the Deputy Administrator, Hans Mark, referred to these kinds of estimates as an inflation of the mission model "beyond any realistic limits in order to reduce the apparent cost per flight of the shuttle." I don't say these things to embarrass anyone. After all, the Congress accepted your rosy estimate.[59]

Actually, there was really no sound methodological basis for arriving at the flight rate figure and payload costs because there was no current system of ELVs carrying payloads into space with which one could properly compare the shuttle and prove it more economical. Yet, Fletcher confidently stated that "by the end of this decade, the nation will have the means of getting men and equipment to and from space routinely, on a moment's notice, if necessary, and at a small fraction of today's cost."[60]

Nevertheless, Fletcher's pitch was well received by Congress. As one observer remarked, "The popularity of the shuttle paying for itself grew rapidly on Capitol Hill; more and more NASA officials began to imply that the shuttles could replace all expendables in the NASA fleet."[61]

This is not to say that there were no skeptics. There were those in the Executive Office of the President (especially in the Office of Management and Budget [OMB]), Congress, and in the scientific community who chided the agency for its vague goals and unrealistic projections of the shuttle program's capability.[62] Sen. Walter F. Mondale and three other senators, including Jacob Javits and William Proxmire, introduced an amendment to the NASA authorization bill for 1972 that would have effectively deleted $137.6 million for the development of the space shuttle. During the NASA appropriations hearings for the 1972 agency budget, Mondale submitted a statement that lambasted the space shuttle program, calling it "another manned space extravaganza" that has no utility to the scientific community, or to the American public:

> The scientific community has not been fooled. In its recent report on the future of the space program, the space science board of the National Academy of Sciences concluded that "it is clear that space science and applications by themselves are insufficient to justify the cost of developing the shuttle."
>
> I do not believe that the American taxpayer will be fooled, either.
>
> This is a classic example of a program and an agency in search of a mission. We are being asked to spend billions—not to meet real and pressing needs—but to give NASA the prestige and visibility which result from multi-billion dollar budgets.

It may be argued that $137.6 million in this year's budget (which will soon increase by 10 and 20 times) is nothing to get excited about. But then I see people in my state and elsewhere—who are losing homes because of spiraling taxes, who cannot afford decent education for their children, and who are experiencing a decline of almost every public service from transportation to police protection.[63]

Instead, he emphasized the proven worth of ELVs "which, for a fraction of the cost of manned space flight, has produced almost every human and scientific benefit resulting from the space program."[64] Nevertheless, in 1972, with the help of certain military, scientific, and business groups that were to become the shuttle's customers, Fletcher won President Nixon's endorsement and substantial congressional support.[65] He undoubtedly oversold the economic benefits of the program to Congress, the White House, and its prospective customers. Given the circumstances in the agency's external environment, Fletcher may have felt compelled to adopt this kind of strategy because he believed that it was the only way to save the agency. Fletcher was, however, probably doing no more than any other politically astute agency leader "in a political system that was 97% hyperbolic—a system based on great expectations, many of which are not met."[66] He naturally wished to save his organization from serious cutbacks and loss of turf. The only way the White House and Congress would even consider a new manned space program would be as the result of arguments consistent with the new public mood of fiscal restraint and economy. Thus, the shuttle program was presented to the White House and Congress in terms of its cost-effectiveness, which would result from a high annual rate of shuttle launches. During an authorization hearing in March 1972, Dr. Fletcher submitted a "Space Shuttle fact sheet" that concluded:

Even though the primary justification for the space shuttle is not economics, for mission models similar to those now in effect the shuttle investment will be returned with billions to spare. If, as is likely, new useful and economically beneficial mission possibilities open up during the 1980s because of the routine and quick access to space the shuttle provides, the investment will be returned many times over.[67]

The key point here is that enough people in both the White House and Congress were willing to believe the launch rate figure of sixty flights a year.

Fletcher's unrealistic launch rate imposed a heavy burden on an agency that was still basically a research and development organization with little experience in managing a quasi-commercial operational program. Yet, NASA had only itself to blame because it was Fletcher who had raised the expectations of outside groups to win their support. In a sense, Fletcher had done too good a job of selling the shuttle and the capabilities of the NASA organization. But, to posture any differently would have caused the agency to lose face with its budget-conscious political and financial backers and threatened the loss of the program it had won "by the skin of its teeth."

Increasing the Launch Pressures on NASA

Meanwhile, Fletcher's successful selling of the space shuttle program unleashed a promotional push from the White House, Congress, and the media—all of whom had very strong stakes in the success of the shuttle as a quasi-commercial operation. The White House, Congress, and especially the media had been subjected to so much hype about the cost savings from frequent launch rates that when these expectations were not realized, they became critical. This only further exacerbated the launch pressures already weighing on the shuttle managers. Let us examine more closely the way in which the agency's cheerleaders clearly indicated their disappointment and frustration with a launch schedule that was continually slipping because of innumerable delays and cancellations.

Members of NASA's congressional oversight committees were constantly questioning the optimistic launch rates projected by the agency. A serious concern of the budget-conscious legislators was whether the space shuttle would fulfill Fletcher's promise of a routine operation that paid for itself. In the early 1980s, when the shuttle became operational, Congress was already aware of a notable gap between agency plans and performance. In 1981, for example, during an appropriations hearing, a skeptical Senator Proxmire asked a senior NASA official, Dr. Alan M. Lovelace, the following question:

> NASA's original 1969 turnaround time allocation was 160 hours. Dr. Frosch, in his 1978 testimony, said that the best time expected in steady state operations was 200 hours. Apparently the current turnaround time assessment is 384 hours, more than double the original estimate. What impact will a 384 hour turnaround time have on the cost of operations, the annual launch rate capability, and the 12 year traffic model? [This predicted that the shuttle traffic would be divided equally between NASA and other agencies, the Department of Defense, and commercial and foreign communication satellites.][68]

Such questions augured the tone of congressional scrutiny in the forth-coming years. Congress was eager to see this manned space program fulfill NASA's prediction that it would pay for itself and, in this way, oversight not only called attention to budgetary issues but also queried the agency about its failure to fulfill its promises to meet its planned flight schedule, which had been reduced from sixty to twenty-four by 1989.[69] Four years later, an exchange between Sen. Patrick Leahy and James Beggs during the Senate appropriations hearings in March 1985 illustrates this point:

LEAHY: We are looking at budgets based on NASA's projections of the number of flights it is going to be able to make per year. Based on that, we determine how much we are going to give them as a commercial payback, how much the military can use it....

Is your 24 flight per year thing unrealistic when you consider the fact it does take a while to work it up? Is it unrealistic? During the next 12 months, will you have 24 flights?

BEGGS: Well, the first year we are projecting a 24-a-year rate is 1989.

LEAHY: Will you do it in 1989?

BEGGS: I believe we will, yes, sir. I think we are on that track.

LEAHY: During the next 12 months, how many flights do you project?

BEGGS: In the next 12 months I think we are projecting 11, in the next 12 calendar months.

LEAHY: You will make the 11?

BEGGS: I believe we will now, yes sir.

LEAHY: Thank you.[70]

Senator Leahy, apparently unconvinced by Beggs's assurances, reiterated his concerns about the projected flight rate, as he said, "So I just want to know how many times it [the shuttle] is apt to go up....You would do a disservice to yourselves if you came in with an overly optimistic thing."[71]

Actually, NASA still managed only four of nine flights in 1984 and eight of twelve for 1985.[72] It had reduced the turnaround time for each of the four shuttles from 100 days to fifty in 1985; it hoped to reduce the latter figure to thirty-five by early 1986, but this aspiration was highly questionable because ground crews were already exhausted from working long hours.[73]

Yet, Beggs was confidently assuring Senator Leahy and the other sub-committee members that by 1989, NASA would have at least twenty-four flights a year. Indeed, when asked by Senator Garn earlier at the same committee hearing if NASA "can handle 24 flights a year with four orbiters," Beggs replied that the agency could do even better than that:

> Late last year, as you know, Mr. Chairman, we flew one a month for 3 months with two orbiters actively in operation. So with that kind of experience, I think it gives us some confidence that we can indeed achieve one flight every two months with an orbiter. That would add up with four orbiters to 24 a year. Indeed, I think we can improve on that. I think we probably could launch one every 6 weeks, once we get to the point where we have mastered the art of turning them around and have the various subsystems to the point where they achieve the durability that we have been designing into them.[74]

Moreover, during a House appropriations hearing later that year, Beggs simply refused to accept Chairman Edward P. Boland's more realistic assessment that by 1989 the flight rate probably would be twenty rather than twenty-four:

> BOLAND: Is the base line still 24 by 1989? Or has that now been dropped to 20?
>
> BEGGS: No, it is still 24 in 1989.
>
> BOLAND: The reason we ask is that staff advises us that the latest information received by the contractors is a flight rate of 20 with a possible surge to 24, which would suggest that you have essentially given up on 24 flights a year.
>
> BEGGS: I think that surge is real.[75]

Beggs, joined by the associate administrator for space flight, Jesse Moore, then went on to reassure Boland that the agency had a very definite chance of reaching this flight rate; not only would they get the required hardware from their suppliers, but they would also improve their turnaround time at Cape Kennedy.[76]

In reality, by 1985, NASA had only achieved an increase in the launch rate to eight flights a year. Yet, Beggs was, in effect, saying that within four years the agency would not only reach twenty-four flights but even surpass that number. By 1985, three years after Reagan had declared the shuttle program operational, a new element of impatience over these delays was evident in the relations between NASA and its closest supporters—Congress and the media. Actually, for an agency that proudly sported its technical expertise of landing a man on the moon, the mundane problems that caused some of the delays must have seemed almost comical as they eluded resolution before liftoff. Imagine, for example, a squirming administrator listening to a very disappointed Senator Garn whose scheduled shuttle was canceled because the bucket of a "cherry picker" crane hit the orbiter Discovery, which damaged the door and the thermal tiles around the door:

> It has been somewhat disappointing and frustrating to all of us because of the delays. There has been a lot of questions asked of me about the delays, and it has obviously brought more attention to those delays because of my involvement....So the delays are disappointing. The decisions are proper....Now I am hopeful that this last one will be able to be fixed and not cause any undue delays. I guess none of us would have anticipated with the technical complexities of the orbiter and the system that we would experience a delay from a cherry picker, something as common as that. Nevertheless, it has taken place.[77]

Furthermore, for about a month before the Challenger launch, the agency had been subjected to ridicule by the press and media over the innumerable launch delays. The Columbia launch, for example, suffered seven delays, which were portrayed by the media as a "running soap opera."[78] Instead of applauding the agency for its caution, the media subjected NASA to relentless ridicule. Dan Rather of CBS reported the aborted launch on January 10:

> The star-crossed space shuttle Columbia stood ready for launch again today and once more the launch was scrubbed. Heavy rain was the cause this time. The launch has been postponed so often since its original date, December 18, that it's now known as mission impossible.[79]

Tom Brokaw reported another Columbia postponement on January 7 in a similarly disapproving tone:

> At Cape Canaveral today, mission commander Robert Gibson said: We have a bad habit going here, a habit of delays. This time, the weather was bad at

[handwritten margin note: Criticisms Prior to Disaster — not pushed future launches pressure]

the Cape and two emergency landing sites. NASA decided the launch would be too risky. It's now aiming for Thursday of this week. These delays are becoming expensive as well. A NASA official said today that the agency loses as much as $300,000 every time there's a postponement.[80]

On the evening of January 27, when the Challenger had been postponed once again, Dan Rather greeted the viewers with the following commentary: "Yet another costly, red-faced-all-around space shuttle launch delay...Bruce Hall has the latest on today's high-tech low comedy."[81] Small wonder that the Kennedy Space Center Director was reported as attributing a large part of the pressure to launch to the media:

> Ninety-eight percent of the pressure to launch came from the news media, which he said ridiculed NASA whenever the agency decided against a launch. Everytime there was a delay, the press would say, "here's a bunch of idiots who can't even handle a launch schedule." You think that doesn't have an impact? If you think it doesn't, you're stupid.[82]

Even a straightforward reporting of the facts behind the delays must have been excruciating to an agency such as NASA that flaunted its "can-do" image. When media coverage portrayed the shuttle managers as bumbling incompetents, such barbs were felt far more acutely. One NASA observer agrees with the shuttle official at Kennedy and waxes strong on the media pressures that were operating on the shuttle managers:

> Now imagine for a moment, that you are a senior NASA official on the morning of January 28. Because you are publicity conscious—indeed, because you may well be a publicity hound—you have been watching all three network newscasts for the past month and reading all the major newspapers.
>
> What goes through your mind as you listen to arguments from meteorologists and technicians about cold weather and O-rings. Do you look for reasons to avoid more of the delays that have "rocked confidence" in NASA? Do you preview in your mind, if only for an instant, what Keystone Kops footage the networks will show tonight after another aborted launch? Do you worry about extending the "comedy of errors" by postponing the Challenger launch yet another day?[83]

The media criticisms were particularly wounding concerning the Challenger because this publicity-conscious agency had much more than usual at stake. This particular launch held the prospect of agency acknowledgment in Reagan's State of the Union Address because it came at the culmination of a year-long public relations campaign promoting NASA's can-do ability. Christa McAuliffe would be the first schoolteacher in space and would give American schoolchildren their first science lesson beamed from outer space.

This idea, which had generated great enthusiasm among teachers and parents, had been accompanied by plenty of press coverage. Following extensive publicity for well over a year, this gimmick for garnering public support had created millions of expectant schoolchildren, parents, and teachers, who were becoming very frustrated with the delays and impatient and disappointed with this agency that bragged that the shuttle was a routine operation. The NBC Nightly News, which was actually the least derisive of the three networks, portrayed an impatient public juxtaposed to a supposedly invincible agency that was dogged not only by bad weather but also by an obstinate door handle:

BROKAW: At Cape Canaveral today, the space shuttle Challenger ran into still more problems and that forced still another delay in efforts to put the first schoolteacher into space. The flight of Christa McAuliffe now has been put off five times. And as NBC's Dan Molina reports tonight, there are worries that it might be put off again tomorrow.

MOLINA: In the end, it was a stiff Florida wind that kept Challenger off the launch pad today. Winds like this would have made an emergency very dangerous. It all started out well. Teacher Christa McAuliffe and her crewmates marched up to the launch pad in the pre-dawn hours. Up at Christa's school in Concord, New Hampshire, they crowded into the cafeteria to watch the big event on television. Then, came the exasperating mishap. A handle attached to the outside of the shuttle hatch had to be unscrewed and removed before takeoff as usual. Today, the threads of one screw were stripped. The call went out for the tools any home handyman would use, a big drill and a hacksaw. They went through two drills. They broke a drill bit. Finally, they got the handle on. But by then, the wind had kicked up.

MAN: We are going to scrub for today, and we'll be letting the crew out of the orbiter, and they will go back to the crew quarters.

MOLINA: The crowd at the launch pad left. As to the students up in New Hampshire:

[margin note: press coverage of teacher]

MAN: We're getting tired of it. We wanted her to go up, so, you know we can find out what it's going to be really like.

WOMAN: (INAUDIBLE)

MAN:....disappointed.

MOLINA: All this, after NASA canceled yesterday's scheduled launch, because the weather forecast looked bad, but turned out fine. Now, the plan is to press ahead with yet another try tomorrow, but subfreezing temperatures are forecast, and that could cause all sorts of problems.[84]

Actually, the White House also had a strong incentive in contacting the shuttle managers and criticizing them for the endless delays with the Challenger: the prospect of including the first teacher in space in President Reagan's State of the Union Message to Congress—and perhaps even engaging in "a telephone hookup to the Challenger astronauts during the State of the Union Address."[85]

Judging from the communication between the White House and NASA during the three or four days before the launch, however, there is absolutely no evidence to support such a theory.[86] According to newspaper reports, "Mr. Larry Speakes, [the White House spokesman] said nine White House staff members had telephoned NASA in the eight days before the launching" but "officials in the White House legal office had found 'no record, no recollection and no indication' that the telephone conversations were related to the launching of the shuttle."[87]

In addition, the Rogers Commission that was investigating the accident found no evidence that the White House had attempted to influence the timing of the Challenger launch. As it states:

Commission investigators interviewed all of the persons who would have been involved in a hookup—if one had been planned, and all stated unequivocally that there was no such plan. Furthermore, to give the crew time to become oriented, NASA does not schedule a communication for at least 48 hours after the launch and no such communication was scheduled in the case of flight 51–L.[88]

Three live telecasts were planned, including Christa McAuliffe's lesson beamed to all the schools, on what it would be like to live and work in space, "but they related in no way to the State of the Union Message."[89]

There was an agency draft submitted to the White House that sought acclaim for Christa McAuliffe's "ultimate field trip," the space station, and the various unmanned space flights such as the Voyager and the Galileo.[90] White House officials denied any knowledge of the draft and stated that they planned to mention NASA in the State of the Union message by using a twenty-one-year-old man, Richard Cavoli, whose "science experiment begun in high school was launched on the space shuttle Challenger."[91] It does seem rather odd that the president—who initiated the Teacher-In-Space Program—would use an obscure twenty-one year-old's experiment in space while totally ignoring the one person who had been given the spotlight by the media and the administration until the Challenger launch.[92] Whatever the motives of the White House, the draft memo strongly suggests that both the White House and NASA had strong self-interested motives for having the Challenger launched in time for Reagan's speech to Congress. Thus, if the White House did not overtly exacerbate the pressures to launch the Challenger, it may have inadvertently added to them by the possibility of including the Challenger mission in the State of the Union Message.[93]

Moreover, the White House had an indirect effect on the launch pressures in another way. From the late 1960s to the late 1970s, OMB cut NASA's budget in half (allowing for inflation).[94] NASA was forced to buy less sophisticated technologies such as the SRBs, but, most important, other changes were made that adversely affected the built-in programmatic safety checks that counterbalanced the promotional drive of the agency. For example, technical personnel were laid off, including 71 percent of the personnel in the quality-control and reliability-assurance functions. Meanwhile, the original independent Safety, Quality and Reliability Assurance organization within NASA was disbanded and its greatly reduced staff was placed under the control of a newly decentralized and compartmentalized operational management. In addition, the stockpile of spare parts was drastically reduced. Cannibalization was rampant. According to one source, sometimes maintenance personnel were literally—and hastily—taking parts from the newly arrived orbiter and placing them on the outgoing orbiter as it was leaving the hangar for the launch pad.[95] Apart from the adverse effects of these measures on safety in general, they must have only increased the frustration when launch schedules were not met.

Ultimately, the evidence indicates that the role of external forces clearly contributed to the launch pressures that were a major cause of the Challenger tragedy. In the first place, external forces failed to provide a safety-oriented counterforce to the launch pressures. They failed to rein in the shuttle managers, or to remind them of the crucial importance of flight safety for the long-term success of the shuttle program. External forces also played an important role in creating these launch pressures. The shuttle program was "oversold" as the first manned space program to be made cost effective through a high number of launches. Cost-conscious external forces were the reason for this hard sell by an agency that was fighting for its life. Simultaneously, external forces indulged an overconfident NASA by accepting this unrealistic launch rate. Furthermore, when it became clear that NASA was failing to achieve these promises, external forces behaved in a way that only intensified the launch pressures on the shuttle managers.

All three of the hypotheses for explaining the Challenger disaster have now been tested. Before assessing the findings, however, the aftermath of the Challenger accident will be briefly examined.

Notes

1. U.S. Congress, House Committee on Science and Technology, *Report of the Committee on Science and Technology: Investigation of the Challenger Accident*, H. Rept. 1016, 99th Cong., 2nd sess., October 29, 1986, p. 123; William P. Rogers, chairman, *Report of the Presidential Commission on the Space Shuttle Challenger*, 5 vols. (Washington: GPO, June 6, 1986), 1:164–167.

2. *Investigation of the Challenger Accident*, p. 123.

3. "Media Stepping Up Its NASA-Watching," *Boston Globe*, May 11, 1986, p. 24.

4. Interview # 75, October 28, 1987.

5. Ibid.

6. Francis E. Rourke, *Bureaucracy, Politics, and Public Policy* (Boston: Little, Brown, and Co., 1984), p. 197.

7. Michael Michaud, *Reaching for the High Frontier: The American Pro-Space Movement 1972–1984* (New York: Praeger, 1986), pp. 22–38.

8. Ibid., pp. 305–314. According to Michaud, since the 1970s numerous citizen groups have formed but these are small, disparate, and uncoordinated with apparently very little political clout.

9. Francis E. Rourke, "Bureaucracy in the American Political Order," *Political Science Quarterly*, vol. 102 (Summer 1987), p. 226.

10. Lawrence Dodd and Richard L. Schott, *Congress and the Administrative State* (New York: John Wiley and Sons, 1979), p. 166.

11. Joel D. Aberbach, *Keeping A Watchful Eye* (Washington: The Brookings Institution, 1990), pp. 87–95. Aberbach concludes that active monitoring or the "police patrol" style of monitoring agencies is the prominent style of congressional oversight. This finding, he contends, is "contrary" to the more passive "fire-alarm model" of congressional information expounded by Mathew McCubbins and Thomas Schwartz in their article "Congressional Oversight Overlooked: Police Patrols and Fire Alarms," *American Journal of Political Science*, vol. 28 (February 1984), pp. 165–179. Aberbach elaborates at length on pages 95–104.

12. Ibid., pp. 83–85.

13. Aberbach, *Keeping A Watchful Eye*, p. 85.

14. Ibid., p. 87.

15. Ibid., pp. 89–90.

16. Dodd and Schott, *Congress*, pp. 157–168; Arthur Maass, *Congress and the Common Good* (New York: Basic Books, Inc., 1983), pp. 120–127, 136–140.

17. Ibid.

18. U.S. Congress, Senate Committee on Appropriations, *Department of Housing and Urban Development—Independent Agencies Appropriations for Fiscal 1986, Hearings before a Subcommittee of the Committee on Appropriations*, 99th Cong., 2nd sess., 1986, p. 29.

19. James Q. Wilson, ed., *The Politics of Regulation* (New York: Basic Books, Inc., 1980), pp. 367–372.

20. Although the key to my argument is that the behavior of certain beneficiaries contributed to the lack of sensitivity toward safety and caution in the space policy arena, there is at least one reason why that is not a perfect "fit" for the distributive policy/subgovernment model that is described in the public policy literature. For example, the beneficiaries extend beyond the characteristically rigid and closed "iron triangle" of the congressional subcommittees, the executive branch agency, and the clientele group, to the White House and the media. Also, although this is a highly technical policy field, I would reserve judgment in characterizing it as an "issue network" of policy experts that "shifts over time" and whose boundaries "are indistinct." (Kay Lehman Schlozman and John T. Tierney, *Organized Interests and American Democracy* [New York: Harper & Row, 1986], p. 277.) The behavior of the role players in this particular case study does not spring from a "common commitment and expertise with respect to a particular issue area," but from enjoying the fruits of an ongoing "successful" shuttle program. Some major works in these areas are Randall B. Ripley and Grace A. Franklin, *Congress, the Bureaucracy, and Public Policy* (Pacific Grove, Calif.: Brooks Cole 1991); Hugh Heclo, "Issue Networks and the Executive Establishment," in Anthony King, ed., *The New American Political System* (Washington: American Enterprise Institute, 1978), pp. 87–124. For

a description of these concepts and a more thorough list of major works in this field, see Schlozman and Tierney, *Organized Interests.*

21. Aberbach, *Keeping a Watchful Eye*, p. 182. He also attributes other reasons for this phenomenon. Some members, for example, may find their jurisdictional subject matter "appealing or interesting" or seek a committee that has "great power in Congress"; see pp.175–183.

22. The impact of "space pork" on Houston, Texas, is described in some detail in the article, "What Houston Won When NASA Came to Town," *Business Week*, September 11, 1965, pp. 90–100.

23. Interview #75, October 28, 1987.

24. Ibid.

25. Ibid.

26. U.S. Congress, Senate Committee on Commerce, Science, and Transportation, *Space Shuttle Main Engine Development, Hearings before the Subcommittee on Science, Technology, and Space*, 95th Cong., 2nd. sess., 1978.

27. "The Shuttle Record: Risks, Achievements," *Science* vol. 231 (February 14, 1986), p. 664.

28. U.S. Congress, Senate Committee on Appropriations, *Special Shuttle and Galileo Mission, Hearings before a Subcommittee of the Committee on Appropriations*, 96th Cong., 1st sess., 1979, pp. 34–36.

29. U.S. Congress, House Committee on Appropriations, *Strategic Programs, Hearings before a Subcommittee of the Committee on Appropriations*, 96th Cong., 2nd sess., 1980, pp. 1–59.

30. For example, U.S. Congress, Senate Committee on Appropriations, *Department of Housing and Urban Development—Independent Agencies Appropriations for Fiscal 1980, Hearings before a Subcommittee of the Committee on Appropriations*, 96th Cong., 1st sess., 1979, pp. 929, 1005; U.S. Congress, Senate Committee on Appropriations, *Department of Housing and Urban Development—Independent Agencies Appropriations for Fiscal 1981, Hearings before a Subcommittee of the Committee on Appropriations*, 96th Cong., 2nd sess., 1980, pp. 1556–1557; U.S. Congress, Senate Committee on Commerce, Science, and Transportation, *NASA Authorization for Fiscal Year 1985, Hearings before the Subcommittee on Science, Technology, and Space*, 98th Cong., 2nd sess., 1984, p. 1092; U.S. Congress, House Committee on Appropriations, *Department of Housing and Urban Development—Independent Agencies Appropriations for Fiscal 1985, Hearings before a Subcommittee of the Committee on Appropriations*, 98th Cong., 2nd sess., 1984, p. 51.

31. For example, U.S. Congress, House Committee on Science and Technology, *1984 NASA Authorization, Hearings before the Subcommittee on Space Science and Applications*, 98th Cong., 1st sess., vol. 2, pp. 2–5; U.S. Congress, House Committee

on Science and Technology, *1985 NASA Authorization, Hearings before the Subcommittee on Space Science and Applications*, 98th Cong., 2nd sess., pp. 741–747.

32. See Aberbach, *Keeping a Watchful Eye*, pp. 93–95 for a discussion on active and reactive monitoring styles.

33. Interview # 87, January 12, 1987.

34. Ibid.

35. Ibid.

36. "Congress and the Challenger," *Washington Post National Weekly Edition*, April 21, 1986, pp. 8–9.

37. One interesting point that Aberbach makes in his book, *Keeping a Watchful Eye* (p. 177), is that "the most senior members, those who are generally most influential in making oversight decisions, often develop a special bias in favor of programs they have helped to shape. They want these programs to continue, indeed to grow and prosper, as monuments to themselves."

38. "NASA Was Trusted to Fix O-Rings," *Washington Post*, February 13, 1986, p. 15.

39. Ibid.

40. "Garn Given Stellar Send-off," *Washington Post*, April 12, 1985, p. 12.

41. "Media Stepping Up Its NASA Watching."

42. "For France's Astronaut It's Pass the Pâté," *Washington Post*, June 19, 1985, p. Bl.

43. "Saudi Arabian Prince Sultan Salmon Saud, His Country's First Man in Space, Meets with Congress, Media, and Saudi and American Aerospace Communities," *Washington Post*, September 12, 1985, p. C2.

44. "Reagan Urges NASA to Be More Visionary," *Aviation Week and Space Technology*, October 24, 1983, p. 25.

45. "President Uses Launch to Attack 'Pessimists,'" *Washington Post*, August 31, 1984, p. A3.

46. Malcolm McConnell, *Challenger: A Major Malfunction* (New York: Doubleday & Co., Inc., 1987), p. 177.

47. Ibid.

48. Ibid., p. 180.

49. Ibid., p. 181.

50. Joseph J. Trento, *Prescription for Disaster* (New York: Crown Publishers, Inc., 1987), p. 108.

51. Ibid., p. 93

52. Herbert Kaufman, *Time, Chance, and Organizations* (Chatham, N.J.: 1985), pp. 27–30.

53. Trento, *Prescription*, p. 106.

54. U.S. Congress, Senate Committee on Appropriations, *Department of Housing and Urban Development—Independent Agencies Appropriations for Fiscal 1972, Hearings before a Subcommittee of the Committee on Appropriations*, 92nd Cong., 1st sess., 1971, p. 638.

55. Trento, *Prescription,* p. 108.

56. Hans Mark, *The Space Station: A Personal Journey* (Durham: Duke University Press, 1987), p. 49.

57. Trento, *Prescription,* p. 118.

58. Ibid.

59. U.S. Congress, Senate Committee on Appropriations, *Department of Housing and Urban Development—Independent Agencies Appropriations for Fiscal 1988, Hearings before a Subcommittee of the Committee on Appropriations,* 100th Cong., 1st sess, 1987, p. 1020.

60. Robert Bazell, "NASA's Mid-life Crisis," *New Republic,* March 24,1986, p. 15.

61. Trento, *Prescription,* p. 110.

62. Barbara Romzek and Melvin Dubnick, "Accountability in the Public Sector: Lessons from the Challenger Tragedy," *Public Administration Review,* vol. 47 (May-June 1987), pp. 227–237; see also, U.S. Congress, Senate Committee on Appropriations, *Department of Housing and Urban Development—Independent Agencies' Appropriations for Fiscal 1972, Hearings before a Subcommittee of the Committee on Appropriations,* 92nd Cong., 1st sess., 1971, pp. 636–638.

63. U.S. Congress, Senate Committee on Appropriations, *Department of Housing and Urban Development—Independent Agencies Appropriations for Fiscal 1972, Hearings before a Subcommittee of the Committee on Appropriations,* 92nd Cong., 1st sess., 1971, p. 638.

64. Ibid.

65. Romzek and Dubnick, "Accountability," p. 232. Even though Nixon gave his support of the space shuttle program, "it was not accompanied by a strong presidential directive to give the program high priority. This allowed OMB to chip away at the program's budget from the start." John M. Logsdon, "The Space Shuttle Program: A Policy Failed?" *Science,* May 30, 1986, p. 1104.

66. Interview #75, October 28, 1987.

67. U.S. Congress, House Committee on Science and Astronautics, *1974 NASA Authorization, Hearings before the Committee on Science and Astronautics,* 92nd Cong., 2nd sess., p. 17.

68. U.S. Congress, Senate Committee on Appropriations, *Department of Housing and Urban Development—Independent Agencies Appropriations for Fiscal 1982,* 97th Cong., 1st sess., 1981, p. 1215.

69. Ibid.

70. U.S. Congress, Senate Committee on Appropriations, *Department of Housing and Urban Development—Independent Agencies Appropriations for Fiscal 1986, Hearings before a Subcommittee of the Committee on Appropriations,* 99th Cong., 1st sess., 1985, p. 33.

71. Ibid., p. 35.

72. *Investigation of the Challenger Accident,* p. 120.

73. *Investigation of the Challenger Accident,* p. 120; Mark, *The Space Station,* pp. 49-50; *Rogers Commission Report,* 1:164–171.

74. U.S. Congress, Senate Committee on Appropriations, *Department of Housing and Urban Development—Independent Agencies Appropriations for Fiscal 1986, Hearings before a Subcommittee of the Committee on Appropriations,* 99th Cong., 1st sess., 1985, p. 30.

75. U.S. Congress, House Committee on Appropriations, *Department of Housing and Urban Development—Independent Agencies Appropriations for Fiscal 1986, Hearings before a Subcommittee of the Committee on Appropriations,* 99th Cong., 1st sess., 1985, p. 123.

76. Ibid. See also, U.S. Congress, House Committee on Science and Technology, *Space Shuttle Requirements, Operations, and Future Plans, Hearings before the Subcommittee on Space Science and Applications,* 98th Cong., 2nd sess., 1984, p. 197.

77. U.S. Congress, Senate Committee on Appropriations, *Department of Housing and Urban Development—Independent Agencies Appropriations for Fiscal 1986, Hearings before a Subcommittee of the Committee on Appropriations,* 99th Cong., 1st sess., 1985, p. 30.

78. "Did the Media Goad NASA into the Challenger Disaster?" *Washington Post,* March 30, 1986, pp. 4–5.

79. "Maybe the Media Did Push NASA to Launch Challenger," *Washington Post National Weekly Edition,* April 14, 1986, p. 20.

80. Ibid., p. 19.

81. Ibid.

82. "Embattled NASA Ends Its Silence," *U.S. News and World Report* (March 31, 1986), p. 19.

83. "Maybe the Media Did Push NASA."

84. "NBC Nightly News with Tom Brokaw," *NBC Transcript,* January 27, 1986, pp. 2–3.

85. U.S. Congress, Senate Committee on Commerce, Science, and Transportation, *Hearings on the Space Shuttle Accident before the Subcommittee on Science, Technology, and Space of the Committee on Commerce, Science, and Transportation,* 99th Cong., 2nd sess., 1986, p. 105.

86. "White House Finds No Pressure to Launch," *New York Times,* April 4, 1986, p. D18; *Rogers Commission Report,* 1:176.

87. Ibid.

88. Ibid.

89. Ibid. See also, *Hearings on the Space Shuttle Accident,* p. 105.

90. *Hearings on the Space Shuttle Accident,* p. 100.

91. Ibid.

92. McConnell, *Challenger*, pp. 636–638.
93. *Hearings on the Space Shuttle Accident*, p. 106.
94. Romzek and Dubnick, "Accountability," p. 232.
95. *Rogers Commission Report*, 1:164–177.

5

The Aftermath:
Internal and External Changes

Did the Challenger accident produce a bureaucratic and political environment that was more focused on safety than it previously had been? This chapter explores the internal organizational changes that resulted from the accident. Then, it considers briefly the postaccident conditions outside the agency that affect its ability to minimize the chances that this kind of accident will happen again.

Postaccident Internal Changes

The Challenger accident spawned numerous investigations from both the executive and the legislative branches. In addition, the Report of the Presidential Commission on the Challenger Accident (Rogers Commission Report) produced many recommendations for improving the overall safety of the space shuttle program. NASA and its contractors spent nearly three years completing these internal changes, which cost $2.4 billion. The changes ranged widely from fixing hardware failures that caused the accident to revamping the prelaunch decisionmaking process and the management structure within the organization.

Resolving the Immediate Causes

It is evident that NASA has made significant strides in compensating for the particular shortcomings that caused the accident. In response to the immediate causes of the Challenger tragedy, NASA did several things. First, the joint was redesigned and subjected to rigorous full-scale testing for a launch date set in late 1988 of orbiter Discovery, Mission 26. A capture feature was added to minimize joint rotation, while a third

O-ring strengthened the seal. Heaters were installed in the SRBs to maintain a seal temperature of at least 75 degrees Fahrenheit along with a weather seal "to prevent water entry into the joint and possible freeze up."[1] Finally, longer pins, new retention bands, and an alternative insulation seal completed the upgrading of this hardware item.[2]

Simultaneously, stringent new weather launch rules and restrictions were imposed. Apparently, these are worded so precisely and are so extensive that "they allow little or no interpretation and virtually eliminate weather risks to launches."[3]

Other Organizational and Procedural Changes

NASA also introduced other organizational and procedural changes that were precipitated by, but actually had no direct causal relationship to, the accident. For example, the agency began to reevaluate all the critical parts on the shuttle whose failures could cause a catastrophe. The overall number has increased from 2,369 to 3,583 with a marked increase in the Criticality 1 components that had no backup safety system, which indicates that NASA now "has a better and more realistic understanding of the winged spaceship and its vulnerability."[4] In addition, the agency ranked these critical items on the basis of which were the most likely to fail, and at the top of the danger list are the highly complex liquid-fueled main engines.

NASA also upgraded the other major components of the shuttle hardware such as the orbiter, the main engines, tires, brakes, and nose-wheel steering systems. For example, it made more than 200 changes in the orbiter and three dozen in the main engines. Attention was also given to the maintenance and inspection of all shuttle hardware parts. The inventory of spare parts was increased to reduce the rate of cannibalization. Any cannibalization that remained would need the approval of the shuttle program director at headquarters and be closely tracked. At any event, it seems that, in relation to the orbiter Discovery, this problem was well controlled. As one official said, "Over 90 percent of the times we go to get spare parts here, we have them. There were very few times on Discovery when we had to cannibalize."[5]

Other organizational changes at NASA were both extensive and highly conspicuous. For example, both the program management and structure were centralized in an attempt to ensure better control and communications with the shuttle program units at the field centers. In this way, safety problems are brought to the attention of the topmost level of the organization. Both the authority and structure of the space shuttle program were reversed from the pre-Challenger days, and Level 2 of the shuttle organization, which provided the technical oversight of the shuttle program, was moved from Houston to headquarters in Washington, D.C. In other words, the "lead center concept" was shelved as the old Level 2 Shuttle Program Office and the program director at JSC were moved back to headquarters under the direct line of the associate administrator for space flight. Replacing the former position of deputy director located at JSC were two new deputy directors, one in charge of planning; the other in charge of operations. Both were located at the field centers at JSC and KFC, respectively, but reported to the program director, who, in turn, reported to the administrator's deputy director for planning. In this way, the various shuttle line-managers of the two program centers, Marshall and Houston, were linked with headquarters through a direct chain of command.

In pulling Level 2 out of JSC and locating it at headquarters, which centralized the line management of the shuttle program, the object was to create better communications and control of the field offices and simultaneously reduce the intercenter rivalry among Marshall, Houston, and Kennedy space centers. The location of Level 2 at JSC was always a source of friction among the three space centers. Various other steps were taken to encourage the cooperation about safety concerns that was previously stymied by past intercenter rivalries. For example, the old isolation of the centers was replaced by daily telephone calls and weekly meetings among safety representatives at Marshall, Houston, and Kennedy. New identification badges for everyone in the organization do not depict their affiliation in the organization; they simply indicate that they are NASA personnel. In addition, new center directors were appointed who showed a marked change in attitude toward the role of their center in the overall NASA organization. One NASA official emphasized strongly that the center directors are "working very hard to break down the destructive competition and build up constructive cooperation—and you can feel it at Marshall. There has been a real turnaround from a very closed shop and a very authoritarian structure where you don't take any bad news up."[6]

Senior NASA officials admitted that there will always be a strong allegiance to the centers. NASA has always encouraged a certain amount of rivalry among the centers because it "believes competition improves quality in the great old American tradition."[7] The key, however, is to strike a balance to avoid the negative outcome of intercenter rivalry.

Thus, on paper, at least, this new organizational program chain of command does not include the two center directors. The Kennedy Space Center is somewhat different because it is a launch center, not a multiprogram center sharing "the spoils" that come down the pipe. As a result, intercenter rivalry is less of a problem. Perhaps for this reason the crew operations manager does not report directly to the headquarters deputy director for operations but to the center director.

Of course, the center directors do play a role in the shuttle program in their capacity as managers of all the resources of the center. As such, they are informed of the program developments by the program managers at their respective centers in the same way as are headquarters personnel. The center directors also play a considerable role in the improved flight readiness briefings that better define decisionmaking responsibilities, especially during the final days of closeout reviews and during the tense forty-eight-hour period before countdown and liftoff. In addition, they also provide an independent assessment of the shuttle program status to the associate administrator of space flight and program director through the monthly meetings of the Office of Space Flight Management Council. This committee, described as an ill-defined and little-used function in the days before the Challenger accident, "is now an important element in active operations and the associate administrator for space flight is said to rely on it for advice, as his senior advisory group."[8]

All of these changes in one form or another were geared to improving safety in the future operation of the shuttle. At the same time, they symbolized a chastened organization that was trying desperately to regain its public credibility as a safety conscious organization. Yet, there were other changes that reflect even more directly on the organization's fundamental change in attitude toward excessive risk taking.

Resolving the Attitudinal Problem

One obvious manifestation of a greater sensitivity toward safety was the design and inclusion of a shuttle crew escape system. A safe escape during the actual launching is virtually impossible because of the speed of the craft and the inability to escape the burning fuel. The agency, however, has devised a crew escape system that enables astronauts to bail out under controlled conditions below an altitude of approximately 20,000 feet.[9]

NASA also took several steps to reduce significantly the heavy operating pressures that pervaded the organization before the Challenger accident. It was decided that the flight rate would be based on a realistic estimate of the agency's resources, so that it reflected "the overall staffing, workshifts, crew training, and maintenance requirements for the orbiter, main engine, solid rocket motor, and other critical systems."[10]

The National Research Council independently calculated a flight rate of eleven in 1991 with the fourth orbiter. This would increase to fourteen by 1994.[11] Furthermore, in August 1986, President Reagan announced a new space policy of having a mixed fleet of expendable launch vehicles (ELVs) and the shuttle. Many of the defense payloads would now be rescheduled on ELVs and no foreign and commercial payloads would fly aboard the shuttle unless they required a manned presence or had national security implications.[12] Finally, new procedures would insulate the shuttle managers from the perturbations of last-minute changes in the cargo manifest.[13]

NASA has acknowledged, however, that pressures of an operational program geared to meeting launch dates will inevitably surface, although they have been realistically tailored to the organizational resources. With this realization, the agency has improved its internal checks on the program management by significantly changing the position of the safety officers in the overall NASA organization. The individual safety officers were removed from the engineering staff organizations and placed together as a separately functioning organization within the space centers. Most important, they were also linked with the headquarters office headed by an associate administrator who himself reports directly to the NASA administrator. One safety engineer commented that "The key difference now is that 'safety' is visible. It's come from the back of the pack…the managers still make the decisions, but we're heard from. Our opinion is asked for."[14] For example, a leak was discovered in the orbiter's maneuvering system that was difficult to reach. The safety engineers raised objections about the safety hazards involved in the projected approach for reaching the leak, and the problem was discussed during conference calls. Before the Challenger accident there would have been no safety representative on the line.[15] Furthermore, there has been a determined effort to encourage people to speak out about safety concerns. For example, the director of the Kennedy Space Center has a picture of the shuttle on his office wall with the words, "If It's Not Safe, Say So."[16]

The directors in each of these safety organizations at the centers report directly to the center directors. They also, however, have direct access to the headquarters associate administrator "to advise him on the mission planning process and readiness for any flight."[17] The headquarters office is independent of the program line organization. It has the appropriate resources for its job of overseeing all aspects of safety throughout the organization. Of course, its control over the reporting and resolution of safety problems is a crucial responsibility. In addition, the office has the help of an anonymous whistleblower system and the newly created Space Shuttle Safety Panel to keep a firm grip on the safety standards in manned space flight. This panel reports to the associate administrator. The fact that this new safety team has free rein in the organization means that it can investigate any possible safety concern and give it high visibility.[18] Indeed, George Rodney, the newly appointed associate administrator of the safety office at headquarters, stated, "I have a specific charter to monitor the situation and to bring it to a head if, in my judgment, I feel that schedule pressure is becoming significant to the overall potential safety."[19] In their role as watchdogs for the program managers, however, these safety representatives will not be especially popular among those efficiency minded individuals that consider these safety representatives to be tiresome nitpickers and promoters of program delays.

It is clear from even such a cursory review of the organizations that this accident produced an extensive array of structural and procedural changes. These were intended not only to rectify the immediate causes of the accident, but also to alleviate numerous other problems highlighted as safety hazards by the various investigations. These changes were simultaneously intended to convince external actors of the agency's rededication to safety, so that normal agency relations could resume. These external forces—especially the media and Congress—were greatly shocked by the accident and made pressing demands on the agency to "clean up its house." Moreover, there was a marked change in the scrutiny given to the agency's safety problems by outside forces.

The Postaccident External Environment

During the post-Challenger period, NASA undoubtedly faced tough scrutiny on safety concerns by its traditional overseers. As one House member remarked, "But perhaps even more painful for the agency, it was the end of the uncritical admiration of the public, the press and many in Congress."[20]

The Media

The press, for example, atoned for its earlier indulgent attitude toward NASA by probing the agency's effectiveness at managing the program and its attentiveness to safety. In the thirteen weeks after the accident, the Kennedy Space Center alone received 108 requests under the Freedom of Information Act. In 1985 the number for the agency as a whole totaled 159.[21] At the same time, two extensive articles in the *New York Times* exposed a long history of waste and mismanagement of the shuttle program. The source for these articles was generally unpublished data from "500 audits of the space agency by its own Office of Inspector General, the General Accounting Office and the Pentagon's Defense Contract Audit Agency," which the newspaper was able to obtain through the Freedom of Information Act.[22]

Other journalistic assessments of NASA criticized the undue haste with which the agency conducted its redesign efforts on the joint. Apparently, the safety analysis and review of the rocket booster components were not keeping pace with the redesign work. Instead of paralleling the redesign work, they arrived "after the fact," which neither provided an impetus for refinements nor was very efficient.[23] Such investigative reporting was scarce before the Challenger accident but is essential to agency sensitivity on safety concerns. This new approach by the media was distinctly felt by the agency, as Dr. James Fletcher, the new agency administrator, complained to his congressional overseers:

> I, too am very appalled and disappointed about the way the press has treated NASA recently.
>
> They seem to have forgotten all of the creative accomplishments that the U.S. space program has made over the last 25 years or so, and they seem to want to focus on all the mistakes and a few problems that the agency has had recently.[24]

Congress

Meanwhile, the postaccident period produced a more rigorous congressional oversight of safety concerns in the way NASA's oversight committees engaged in a systematic follow-through of the agency's post-Challenger reforms. For example, during the authorization hearings in the spring of 1987, committee members were evidently eager to hear that the launch date for the first flight after the accident was still on schedule. Yet, they were extremely interested in whether the agency had finally understood "the behavior of these joints and the O-rings" to ensure effective modifications.[25] They also cautioned the agency against becoming the prisoner of a new launch schedule fever and displayed much interest in the new headquarters safety organization—the Office of Safety, Reliability, Maintainability and Quality Assurance (SRM&QA), which functions as a safety check when launch schedules are tight and pressures increase.

In particular, committee members wanted reassurances from Associate Administrator George Rodney, the head of SRM&QA, that he and his people would participate in the "whole tier of events that build up to the launch" and that he would have direct access to the agency administrator for purposes of recommending aborting the launch.[26] An exchange between a committee member and Mr. Rodney highlights this concern of the committee:

VOLKMER: Now, remember we're 15 minutes before launch time, and the countdown is going, what can you do about it?

RODNEY: What can I do? If I am convinced that we have to abort launch, I can tell the Administrator that we have to abort the launch.

VOLKMER: You have to review whatever is going on down there. If you feel that it has to be reviewed, you'd have the authority to go to the Administrator then and request abort?

RODNEY: Yes, sir.[27]

The committee grilled Rodney on what his behavior would be in certain sensitive situations, such as if "there are icicles all over the launch pad." It also sought assurances from him that even though his responsibilities were to Dr. Fletcher, he would "directly inform" members of Congress of these safety problems.[28]

This new congressional toughness toward NASA showed a sensitivity about safety in the long-term health of the shuttle program. It was tempered, however, by an acknowledgment of its own role in causing the Challenger accident. As one House member remarked, "This has been a difficult time for Congress as well. We have also taken considerable criticism for our role in this tragedy—for helping to create the environment that pushed NASA into taking the chances they did."[29] In addition, Senator Proxmire, from the agency's Senate appropriation committee, admitted that Congress had expected too much from NASA with relatively limited resources.[30]

This last point was not lost on the White House, which, along with Congress, had been guilty of the same outlook. After the accident, however, there was a 30 percent increase in NASA budget figures submitted to Congress. This apparently was the result primarily of direct presidential input. So, although Reagan did not exactly change his restrained behavior toward the manned space program before the successful mission of the Discovery in 1988, his actions indicated his endorsement.

Conclusion

The heightened sensitivity of the NASA organization toward safety concerns has important implications for this enquiry. It indicates that it sometimes requires a highly visible and embarrassing accident for bureaucrats to respond appropriately to critical safety problems, which raises the additional question of whether or not organizations can avoid similar problems in the future. Yet, NASA has surely taken the first steps: the flawed joint was redesigned, a more realistic launch schedule was put in place, and important internal and external safety checks were already established as a counterpressure to the natural promotional bent of the program management. Not even mentioned are the numerous changes undertaken by NASA that generally upgrade safety in its overall endeavor. Yet these changes still beg the question of whether or not they will suffice to maintain a sensitivity toward long-range safety concerns. This line of enquiry must wait for futher elaboation in the concluding chapter. Now, the TMI case merits closer examination— applying analytical methods similar to those used in the Challenger case.

Notes

1. U.S. General Accounting Office, *Briefing Report to the Chairman, Committee on Science, Space, and Technology, House of Representatives, Space Shuttle Accident: NASA's Actions to Address the Presidential Commission Report* (Washington: GPO, October 1987), p. 11.
2. Ibid.
3. "NASA to Launch Discovery under Stringent New Weather Restrictions," *Washington Post*, September 22, 1988, p. A3.
4. "Doubts Remain about Shuttle as Launching Draws Near," *New York Times*, September 26, 1988, pp. A1, B6.
5. "Path to Orbit Paved with Paperwork," *Washington Post*, September 26, 1988, pp. A1, A4.
6. Interview # 71, April 13, 1988.

7. Interview # 70, April 4, 1988.

8. "NASA Overhauls Shuttle Launch Process," *Aviation Week and Space Technology,* May 23, 1988, p. 20.

9. "Bailout System, Engine Limits Shape Shuttle Abort Philosophy," *Aviation Week and Space Technology,* September 26, 1988, p. 63-64. "NASA Selects Telescoping Pole for Shuttle Crew Escape System," *Aviation Week and Space Technology,* April 11, 1988, p. 31. See also, U.S. General Accounting Office, *Briefing Report to the Chairman,* pp. 30-33.

10. Report to the President, *Actions to Implement the Recommendations of the Presidential Commission on the Space Shuttle Challenger Accident* (Washington: GPO, July 14, 1986), p. 8.

11. U.S. General Accounting Office, *Briefing Report to the Chairman,* p. 35.

12. U.S. Department of Transportation, Office of Commercial Space Transportation, *Annual Report to Congress, Activities Conducted under the Commercial Space Transportation Act,* Fiscal Year 1987, p. 3.

13. U.S. General Accounting Office, *Briefing Report to the Chairman,* p. 36.

14. "Revamped Safety Program Casts Critical Eye on Systems," *Washington Post,* September 27, 1988, pp. A1, A9.

15. Ibid.

16. Ibid.

17. U.S., General Accounting Office, *Briefing Report to the Chairman,* p. 22.

18. U.S. Congress, House Committee on Science, Space, and Technology, *1988 NASA Authorization Hearings before Subcommittee on Space Science and Applications of the Committee on Science, Space, and Technology,* 100th Cong., 1st sess., 1987, vol. 2, p. 787. See also Actions to Implement the Recommendations of the Presidential Commission of the Space Shuttle Challenger, p. 14.

19. Ibid., p. 802.

20. Ibid.

21. "Media Stepping Up Its NASA Watching," *Boston Globe,* May 11, 1986, p. 24.

22. "NASA Wasted Billions Federal Audits Disclose," *New York Times,* April 23, 1986, pp. 1, 14; "NASA Cut or Delayed Safety Spending." *New York Times,* April 24, 1986, pp. 1, B4.

23. "NASA Safety Effort Beset with Doubts," *Dallas Morning News,* May 26, 1988, pp. 4, 16.

24. U.S. Congress, House Committee on Appropriations, *Department of Housing and Urban Development—Independent Agencies' Appropriation for Fiscal 1987. Hearings before a Subcommittee of the Committee on Appropriations,* 99th Cong., 2nd sess., 1986, p. 7.

25. U.S. Congress, House Committee on Science, Space, and Technology, *Hearings before a Subcommittee on Space Science and Applications of the Committee on Science,*

Space, and Technology, 100th Cong., 1st sess., 1987, vol. 2, p. 108; see also, "Congress Shuns Its Role as NASA's Cheerleader and Steps Up Scrutiny after Shuttle Tragedy," *Wall Street Journal,* April 4, 1986, p. 44.

26. *Hearings before a Subcommittee on Space Science and Applications of the Committee on Science, Space, and Technology,* p. 784.

27. Ibid., p. 808.

28. Ibid., p. 795.

29. Ibid., p. 3.

30. U.S. Congress, Senate Committee on Appropriations, Department of Housing and Urban Development, and Certain Independent Agencies for Fiscal 1988, *Hearings before a Subcommittee of the Committee on Appropriations,* 100th Congress, 1st sess., 1987, p. 1020.

The Nuclear
Regulatory Commission

6

The Accident at Three Mile Island and the Early Warnings

The NRC was also forewarned about its organizational failure, the accident at TMI. The early warnings focused on a particular safety problem that exacerbated the accident at TMI. Specifically, the safety problem involved human factors inasmuch as plant operators were ill-prepared for the sequence of events that unfolded at the reactor during the early morning of March 28, 1979. Let us first describe the accident and the operator error in greater detail and then demonstrate the way in which the information on this particular operator behavior repeatedly reached key officials in the NRC organization.

The Accident at Three Mile Island

The accident at Three Mile Island (see Fig. 6–1) occurred when the pressurized water reactor in Metropolitan Edison's Unit-2 came very close to a core meltdown. (A core meltdown occurs when the fuel, no longer cooled by the flow of water, begins to melt. The molten fuel could ultimately melt its way through the reactor vessel and containment building floor and into the earth, which results in catastrophic consequences as large quantities of radioactive materials inflict untold damage upon the environment as well as sickness and death on the public.)

Several hours elapsed before the reactor was finally brought under control. A malfunction in both main feedwater pumps stopped the flow of the secondary water system to the heat exchanger, causing the reactor coolant system (RCS), which consists of water that cools the reactor core and carries away heat, to overheat and expand. This malfunction pushed the water into a surge tank, called the pressurizer, and then through a

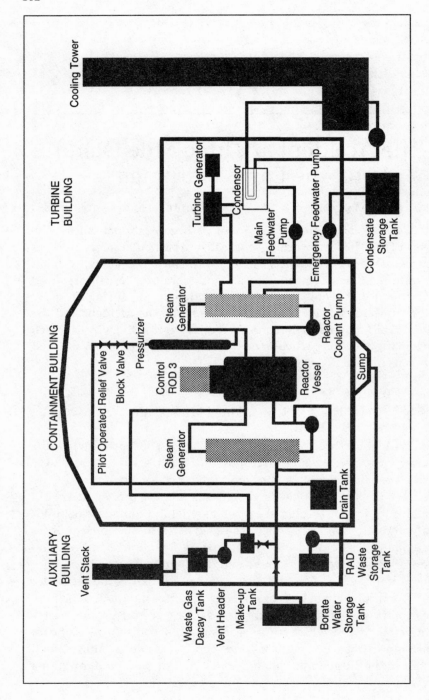

FIGURE 6–1 Pressurized Water Reactor Diagram

Source: John G. Kemeny, *The Report of the President's Commission on the Accident at Three Mile Island* (Washington: GPO, 1979)

valve called the pilot-operated relief valve (PORV) that had opened to relieve the increase in pressure. Seconds later, the TMI–2 reactor scrammed (as it was designed to do): its control rods dropped automatically down into the reactor core to halt its nuclear fission.[1]

Then, two high-pressure injection (HPI) pumps automatically began pumping one thousand gallons of cold water per minute into the RCS, which produced a cooling effect. The pressure in the RCS dropped, at which time the PORV should have closed. It did not, however, and remained stuck open, which, moreover, went undetected by the operators.[2] A stuck open PORV meant that there was a leak of one-half to one inch in diameter in the primary coolant system. A small-break loss-of-coolant accident (LOCA) was in progress, and the control-room operators were totally unaware of it.

This was crucially significant because, although the rods had stopped the fission process, the reactor core was still in danger of overheating from the decay heat, and, all the while, the coolant water was pouring through the pressurizer and out the PORV. The operators misinterpreted the rising pressurizer level as an indication that the RCS had plenty of water and that the HPI were excessively raising the dangerous possibility of having a solid system, which occurs when the entire RCS, including the pressurizer, is filled with water. The pressure within the RCS becomes more difficult to control and may cause damage to the RCS itself.[3] As a result, they released some of the coolant water through a "let-down" system and, only two-and-a-half minutes after the HPI pumps were activated, they shut down one and reduced the flow from the other pump to 100 gallons a minute.

As the water level and the pressure dropped in the RCS, the water began to boil. The saturation point was reached after five and a half minutes, and steam bubbles began to form in the RCS, pushing the water in the reactor vessel itself into the pressurizer, sending its level even higher, which continued to suggest to the operators that there was plenty of water in the RCS. In reality, with more water leaving the system than was being added, "the core was on its way to being uncovered."[4]

For two hours and twenty-two minutes, 32,000 gallons of slightly radioactive water mixed with steam (over one-third of the entire capacity of the RCS) escaped through the open PORV into the drain tank on the containment building floor. (When this tank was full, the water overflowed into a sump tank that was pumped into another tank in the auxiliary building. This was the major source of most of the radioactive releases at the site.)[5] Finally, one of the operators was advised to close the block valve between the pressurizer and the PORV, in the event that the PORV was stuck open. The LOCA stopped, and pressure began to rise, yet water in the reactor was below the top of the core.[6] It was another hour before the operators turned on the HPI pumps, which seems to indicate that the operators still had not fully realized the magnitude of the situation. It took another two hours to cover the core completely.

Although the accident was initiated and aggravated by hardware failures, the single factor that rendered it such a serious public health and safety threat was the behavior of the plant operators. They interfered with the emergency core cooling system by greatly reducing the HPI flow that kept the reactor cool. Yet, this action was not, strictly speaking, an operator error because the operators were correctly following established guidelines and procedures. The problem was that they misperceived the event because they had never been trained for this kind of scenario involving a small-break LOCA (a small leak in the reactor core).

In any case, a core meltdown had been averted. There was significant fuel damage and some uncovering of the core, which involved an expensive and potentially dangerous cleanup operation that has yet to be completed. No lives were lost, however, and the amount of radioactivity released into the environment proved not to be a serious health hazard.[7] Yet, this accident raised the ominous question in the minds of government officials and the public alike of what might have happened had the cause of the LOCA not been detected in time to prevent a full-scale meltdown of the core.

Early Warnings at the NRC

The NRC had early warnings of the operator error that occurred at TMI long before this accident occurred. One set of early warnings was generated from the "transient" (an abnormal condition or event) that occurred at Toledo Edison's Davis-Besse plant on September 24, 1977, which virtually duplicated the circumstances at Three Mile Island.[8] In a preview of the TMI accident eighteen months later, the operator turned off the HPI before the leak was secured. The major difference in this case was that the accident was contained, primarily because the leak was detected within minutes after the HPI pumps were turned off and the plant was operating only at 9 percent power.

Information about this "abnormal occurrence," to use the agency terminology, reached the appropriate offices at headquarters through the standard reporting procedure for licensees and the agency's own reporting procedures for its regional inspectors. The licensee submits a Licensee

Event Report (LER) in all events with "safety significance."[9] In mid-October, Toledo Edison sent to both headquarters and the regional inspector a report that described the event and proposed the corrective action. The regional inspector personally sent several reports to headquarters assessing the event. One report detailed the chronology of events and described the way in which how the operator had turned off the HPI several minutes before the leak was secured. In the regional inspector's final report in late November 1977, he recorded that the licensee had taken the appropriate corrective action and, thus, had complied with the regulations.[10]

These reports flowed through several important offices at headquarters. In particular, they reached the officials in the program office of Inspection and Enforcement (I&E) and were distributed further to other parts of the headquarters organization, including the office of Management and Policy Analysis and the Division of Operating Reactors and the Division of Systems Safety (DSS) in the program office of Nuclear Reactor Regulation (NRR) (see Figure 6–2). For a more complete description of the NRC organization and its communication flows, the reader should refer to the Appendix.

In any event, this process was preempted by a fact-finding team that was sent from DSS six days after the incident. The team visited the Davis-Besse plant and presented a report to a joint meeting of officials from NRR and I&E. Gerald Mazetis, the official who gave the briefing from his set of notes, indicated not only the hardware problems associated with the event, but also the operator error. As a result of this meeting, Gerald Mazetis' superior, Denwood Ross, sent a memorandum to the appropriate senior official, Karl Seyfrit, at I&E, advising him that this problem should be addressed at Davis-Besse.[11]

At approximately the same time that these events were occurring, other warnings were surfacing in another part of the organization. In early September 1977, Carlyle Michelson, a Tennessee Valley Authority engineer and consultant to the Advisory Committee on Reactor Safeguards (ACRS), gave a copy of his handwritten report of his analysis of very small leaks in a plant's reactor core to his close friend Jesse Ebersole, a member of the ACRS.[12] Leaks or "breaks" in the reactor core vary in size from a very small break to a large break. Any leak in the reactor core is significant because the core is in danger of overheating. Thus, any leak—large or small—is serious and is defined as a loss-of-coolant accident (LOCA).

Michelson noted that these kinds of accidents are very slow moving in contrast to a large break. In some ways, they are even more dangerous than the large breaks because they are difficult to detect. They can cause

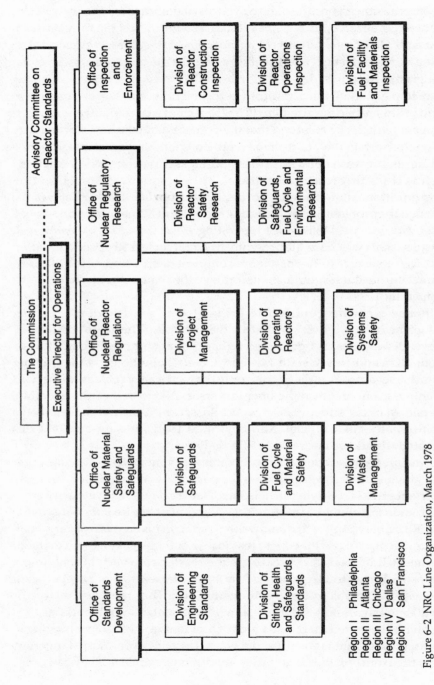

The Commission

Advisory Committee on Reactor Standards

Executive Director for Operations

Office of Standards Development

Division of Engineering Standards

Division of Siting, Health and Safeguards Standards

Office of Nuclear Material Safety and Safeguards

Division of Safeguards

Division of Fuel Cycle and Material Safety

Division of Waste Management

Office of Nuclear Reactor Regulation

Division of Project Management

Division of Operating Reactors

Division of Systems Safety

Office of Nuclear Regulatory Research

Division of Reactor Safety Research

Division of Safeguards, Fuel Cycle and Environmental Research

Office of Inspection and Enforcement

Division of Reactor Construction Inspection

Division of Reactor Operations Inspection

Division of Fuel Facility and Materials Inspection

Region I   Philadelphia
Region II Atlanta
Region III Chicago
Region IV Dallas
Region V   San Francisco

Figure 6-2 NRC Line Organization, March 1978

Source: U.S. Nuclear Regulatory Commission, 1975 Annual Report (Washington: GPO, April 1976).

great confusion among the plant operators, if the latter are not adequately trained. He observed that during a small-break LOCA, the operator can be misguided by the rising pressurizer level: "Note the presence of a rising pressurizer level is not an indication that adequate core coverage is being achieved."[13]

Ebersole passed along this information in two ways. He first gave a copy of this report informally to a friend, Sanford Israel, in the reactor systems branch of DSS. Israel later wrote a memorandum alerting the engineers within the branch office. He described the operator problem, noting that it was common to all Babcock and Wilcox (B&W) reactors, such as the Unit-2 reactor at TMI.[14]

In addition, after receiving a typed draft from Michelson that further detailed the problem of the operator's misinterpretation of the pressurizer level, Ebersole in late 1977 used it to form several on a list of twenty-six questions that was submitted by the ACRS and routed through the reactor systems branch of DSS to the license applicant of the Pebble Spring power plant. The question specifically asked the applicant whether he realized that a rising pressurizer level could mislead the operators about conditions in the reactor vessel.[15]

Finally, in late summer of 1978, an I&E inspector from Region 3, James Creswell, was inspecting the data from another abnormal occurrence at Davis-Besse on November 27, 1977.[16] Creswell engaged in a very frustrating and time-consuming process to alert I&E, B&W, and the utility, Toledo Edison, of the safety problems associated with this transient.[17] In the course of his investigation, however, Creswell reviewed the data on the September 24, 1977, transient and noted that the operators had terminated the HPI while the LOCA was still in progress. In his inspection report for I&E headquarters, dated October 25, 1978, he noted that:

> The licensee is reviewing the operator action of…securing high pressure injection to determine if different actions would be advisable in the future should a similar set of conditions arise. The matter is unresolved.[18]

Creswell also took advantage of the agency's open door policy. He sent a copy of his inspection report to commissioners Bradford and Ahearne and also had several phone conversations with Commissioner Bradford. Only nine days before the accident at TMI, on March 21, 1979, Creswell met with the commissioners to air his concerns about the overall operation of the Davis-Besse facility—and these concerns included the operator error of turning off the HPI during the abnormal event on September 24.[19]

Other Early Warnings That Were Blocked

It would appear that communication blockages from either poor monitoring procedures or structural deficiencies played no role in explaining this organizational failure because the early warnings successfully penetrated the NRC organization. For example, the NRC lacked a tracking system for highlighting safety problems. The General Accounting Office (GAO) had repeatedly criticized the NRC for lacking an individual or group to coordinate the review of these events at the plants.[20] Less than a year before TMI, it advocated "an overall trend analysis system [to] help insure all important trends are identified and corrective action taken."[21]

One could argue, therefore, that because the early warnings were mixed with a host of other safety concerns, it was understandable that these officials overlooked the particular safety problem that anticipated the accident at TMI. One scholar observed from her own research on the failed warnings that predicted the Pearl Harbor attack:

> It is much easier after the event to sort out the relevant from the irrelevant signals. After the event, of course, a signal is always crystal clear, we can see now what disaster it was signaling, since the disaster has occurred.[22]

Yet, this problem did not have any adverse effect on the communication of these early warnings. Information on the operator error passed under the very noses of these NRC officials, not once or twice, but several times. It reached I&E at headquarters through an LER, various inspection reports, and an interprogram office briefing, and it passed through RSB in NRR as a result of the Davis-Besse transient, the Michelson Report, and the Pebble Spring licensing questions. Furthermore, a number of officials, including Gerald Mazetis and Denwood Ross, were aware of the problem. One, Sanford Israel, was sufficiently knowledgeable to recognize the generic implications of the information. Both Ross and Israel wrote a memorandum that would seem to indicate that they understood the significance of the problem. Therefore, although there was no trend analysis of safety problems, it would not have made any difference because the early warnings still reached the desks of the appropriate officials.

Structural deficiencies may have played a role in the interrupted flow of one early warning, but, even if it had reached its destination, it would not have caused any significant changes at the nine B&W plants, one of which was Unit-2 at TMI. The memorandum from Denwood Ross, a senior official in NRR, to Karl Seyfrit, a senior official in the Division for Operating

Reactors Inspection, apparently was lost. It was meant to be conveyed to Thomas Tambling, the regional inspector at Davis-Besse, advising him to alert the operators of the conditions that can lead to the operator error. Neither Seyfrit nor Tambling, however, remembers receiving the memo.[23]

This confusion over the lost memo may have been rooted in the structure of the headquarters organization. The headquarters organization was divided into five highly specialized program offices. The ensuing rivalry and jealousy that existed between the five headquarters divisions hindered the cooperation and coordination of personnel. A GAO Report in 1975 found that "staff members within each of the Commission offices, tended to retain information in their own offices.[24]

This insularity among the five program offices was exacerbated by the geographic spread of the agency itself. Before TMI, it was housed in eight separate buildings in four geographic locations in Washington, D.C., and Montgomery County, Maryland. Obviously, such a situation only impairs cooperation and communication within the agency. If the program offices were at least close together in one major building complex, as one long-time employee stated, there would be "more meetings and more rapport" among the bureaus instead of an attitude of "those guys over there."[25]

In any event, whether the loss of the memo was owing to poor coordination between NRR and I&E is really immaterial to the case at hand because the memo only addressed the operator error at one particular power plant. Therefore, even if the memo had reached its destination, and the problem had been consequently solved, the accident at TMI would not have been prevented.[26] (Actually, the Davis-Besse problem was solved in 1978, owing to the efforts of the NRC regional inspector, James Creswell.)

Even so, one could advance a counterargument that, if this memorandum had reached regional inspector Tambling, he would have directed it to the utility, Toledo Edison, which, in turn, would have forwarded it to B&W, the company that built the reactor. At this point, B&W would have informed its other customers—including Metropolitan Edison's TMI facility—and given them some guidelines on the problem. In this way, the accident at TMI might have been either minimized or completely averted.

Early Warnings in the Industry

Actually, B&W was aware of this problem concerning operator misinterpretation of the pressurizer level. Joseph Kelly was sent to the Davis-Besse plant to scrutinize the incident of September 27, 1977, and, after further discussion of the "event" with other staff, the significance of the operator error was pointed out to him: "Bert Dunn told me that he was concerned because they had turned off high-pressure injection and he said that he could postulate scenarios that would lead to possible fuel damage if they turned the high pressure injection off too soon."[27]

As a result, Kelly sent a memo, dated November 1, 1977, to several of his superiors in the B&W organization, which alerted them to this problem and recommended that new guidelines be sent to the other operators at B&W reactors. Later, Dunn also wrote a memorandum, dated February 9, 1978, to senior management in which he described how the operator had prematurely turned off HPI and the highly damaging effect this would have had had the plant been operating at full power.[28] He concluded that "The incident points out that we have not supplied sufficient information to reactor operators in the area of recovery from a LOCA. I believe this is a very serious matter and deserves prompt attention and correction."[29]

There were several other occasions on which B&W was alerted to this particular problem: when it received a copy of the report from Michelson in the spring of 1978 as well as when it received the ACRS list of safety questions associated with the license application for the Pebble Spring nuclear plant. Question six specifically asked the company for its solution to the very scenario that had already occurred at Davis-Besse.

Although the NRC did not know what was happening within the B&W organization, however, does not detract from what it did know. The fact that the reactor manufacturer was aware of the operator error was hardly an excuse because of what the NRC knew from its own early warnings about the problem. The NRC had the knowledge to fix the problem in all of the B&W plants including the Unit-2 reactor at TMI. Yet, it rectified the situation in only one of them.

In sum, two major early warnings, the Davis-Besse incident and the Michelson Report, penetrated the NRC organization with important effects. They produced a significant response from regional and headquarters officials, in addition to alerting two of the NRC commissioners. Why, then, if these officials knew of the problem, did they not take the appropriate action and send an I&E bulletin requiring those plants with B&W reactors to devise new procedures preparing the operators for this possible condition? One explanation could be that the officials simply did not recognize the seriousness of the operator error. In other words, when these officials were informed about the operator error, they did not recognize that it presented a serious risk to the safe operation of nuclear power plants. The next chapter explores this possibility by examining the response of these officials to the early warnings.

Notes

1. John G. Kemeny, *Report of the President's Commission on the Accident at Three Mile Island, The Need for Change: The Legacy of TMI* (Washington: GPO, 1979), pp. 110–114.

2. Ibid., p. 111.

3. Ibid., p. 114.

4. Ibid.

5. Ibid., p. 111.

6. Ibid., p. 120.

7. U.S. Nuclear Regulatory Commission Special Inquiry Group, *Three Mile Island, A Report to the Commissioners and to the Public*, vol. 2, pt. 1 (Washington: GPO, 1980) pp.149–150, 155.

8. Ibid., pp. 149–152.

9. *Staff Report to the President's Commission on the Accident at Three Mile Island*: The Nuclear Regulatory Commission (Washington: GPO, 1979), p. 97.

10. NRC Special Inquiry Group, p. 151.

11. Ibid., p. 151.

12. Carlyle Michelson, "Decay Heat Removal Problems Associated with Recovery from a Very Small Break LOCA for B&W 205-Fuel-Assembly PWR," Tennessee Valley Authority, September 9, 1977.

13. Ibid., p. 9.

14. T. M. Novak, NRC, "Loop Seals in Pressurizer Surge Line," Letter to RSB Members, January 10, 1978.

15. *Staff Report to the President's Commission on the Accident at Three Mile Island: The Role of the Managing Utility and Its Suppliers* (Washington: GPO, 1979), p. 144; Memorandum, November 7, 1977, S. A. Varga, NRC, to all divisions of the Systems Safety Branch, "ACRS Questions on Pebble Springs."

16. Creswell was actually invited by Thomas Tambling to review the data on an event that had occurred at Davis-Besse on November 27, 1977. See NRC Special Inquiry Group, p. 165.

17. Ibid., pp. 164–171.

18. J. S. Creswell, Report of Inspection of the Davis-Besse Nuclear Plant, Unit 1, September 5–8, 1978, NRC Inspection Report No. 50/346/78–27, October 25, 1978, p. 3.

19. *President's Commission on the Accident at Three Mile Island*, Deposition of James Creswell, October 12, 1979, p. 89.; see also, *Staff Report to the President's Commission on the Accident at Three Mile Island*, p. 109.

20. U.S. General Accounting Office, EMD 78–29, p. 13.

21. Ibid.

22. Gloria Wohlstetter, *Pearl Harbor: Warning and Decision* (Stanford: Stanford University Press: 1962), p. 387.

23. NRC Special Inquiry Group, Deposition of Thomas Tambling, August 22, 1979, p. 26; *President's Commission on the Accident at Three Mile Island*, Deposition of Karl Seyfrit, p. 15.

24. U.S. General Accounting Office, *Licensing Practices of the Nuclear Regulatory Commission*, Report No. 105662B1226189, April 18, 1979, p. 5.

25. Interview #5, August 11, 1986.

26. NRC Special Inquiry Group, p. 167.

27. *President's Commission on the Accident at Three Mile Island*, Deposition of Joseph Kelly, July 7, 1979, p. 17.

28. *Staff Report: The Role of the Managing Utility and Its Suppliers*, p. 159; NRC Special Inquiry Group, p. 132.

29. NRC Special Inquiry Group, p. 159.

7

Explaining the Accident: Misperception of Received Communications

Because the early warnings reached key people in the NRC organization, one could easily conclude that these officials were incompetent in failing to rectify the operator error. Yet, a careful examination of their reaction to the early warnings might lead to a better understanding of this failure. It could be that the NRC regulators were laboring under some psychological block that prevented their recognizing the gravity of the operator error. This could be because of a professional bias at the NRC that focused attention entirely on the importance of hardware in matters of plant safety. As a result, human factors were discounted as serious threats to plant safety. Moreover, the fact that an accident had never been beyond control may have only confirmed the agency's confidence in its regulatory approach to ensuring plant safety. This chapter initially elaborates on the nature of such selective attention and then demonstrates the way in which it was manifested by the regulators' reaction to the information on the operator error.

A Professional Bias at the NRC

Before the accident at TMI, the NRC simply ignored the role of human factors in nuclear plant safety. The thrust of the agency's regulatory policy was to establish certain requirements for all hardware and safety systems. Provided that these were enforced, a serious accident was considered highly unlikely. The problem with this outlook was not that the reasoning behind the hardware solution was faulty. In fact, if the operators had not interfered with the safety system (known as the emergency core cooling system) at TMI, the accident probably never would have escalated. The flaw in this outlook was the notion that the hardware solution alone was enough to eliminate the threat of a serious accident.

In the late 1980s, with the significant growth in the field of human factors engineering, it is generally known that operating "failsafe" equipment is no straightforward matter. Human factors receive the attention they deserve because of their acknowledged role in causing serious accidents. For example, airline safety specialists are now aware that two of every three commercial jetliner crashes are caused by some kind of flight crew error.[1] One observer of the airline industry remarked that human factors research

> was resisted in its infancy by hard engineers—those who designed and built engines and wings and other aircraft parts that behaved in controllable, predictable ways. The biggest battle was to convince engineers there was something to this human factors stuff.[2]

Thus, it is reasonable to expect that when engineers dominated a government agency, a similar kind of blind spot might have surfaced in the agency's policymaking. In the National Traffic and Highway Safety Administration, engineering professionals ignored the role of the driver in causing highway deaths and injuries. Instead, it defined its goal of "reducing highway death and injuries" by improving the safety standards of vehicles.[3]

In addition, professionals in the Occupational Safety and Health Administration (OSHA) viewed safety in the workplace from the standpoint of engineering controls rather than personal protective equipment (such as earplugs, earmuffs, and respirators).[4] Most of the professionals were from the fields of safety engineering and industrial hygiene, whose justification for their particular approach included the particular hardships that protective equipment imposed on the workers. There was also, however, a belief that relinquishing safety in the workplace to personal protection devices was a professional "copout"—an indication of failure. As one scholar remarked, "As much as it may be unpleasant to the workers, personal protective equipment is insulting to the engineer."[5]

Similarly, in the late 1970s at the NRC, the general indifference to human factors may have reflected a general orientation of the engineering profession. Thus, predictably, when other early safety warnings were geared to hardware items, the NRC did "bother" the industry, and industrywide corrections were distributed in the form of the NRC's Inspection and Enforcement (I&E) bulletins, which compelled the industry to make the appropriate changes. From 1971 to 1978, apart from the three issued after a cable fire at Brown's Ferry, these bulletins focused upon hardware problems.[6]

This professional bias was reinforced by the fact that no accident had yet shaken the regulators' confidence. Reports on the post-TMI investigations of the agency emphasized this amazingly confident outlook by agency officials.[7] Indeed, almost ten years after the accident, agency officials readily admitted that they exhibited a mindset that a serious accident was "highly improbable" or "simply couldn't happen," because of their absolute faith in the hardware design. As one agency official stated: "we can think of all the possible thing that can go wrong and design them away."[8] Actually, the agency and industry alike believed that the major threat to the integrity of the reactor core came from large-break loss-of-coolant accidents (LOCAS). This was because breaks in large pipes had the potential of leaking greater amounts of radioactivity into the atmosphere than did breaks from smaller pipes or malfunctioning valves like the pilot operated relief valve (PORV). Automatic failsafe redundant safety systems were the answer to serious threats to reactor safety, and in such a fast moving scenario, the operator was virtually an onlooker. As a result, hardware design as opposed to human factors was the focus of attention.

Also, small-break LOCAS were viewed as no cause for concern and consequently given little attention because the reactor's safety systems were designed to contain large-break LOCAS, so smaller breaks were automatically "bounded" by them. In this way, small leaks from such things as small pipes or a malfunctioning PORV presented no serious threat because the high pressure injection pumps of the Emergency Core Cooling System would be automatically activated and would keep the reactor core cool until the operator detected the leak. Moreover, with smaller breaks, conditions in the reactor core were not so immediately critical so there was more time for the operator to respond appropriately. One agency official states:

I think that initially our thinking preceding Three Mile Island 2 was that this (a stuck-open PORV) was not a problem, that indeed you can fail a valve like this and create a small leak and either operator action or operation of other systems would terminate this event into a situation where it would be a rather mild, uneventful transient.[9]

A division chief made this point even more succinctly when he described this ingrained agency outlook as a mindset in which "accidents wouldn't happen" provided one had "well-engineered, well-designed, well-analyzed safety systems."[10] Unfortunately, he added, this attitude "forgot about the people who could stand by and defeat them if they didn't have the right training."[11]

The very structure of the organization indicated that the operator's role hardly figured in the agency's overall regulatory mission. Before TMI, there was no branch or even a section in the areas of licensing, inspection, and enforcement that actually reviewed operator procedures and analyzed the human-machine interface aspect of nuclear plant operations.

After the accident at TMI, one of the NRC's division chiefs explained the agency's earlier resistance to the idea that human factors play a prominent role in reactor safety, when he described the agency's reaction to the official findings from a pre-TMI agency-sponsored research team:

> If you go into the Rasmussen Report [another name for this is WASH-1400, which attempted to quantify the risks of operating a nuclear reactor] and look at every point where the operator makes an error in the [accident] sequence and you make that operator do the right thing, the overall risk drops by a factor of almost 10. That tells you operator error is an important element of many many many of the sequences of the Rassmussen [sic] report. Yet the area of operator error was not given attention by the regulatory process or by the research program at any time up to Three Mile Island.[12]

The Rasmussen Report also pointed out the serious risk to reactor safety from small-break LOCAs—especially the extremely small ones (1/2 inch to 2 inches in diameter), but, as a post-TMI special inquiry report pointed out, "despite the emphasis in WASH–1400 on the significance of small LOCAs, the NRC continued to place a great deal of emphasis in the licensing process and in research allocations, on large LOCAs."[13]

Ignoring the Early Warnings

In light of the preceding discussion, we will examine the evidence that demonstrates the way in which the NRC staff responded to early warnings about one particular human factors problem, the operator error that exacerbated the accident at TMI. As described in chapter 6, the event at Davis-Besse and the Michelson Report generated a series of warnings about the same operator error problem. The following discussion once again traces the flow of the early warnings as they penetrated the organization and were received by various NRC officials located at the regional and headquarters level.

The Event at Davis-Besse

The first early warning came with the event at Davis-Besse that occurred on September 24, 1977, when the plant was operating at only 9 percent power—an accident whose features were replicated (except for the power level) by the accident at TMI eighteen months later.[14] (In technical terms, those features were a total loss of the secondary feedwater flow, a failed PORV, a high pressurizer level and a low reactor coolant pressure, and a premature termination of HPI pumps.)[15] This event alarmed the NRC, and it was investigated by both regional inspectors and by headquarters personnel. Yet, it resulted in absolutely no agency action in terms of requiring the industry to implement new operator procedures. (For a better understanding of where these officials were placed at headquarters the reader may wish to read the Appendix, which describes the organization's structure and communication flows.) The reaction of the regional inspectors will be examined first.

The Regional Inspectors. Two NRC regional inspectors, Terry Harpster and Thomas N. Tambling, contributed to the report that was sent to headquarters. In both cases, the significance of the operator error was not recognized. Terry Harpster, who made the initial review, gave most of his attention to what he believed was his primary concern, "the plant physical problems. I would have to go back to the report and see what I said exactly about operator response. But I don't know that I felt that it was a major problem at that time."[16] He did note, however, that during the incident the operators were relying too heavily on the pressurizer level, but he never followed through on this insight.

> Obviously, at that time, I did not feel operator response was nearly as significant a short-term problem as was the physical problems presented by the transient across the fuel, the effects on the steam generator, things like this.
>
> This is the way I had prioritized the concerns at that time. I felt the rapid depressurization and cool down on the primary system was much more important.
>
> You can see from these notes and my logic at the time operator response wasn't nearly the major consideration that some of these physical problems were.[17]

Tambling, who took over from Harpster, completely missed the operators' action of turning off the HPI before the leak was found. He argued that their action was correct because they wished to avoid a dangerous condition in which the reactor core fills up with too much water. This condition, known as "going solid," makes it very difficult for the operators to control the reactor:

TAMBLING: The securing of the HPI pump...I felt that the action that he was taking at the time appeared appropriate, because he was back in his operating range on the pressurizer level. In other words, he had gotten—the pressurizer level was starting to come back up when he secured the pump. There appeared to be no problem with its securing at that time.

We all were—had the problem of associating the pressurizer going solid and the concerns you have with that problem. This is what we were concerned with at the time.

HEBDEN: So then to some extent you feel that you did address the issue securing the HPI flow?

TAMBLING: That's right. At that time I had no problem with the action that the operator had taken.[18]

Yet, it is remarkable that Tambling accepted the operators' action as proper because the fear of the reactor "going solid" assumes there is no leak. His inspection report of November 1977 shows that he knew there was a leak and that the operators turned off the HPI two minutes and nineteen seconds before the leak was found.[19] One can only conclude that he failed to grasp the significance of their behavior, as the following exchange before the president's commission suggests:

HEBDEN: Did you realize that the operators secured the high pressure injection before they identified and isolated the leak?

TAMBLING: I guess I would have to say that I realized that, but I did not apparently at that time associate it with any major problem.

HEBDEN: Did you consider that to be a proper operator action?

TAMBLING: In view of when they secured them and the way the pressurizer level was coming back at the time, I would say yes, it was, because again, unfortunately, we were using—we were relying very heavy on pressurizer level as an indication of system inventory.

HEBDEN: In hindsight, would you consider that to be a proper operator action?

TAMBLING: In hindsight, no.

HEBDEN: Why?

TAMBLING: From what I've learned from TMI-2, you have to consider if you reach saturation temperature of the coolant, you can have voiding in the system. Therefore, you should leave them on until you've identified and possibly isolated the leak.[20]

He also "saw" various indicators of leakage in the reactor core—boiling of the water in the reactor coupled with a sharply rising pressurizer level—but did not recognize their import. In short, all of this passed him by.[21]

Tambling and Harpster were not alone in their omissions. Other regional inspectors, according to Harpster, had the opportunity to review the data during a training session after the incident. Yet, no one called attention to the serious mistakes that were made during the incident:

HEBDEN: I guess that's what's causing me a lot of confusion. We've talked now about the fact you looked at this incident. You held a training session where, apparently, a large number of other inspectors looked at this particular incident.

You had two points: One, the fact that the operators secured the high pressure injection system while they still had a LOCA in process; and secondly, the fact that the pressurizer level, which was a key indication to the operators, of what was going on in the plant during a loss of coolant accident, responded in a very anomalous fashion. It went up to the high level in the pressurizer and pegged high and stayed there for a period of about 20 minutes, during which the plant was cooling down and there was a valve stuck open relieving water out of the primary with no input going in.

I don't understand why these issues didn't seem to bother anyone. They didn't seem to come up as a concern to anyone.

HARPSTER: Well, in retrospect, that's a very good question.

HEBDEN: Do you have any feel for why they weren't a concern.

HARPSTER: No. I can only speak for myself. At the time I did not see it as a generic problem. I can't go back in my memory and tell you exactly how I explained that particular part of it, although I'm sure that all of us, in retrospect, would take a hard look at what we concluded from that.

But no, I can't tell you why we didn't identify that. However, a lot of people looked at that and no one seemed to have identified it as a problem.[22]

Yet, in the late summer of 1978, one particular inspector, James S. Creswell, recognized the significance of the operators' error. He had occasion to review the analysis of the September 24 transient and recorded this discovery in his report of October 25, 1978.[23] In any event, Creswell discussed this matter with his supervisor John Streeter, who ultimately succeeded, by September 1978, in persuading the utility, Toledo Edison, to approve a modification in the procedures at Davis-Besse for operating high-pressure injection pumps. After a review by Streeter and Creswell, this new procedure stated:

Prior to securing HPI, insure that a leak does not exist in the pressurizer such as a safety valve or an electromagnetic relief valve [PORV] stuck open. A minimum decay heat flow of 2800 gpm is required prior to securing HPI. If the leak has been isolated, the HPI Pump can be shutdown after RCS pressure increases above the shutoff head pump.[24]

However, even in this review, neither Creswell nor Streeter recognized the generic implications of the problem. It evidently did not occur to them that other reactors with the same manufacturer, Babcock and Wilcox (B&W), such as TMI-2 could have benefited from the new procedure instituted at Davis-Besse.

Six months later, during the last week of March 1979, only eight days before the accident at TMI, this issue was not raised as a generic item when Creswell met with commissioners John Ahearne and Peter Bradford and their technical assistants, Mr. Hugh Thompson and Mr. George Sauter. Creswell was generally unhappy with the overall management at Davis-Besse and wanted the plant closed, "because of the weakness of the Davis-Besse management."[25] He included the operator problem that caused the September 24 transient in his list of serious plant deficiencies.[26] Apparently, Creswell cited "the operator disabling the high-pressure injection system during a LOCA."[27] Unfortunately, the accident at TMI occurred while the commission was in the process of checking on Creswell's claims.

In any event, the headquarters officials who investigated the incident at the Davis-Besse plant fared no better than their regional counterparts in recognizing the generic implications of the operators' error.

The Headquarters Officials. Because there was no response from headquarters after Creswell filed his report, one can conclude that either no one read it, or, if someone did, he saw nothing unduly worrying in the document. In fact, long before any inspection reports were filed on the Davis-Besse incident, headquarters officials were given a more direct opportunity to respond to the operator error problem when a group of Nuclear Reactor Regulation (NRR) officials was sent to the Davis-Besse plant site on a fact-finding trip shortly after the incident occurred.

On October 3, Gerald R. Mazetis, an official from the Reactor Systems Branch (RSB) in NRR, briefed officials from NRR and I&E on his fact-finding trip to the Davis-Besse plant site (several of those in attendance at the meeting, such as Leon Engle, the project manager for Davis-Besse, had gone along with him). Mazetis recognized the operators' behavior of turning off the HPI prematurely but did not view it as a "contributor to the transient."[28] Although "it wasn't obvious that they were safety problems," he thought it was "an area to pursue," because "it wasn't clear [he] had discovered anything."[29]

Indeed, in Mazetis's three part report, the operator error was mentioned only once—in the second part at the conclusion of the "event scenario."[30] It is significantly absent from the first section (a summary of the incident) and from the third section (on the "system failures"). Thus, it seems that operator error was perceived as a peripheral issue, and that hardware problems were the predominant focus of Mazetis's report. Indeed, he states that with "the 10 or 15 areas which needed follow-up, it just wasn't obvious" that the operators' behavior was a safety problem. It did bother him enough at the time, however, that he "felt somebody should look into it."[31]

Someone did. His boss, Denwood F. Ross, attended the meeting and sent a memorandum to Karl V. Seyfrit at I&E who was leading the investigation. Ross advised that certain factors should be "factored in" the investigation, one of which was that "the operator's decision to secure HPI flow based on pressurizer level should be explained."[32] Neither Seyfrit nor Tambling, the inspector to whom Seyfrit would have conveyed this memo, remembers receiving it.[33] Even if the memo had reached Tambling, it probably would not have produced any positive results at other B&W reactors, because no one apparently viewed this problem as a generic one. In other words, it did not occur to these officials that other operators working in a host of pressurized water reactors might be faced with the same kind of problem and respond in a similarly inappropriate way.

Furthermore, there were no other individuals at the October meeting who realized the generic implications of the problem. Many of them did not even recall the operators' errors being mentioned. For example, Roger J. Mattson, the deputy director of the Division of Systems Safety in which RSB belonged, recalls that the "meeting was more a hardware-oriented meeting, and I recall no discussion of operator error. There may have been some and my memory doesn't serve me."[34] In this way, he suggests that the people there viewed the accident "more from a standpoint of boiling a steam generator dry and having a rapid cooldown than from deception by the pressurizer level indicator."[35] Tom Novak, Mazetis's boss, recalls that the discussion was "more of the equipment malfunction and the end product of the event."[36]

In sum, the incident at Davis-Besse on September 24, 1977, created a substantial amount of concern among NRC officials. Yet, not one of them reached the first step of recognizing the significance of the operators' error: that it could very well lead to a core meltdown. This occurred because the NRC officials at the regional level and at headquarters were focusing on the hardware problems, which they perceived to be the most important safety item. When the operator error was finally acknowledged, it was still considered sufficiently serious for them to assess the generic implications. The regional inspector, Creswell, and the headquarters' official, Ross, concentrated on solving the problem solely at Davis-Besse.

The NRC organization had another opportunity to comprehend the generic implications of this safety problem through the early warning contained in the Michelson Report. The latter penetrated the organization at approximately the same time that the Davis-Besse event occurred in the Fall of 1977.

The Michelson Report

In early September 1977, Carlyle Michelson, a Tennessee Valley Authority engineer and a consultant to the Advisory Committee on Reactor Safeguards (ACRS), gave a copy of his handwritten report to his close friend Jesse Ebersole, who was a member of the ACRS.[37] Michelson had been studying "the problems of small breaks on pressurized water reactors" for approximately two years and had reached the conclusion, counter to the prevailing norm of the agency, that "if pipe breaks were to be experienced, they would likely be small ones, as opposed to large ones."[38] In this same report, he drew attention to the operator's role, noting that the pressurizer level could not be relied upon to give an accurate measure of the condition in the reactor.[39]

This report had important repercussions in the organization because Ebersole decided to use it himself in an upcoming license review of a plant. Ebersole passed along the report to a friend, Sanford Israel in RSB, who wrote a memo recognizing the generic implications of the problem.

First of all, in November 1977, Ebersole used the warning about the operator error in the Michelson Report to review the license application of the Pebble Springs power plant of the Portland General Electric Company. The warning was contained in the sixth of twenty-six questions that were routed through the RSB:

Does applicant know that time-dependent levels will occur in pressurizer, steam generator, and reactor vessel after a relatively small primary coolant break which causes coolant to approach or even partly uncover fuel pins [the reactor core]? What does operator do in respect to interpreting level in the pressurizer?[40]

All twenty-six questions were sent to the manufacturer of the reactor, B&W. In response, the company gave Ebersole "no direct answer."[41] In fact, he describes B&W's answer as "an inadequate answer. It was gobbledigook, I guess."[42] The sixth question, along with the others, was rerouted through RSB for the review team headed by Mazetis, the same official who had led the fact-finding team to Davis-Besse in late September. This provided yet another opportunity for the officials from RSB to be exposed to the early warning on the operator error. It is true that the RSB staff in Mazetis's section had already finished its own work on the Pebble Spring construction permit, and since Ebersole had actually formulated the questions, the review group felt less responsible in evaluating the responses.[43]

In any case, Mazetis states that he "looked through [them] quickly understanding that the responses covered a variety of expertise."[44] Question six raised the same issue that was raised (although peripherally) at the October 3 meeting, which later prompted the Ross memorandum to Seyfrit. It appears from his testimony, however, that neither the question nor the response had any impact upon him:

Q: The question I have is did the applicant anywhere in the response to question number 6 answer this question: What does operator do in respect to interpreting level in pressurizer?

MAZETIS: No.

Q: Did that fact come to your attention? Were you aware of that when you or the members of your team reviewed the question and the response from applicants?

MAZETIS: I just don't recall. It may, may not. I just don't recall. Because I don't recall, I would assume that it just didn't register at the time, but I just don't recall.

Q: Had it registered at the time, there would have been some procedure that you would have followed to insure that the applicant did respond to that portion of question 6?

MAZETIS: I would assume we would have called the applicant or requested him to revise his response.[45]

Even if Mazetis had missed the omission on question six, he had the opportunity, along with the other NRR officials such as Sanford Israel, to hear Ebersole ask the utility during the actual ACRS hearing on this very question. What transpired at the meeting is succinctly paraphrased by a Post-TMI special inquiry group:

A lengthy discussion of the various questions was conducted which included specific reference to question 6. Ebersole again raised the issue of how the operators would interpret pressurizer level. The initial argument was that this subject would be covered in their training. However, Ebersole stated that he thought this event would not be accurately simulated by the simulator used for operator training. This assertion was not challenged by any individual at the meeting. No subsequent discussion of this issue was conducted and the meeting proceeded to the next question.[46]

Ebersole seemed satisfied that he had raised this issue in front of everyone at the ACRS meeting, but the NRC staff who attended the meeting (including Mazetis and Israel) "did not recall the discussion of the operator interpretation of pressurizer level" and "their overall impression was that the ACRS discussion did not raise any concerns."[47]

Ebersole's Warning. In any event, Israel was given another opportunity to be informed of the operator error when he received the Michelson Report on October 10, just seven days after he attended the briefing on the event at Davis-Besse. The report was given to Israel informally, and Ebersole probably chose Israel because he was "one of the better known individuals involved with emergency core cooling design."[48]

Actually, according to Israel, the report had absolutely no impact on him. His explanation was that he quickly laid it aside when he realized that it did not contain the specific technical information that he was seeking.[49] However, he apparently remembered seeing a diagram of a loop seal that was several pages beyond the two places in the text where the warnings appeared.[50]

Yet, this does not explain Israel's memorandum, dated January 10, 1978, and signed by his boss, Novak. It included a specific warning that the operator can be misled by the rising pressurizer level into prematurely turning off the HPI.[51] Most important, he made a point of stating that this problem was common to a large number of plant reactors:

The uncertainty associated with unknown vessel level, the adequacy of emergency operating instructions and operator training for this event,...These very small break LOCA appear to be generic for pressurized water reactors although it may be more severe for the B&W 205-Fuel-Assembly plant because of the once-through steam generator configuration.[52]

He observed that this problem had already occurred at Davis-Besse and advised his staff to review "procedures...to ensure adequate information before the operator terminates makeup flow."[53] Although the memo was distributed to the fifteen RSB engineers whose job it was to review the design of nuclear reactors before they came on line, neither Israel nor his superior sent it beyond his own area of responsibility. It simply did not occur to them, for example, to send it over to I&E for further scrutiny regarding reactors already in operation:

HEBDEN: Is there any reason why you didn't send a copy of your memo to I&E to alert them?

ISRAEL: I don't have an answer to that. I was probably pushing our frontier a little bit ahead to try to get a better understanding of what was going on. At the time I guess my consciousness wasn't raised to the fact that, hey, there was a serious problem up there, that there was a serious problem gap in what was going on. That's where I stood at the time.[54]

The simple explanation for this evident lack of concern is that both Israel and Novak believed there was no actual safety problem at issue. In other words, they confidently assumed that the operators would not be misled by the pressurizer level. Although the memo stresses the fact that operators could be misled by the pressurizer level to turn off the HPI, Israel raised the operator error issue purely as a tactical device so that his own engineers would actually read the memo, and not just file it away. At the same time, he evidently did not believe that the operators would actually behave in the way he described.

ISRAEL: But the way the memorandum was written, my fixation was with the manometer effect [of the loop seal on the pressurizer level]. And all of our memos, we get into a routine of trying to develop interest in considering whatever these memos are, and one of those is to add safety concern. So I probably overstated the safety concern so that others would pick it up.

Basically, at the time, I am pretty sure my perception was the operator was sensitive, unless it—if I truely [sic] believed what the operator was going to do was fixate on the pressurizer level, I find it hard to believe we would have handled it that way. I hope I would not have handled it in such a casual manner.

Q: I understand that concern of yours. But once again, I am not interested in your subjective thought processes at the time of the memorandum. I am concerned with what the memorandum says.

You emphasized the safety concern in the memorandum?

ISRAEL: Yes. But the purpose of the memorandum was to get the reviewers to take a look at the situation, on plants that would be coming in at that time. We did not have any—at that time we weren't actively reviewing any B&W plants. And I didn't want to forget about it, so this was a mechanism.[55]

Q: That is the reason you expressed the safety in the memorandum?

ISRAEL: That is correct. That is the reason I added the last couple of paragraphs, was to maintain some interest on the part of the reviewers.[56]

This also explains the reason that Israel did not circulate the memo beyond his department although he acknowledged that the operator error problem was common to all B&W reactors. He evidently believed that it was not that serious because in "upset conditions," such as a stuck-open PORV, an inaccurate pressurizer level would not lead the operators astray; they would not misinterpret it, but, rather, catch the leak and bring the plant to a safe shutdown. Such a confident assumption is amazing especially because they did not even bother to check whether there were operator procedures that covered such a scenario. The fact that the operators at Davis-Besse had caught the stuck-open PORV and brought the plant to a safe shutdown may have only reinforced Israel's own convictions.[57]

Indeed, Israel believed that there were already adequate operator training procedures in this area, and his recommendation at the end of his memo that "OL [operator license] procedures should be reviewed to ensure adequate information before the operator terminates makeup flow," was an exhortation to the engineers in both sections to gain knowledge of these supposedly preexisting operator guidelines:

> The rationale there [alluding to recommendation to review operating procedures] was for the reviewers to get a better understanding of what it was the operator was trained, or by procedures were doing to bring the plant to a safe shutdown in a situation.
>
> In other words, I was trying to get more information in an area that I thought was already there. It was already my perception that the operator might have known how to bring the plant to a safe shutdown under these situations. There was nothing that we had, that we were reviewing, in this area, and I was trying to generate interest in reviewers to pick this up and go into this area a little bit.[58]

If the memo, however, had been distributed beyond RSB—to the project managers in the Division of Operating Reactors Inspection in I&E, for example—it could have had important repercussions, as Israel states:

> The importance of the memo is that if somebody [may have] started pursuing the loop seal and discussed what instructions they had on training or whatever, how they were sensitive, it may have come out as a peripheral type thing; what instructions should have been given to operators, the training they should have, turning off HPI.
>
> So in that respect, if a reviewer has carried it far enough, he may have been able to pick that up and that may have been disseminated to the operating plants, depending upon how exactly it was handled. So it may have prevented that aspect of Three Mile Island from a gross loss of inventory.[59]

Thus, although the Michelson Report generated a number of warnings that converged on officials in RSB, nothing constructive was achieved in terms of resolving the operator error problem. Only one official, Israel, recognized the generic implications of the operator error, and this was not, apparently, as a result of his exposure to the Michelson Report. He only alerted his own engineers in RSB to this problem, however, because he actually believed that the operator error simply would not happen— that the operator would realize what was happening and secure the leak. After all, this was what had happened at Davis-Besse.

Therefore, the NRC officials did not respond to the early warnings on the operator error because of a selective attention that was entirely focused on the hardware aspects of plant safety. They failed to recognize the risk associated with the operator error because of an engineering bias, which was derived from a professional insensitivity toward the role of human factors in causing plant accidents. The early warnings demonstrated that in certain plant conditions the operators could inadvertently cause a core meltdown. The NRC staff did not respond by alerting other B&W reactors because they did not believe that such a situation would actually occur. The belief was that well-designed hardware would take care of all contingencies that threatened the safety of plant operations. This regulatory approach was followed by the agency and its predecessor, the Atomic Energy Commission, until the accident at TMI.

Although such internal factors may have contributed to the inattentiveness of the NRC staff to the operator error, the role of external forces has yet to be examined. It may be, for example, that the attention of the NRC staff was focused on accommodating the promotional forces in the agency's external environment and, as a result, did not respond to the early warnings because of the concomitant cost to the industry. The next chapter addresses these considerations.

Notes

1. "Sifting through Tragedy," *Washington Post*, October 6, 1987, p. A19.
2. Ibid.
3. Charles Pruitt, "People Doing Their Best: Professional Engineers and NHTSA," *Public Administration Review*, July-August 1979, pp. 363–371.
4. Steven Kelman, "Occupational Safety and Health Administration," in *The Politics of Regulation*, ed. James Q. Wilson (New York: Basic Books Inc., 1980),

pp. 236–266.

5. Ibid., p. 252.

6. NRC's listing of I&E Bulletins, 1986, NRC Public Documents Room.

7. U.S. Congress, House Committee on Government Operations, *Nuclear Regulatory Commission: The Rogovin Report, Hearings before a Subcommittee of the House Committee on Government Operations,* 96th Cong., 2nd sess., 1980, p. 9; U.S. Congress, House Committee on Science and Technology, *Oversight, Kemeny Commission Findings, Hearings before the Subcommittee on Environment, Energy and Natural Resources of the House Committee on Science and Technology,* 96th Cong., 1st sess., 1979, pp. 6–7.

8. Interview #13, August 18, 1986.

9. *President's Commission on the Accident at Three Mile Island,* Deposition of Robert L. Tedesco, August 22, 1979, pp. 87–88.

10. *President's Commission on the Accident at Three Mile Island,* Deposition of Roger Mattson, August 6, 1979, p. 218.

11. Ibid.

12. *President's Commission on the Accident at Three Mile Island,* Deposition of Robert J. Budnitz, August 27, 1979, pp. 30–31.

13. U.S. Nuclear Regulatory Commission Special Inquiry Group, *Three Mile Island, A Report to the Commissioners and to the Public,* vol. 2, pt. 1. (Washington: GPO, 1980), p. 142.

14. Ibid. pp. 149–160.

15. Ibid.

16. *President's Commission on the Accident at Three Mile Island,* Deposition of Terry Harpster, August 30, 1979, p. 30.

17. Ibid., p. 32.

18. NRC Special Inquiry Group, Deposition of Thomas Tambling, August 22, 1979, pp.28–29.

19. Thomas Tambling, Report of Inspection of the Davis-Besse Nuclear Plant, Unit 1, November 22, 1977, NRC Inspection Report No. 50–346–763, November 22, 1977, p. 5.

20. Ibid., p. 47.

21. Ibid., pp. 28–29.

22. *President's Commission on the Accident at Three Mile Island,* Deposition of Terry Harpster, pp. 53–54.

23. J. S. Creswell, "Report of Inspection of the Davis-Besse Nuclear Plant, Unit 1, September 5–8, 1978," NRC Inspection Report No. 50/346/78–27, October 25, 1978, p. 3.

24. NRC Special Inquiry Group, p. 167.

25. NRC Special Inquiry Group, p. 171.

26. *President's Commission on the Accident at Three Mile Island*, Deposition of James S. Creswell, October 12, 1979, p. 89.

27. Ibid. However, Creswell did not mention the role of the pressurizer level in confusing the operators.

28. *President's Commission on the Accident at Three Mile Island*, Deposition of Gerald R. Mazetis, August 13, 1979, p. 27.

29. Ibid., p. 43.

30. Gerald Mazetis, NRC internal document, "Trip Report, Davis-Besse Abnormal Occurrence," September 27, 1977, p. 6.

31. *President's Commission on the Accident at Three-Mile Island*, Deposition of Gerald Mazetis, August 13, 1979, p. 43.

32. Memorandum, from Denwood F. Ross, NRC, to Karl V. Seyfrit, "Davis Besse 1 Abnormal Occurrence (9/24/77)," October 20, 1977.

33. *President's Commission on the Accident at Three-Mile Island*, Deposition of Thomas Tambling, August 22, 1979, p. 26; Ibid. Deposition of Karl Seyfrit, p. 15.

34. Ibid. Deposition of Roger J. Mattson, August 6, 1979, p. 63.

35. Ibid., p. 67.

36. Ibid. Deposition of Thomas Novak, July 31, 1979, p. 27.

37. Carlyle Michelson, "Decay Heat Removal Problems Associated with Recovery from a Very Small Break LOCA for B&W 205-Fuel-Assembly PWR," Tennessee Valley Authority, September 9, 1977, p. 9.

38. *President's Commission on the Accident at Three Mile Island*, Deposition of Carlyle Michelson, September 6, 1979, p. 9.

39. Ibid., p. 9.

40. *Staff Report to the President's Commission on the Accident at Three Mile Island: The Role of the Managing Utilities and its Suppliers*, pp. 236–266.

41. *President's Commission on the Accident at Three Mile Island*, Public Hearing, testimony given by Jesse C. Ebersole, August 22, 1979, p. 123.

42. Ibid.

43. Ibid. Deposition of Sanford Israel, July 31, 1979, p. 40.

44. Ibid. Deposition of Gerald Mazetis August 3, 1979, p. 65.

45. Ibid., p. 68.

46. NRC Special Inquiry Group, p. 163.

47. Ibid.

48. *President's Commission on the Accident at Three-Mile Island*, Deposition of Carlyle Michelson, July 26, p. 45.

49. Ibid. Deposition of Sanford Israel, pp. 27–28.

50. Ibid. Deposition of Sanford Israel, July 31, 1979, p. 4.

51. T. M. Novak, NRC, "Loop seals in Pressurizer Surge Line," Letter to RSB Members, January 10, 1978.

52. Ibid.

53. Ibid.

54. *President's Commission on the Accident at Three-Mile Island*, Deposition of Sanford Israel, July 31, 1979, p. 12.

55. Ibid. Deposition of Sanford Israel, July 26 1979, p. 7.

56. Ibid. Deposition of Sanford Israel, July 26 1979, pp. 41–42.

57. Ibid. Deposition of Sanford Israel, July 31, 1979, p. 7.

58. Ibid. Deposition of Sanford Israel, July 26, 1979, pp. 43–44.

59. Ibid. Deposition of Sanford Israel July 31, 1979, p. 11.

8

Explaining the Accident:
External Forces

Although the early warnings reached key people in the Nuclear Regulatory Commission (NRC) organization, NRC officials apparently failed to recognize the risk associated with the operator error. Evidence in an earlier chapter indicated that a professional bias might be one explanation for this phenomenon, another possible explanation lies in the agency's relations with its external environment. It is possible for example, that the behavior of the officials at the agency was also shaped by the presence of powerful promotional pressures within the White House, Congress, and the nuclear power industry. In other words, the seriousness of early warnings was not given sufficient attention because of the determination to accelerate the plant licensing process. At the same time, however, conspicuous counterpressures were attempting to sensitize the agency to safety concerns when the early warnings were penetrating the NRC organization. Some extremely vocal interest groups, for example, were deeply concerned about the radiation hazards of nuclear power plant operations. The White House and Congress, while emitting promotional cues to the NRC, also communicated safety-oriented signals. Thus, it could very well be that the safety-oriented forces were simply not sufficiently strong to counter the greater influence of the promotional forces on the agency. This chapter begins exploring the validity of this explanation by examining more closely the safety-oriented forces operating on the NRC. First, however, it is necessary to trace the source of the opposition to nuclear power that the newly created NRC inherited in 1975.

The Commercialization of Nuclear Energy

As one scholar observed, "the sobering experiences of Hiroshima and Nagasaki were grim reminders that these achievements also had unleashed a terrible new destructive force upon the world in the form of atomic weapons."[1] There were two important results from the explosion of the two atomic bombs—one was an extremely strong desire among the political and scientific communities to promote, through generous government subsidies, the rapid development of nuclear energy for peaceful civilian purposes: the other was to establish a firm government control over such development in the private sector. The Atomic Energy Act of 1946 was passed with these two goals in mind, and it established the Atomic Energy Commission (AEC)—the predecessor of the NRC—consisting of a five member executive whose accountability "would be achieved primarily by means of a Congressional Joint Committee on Atomic Energy (JCAE), which had wide-ranging watchdog and surveillance privileges over the AEC, as well as broad political powers over all aspects of nuclear energy policy in the United States."[2] Although the AEC was firmly committed to commercializing civilian nuclear power, it still devoted much of its energy to overseeing military applications of nuclear development programs.[3] In any case, with regard to the civilian aspect of its mission, the JCAE, with strong support from the AEC, the industry, and utility companies, boosted the chances of commercializing civilian nuclear energy by legislating the Price-Anderson Bill which limited "public liability claims arising from nuclear accidents" to $560 million.[4] It was passed in 1957. Later, in 1963, with strong support from the private sector, the government permitted the ownership of nuclear fuels by private industry. Such action would apparently ease the tax burden for the American citizen and lower "future power costs and price predictions."[5]

Meanwhile, in the attempt to make nuclear fission economically competitive with fossil fuels, power companies, beginning with General Electric, introduced the novel idea of offering "turnkey" contracts to the utilities whereby the plant was built for a fixed price (allowing for inflation) so that "once the plant was completed, [all one] had to do was put the key in the door and crank up the generating equipment."[6] Most important, the plan was to build larger reactors so that the subsequent economies of scale would considerably reduce the cost of building and operating the plants. Although these turnkey plants actually did not produce any cost savings, they partly contributed to the significant increase in the number of nuclear power plant orders from the utilities. As one observer, Elizabeth S. Rolph, states, "after one lean year in which utilities seemed to be taking stock, orders jumped from eight in 1965 to twenty-one in 1966 and then twenty-seven in 1967."[7] The year between 1966 and 1967 was justifiably described by another observer as "the great order surge."[8]

The new plant orders also were accompanied by an increase in the reactor size. Rolph comments that "between 1963 and 1967 the average reactor capacity jumped from 550 MWe [megawatts of electrical energy] to 850 MWe, the latter design representing almost a four-fold increase over the first commercial scale reactors that came on line just a few years earlier."[9]

The tremendous growth, however, in the size and number of nuclear power plants from the mid 1960s to the early 1970s produced an agency in turmoil—both in trying to keep pace with the increased licensing and regulatory responsibilities, and in trying to resolve internal dissension among the staff and with the ACRS over meeting new safety criteria and standards that accompanied such rapid commercialization.[10] In sum, the rapid pace of the commercialization of nuclear energy meant that the nuclear industry was ill-prepared to manage a "technology that was both complicated and, even today experimental."[11] There were no siting criteria for urban areas or for those that had seismic activity, for example, and equally serious were the findings of the 1967 Ergin Task Force (composed of the AEC's own scientists) that the reactor vessel design and the emergency core-cooling system needed improvement. Even more important, however, the lack of focus on safety aspects during these years of rapid nuclear commercialization created an agency image of incompetence and poor credibility. Such inadequacy fueled the growing public concern about the uncertainty of risks associated with nuclear energy. The agency's amended licensing and regulation procedures of the 1954 AEC Act allowed for public participation of individuals and groups (known as intervenors) through mandatory public hearings at the construction permit and the operating license stage. (This last provision was dropped in 1962 in an effort to expedite the licensing process, although an intervenor could request a hearing.) Initially, these hearings were essentially window dressing in which the role of the intervenors was largely "perfunctory."[12] The concerned citizenry, at least in these early years, were seriously handicapped by a lack of technical expertise, and the process of building the plant was well under way by the time they were afforded the opportunity to air their concerns.[13]

The new chairman of AEC, James R. Schlesinger, who was appointed in 1971, worked hard to improve the credibility of the agency by increasing the regulatory staff, by promulgating new safety standards and criteria for plant design and safety systems, and by resisting attempts from some sources to restrict public participation in the plant licensing process. It was still to no avail, as one observer states, "As orders for new power plants streamed in, the AEC still appeared in a promoter role, deeply committed to the rapid proliferation of nuclear power."[14]

By the early 1970s, there was such public skepticism about the agency's commitment and competence in safeguarding the public against radiation that Congress passed the Energy Reorganization Act of 1974, which separated the AEC's promotional from its regulatory responsibilities. The Energy Research and Development Administration was responsible for promoting nuclear energy, and the Nuclear Regulatory Commission was given the regulatory task of the old AEC.[15]

Opposition to nuclear energy and distrust of government bureaucrats persisted, however. Critics charged that the only essential change was the name of the agency because the regulatory staff remained the same:

> Although the NRC is out from under the shadow of the AEC's developmental wing, it is mostly staffed by those who staffed the AEC during its last years. It has inherited the same regulatory traditions, it faces the same technical problems and uncertainties that plagued its predecessor, and its basic approach to safety...has not changed.[16]

It was not surprising, therefore, that the NRC received the same kind of criticism of its safety record as had the AEC. The NRC inherited the legacy of public distrust and cynicism from the AEC; in addition, the mission of this regulatory body was based on the assumption that nuclear power, if properly regulated, was a viable source of energy for the nation. Thus, in the eyes of safety-oriented forces, the agency was already tagged with the proindustry label. Yet, the agency was apparently no love child of the nuclear power industry. As one former NRC commissioner stated,

> The single goal [of the agency] is to ensure adequate protection to public health and safety, but what is adequate? The industry says the NRC goes too far and [imposes regulatory] requirements that are not necessary. The antinukes say that the NRC has not gone far enough. Where is the marker?[17]

And so, in contrast to NASA, the external environment of the NRC was one of conflicting forces buffeting the agency—unsatisfied with its performance and reflecting the deepening controversy over nuclear energy in the 1970s. Let us turn to the safety-oriented pressures that were operating on the agency during the early warning period before the accident at TMI.

Safety-Oriented Pressures on the NRC

Safety-oriented forces in the White House, Congress, and the grass-roots antinuclear movement sent conspicuous signals to the NRC. The following elaborates further on this point. One must try to decide whether these signals shed sufficient light on the agency's nonresponse to the early warnings on the operator error. Let us first examine the White House role in influencing the NRC to become more safety-oriented.

The White House

Because independent regulatory commissions are "more the creatures of Congress than the Executive branch," it was probably difficult for the White House to exert the direct overt pressure on the NRC that Congress can.[18] As one agency source stated, when President Ford met with the commission at the beginning of his term, he remarked, "This is the first and last time that I see you."[19] According to one observer, Presidents have been known to speak "directly to regulators both openly and secretly".[20] Thus, theoretically, there was nothing to stop presidents Ford or Carter or, more realistically, members of their staffs, from picking up the phone and telling a commissioner of the urgent need for improving safety at nuclear power plants. As one former commissioner observed, it really depends on how much attention a president desires to give to NRC matters because these have to vie with other, more pressing issues on the president's agenda.[21]

Actually, it was through commission appointments by President Carter, whose administration from 1977 to 1980 covered much of the early warning period, that one sees strong safety-oriented signals directed at the NRC.

President Carter accepted the short-term necessity of nuclear energy, although his staff was still not convinced of its viability.[22] During Carter's 1976 election campaign, nuclear energy was presented as the energy of the last resort, and Carter made a point in his energy program of "insisting that the safety and inspection standards for reactors be strengthened."[23] Furthermore, all three of his commission appointments—Joseph Hendrie, Peter Bradford, and John Ahearne—were accepted by various environmental groups before they won the Senate vote of approval.[24] Bradford, in particular, defined himself as "the protector of the public health and safety who takes a 'let the chips fall where they may' approach to the repercussions of his decision."[25] In addition, he believed that the "NRC should be blind to any goals or quotas—set elsewhere in the government—for increasing nuclear power capacity."[26]

After these appointments, the commissioners "took the initiative and cooperated sincerely with the citizen groups who had previously been excluded."[27] Meanwhile, the staff "reluctantly began extending routine informational courtesies" to them.[28]

Congress

In contrast to NASA, the NRC's congressional committees were very active in exerting safety-oriented pressures on the agency. This could have been a result of the vigor and saliency of the anti-nuclear groups in the regulatory policy arena, or it could have been owing to the general increase in oversight activity of Congress during these years.[29] In any event, the committee staffers intelligence network that is described in an earlier chapter was certainly reluctant to raise safety concerns for congressional review. Even the Joint Committee on Atomic Energy (JCAE)—the self-proclaimed cheerleader of commercial atomic energy—was by no means timid in reviewing the agency's record on safety problems. This committee and the Senate Government Operations Committee held joint hearings on February 5, 1975, to discuss pipe cracks in twenty-three reactors.[30] Two weeks later, on February 20, when the same committee was examining a supplementary authorization request, agency officials were asked for an update on the NRC's directive to shut down these reactors within twenty-three days. Senator Montoya asked for "the result of the pipe inspections and findings of the inspection task force as to the source of the pipe cracks."[31]

In addition, there were other oversight hearings on questionable activities of the NRC regarding safety concerns. In December 1976, for example, the Senate Committee on Governmental Operations held hearings concerning the allegations that the NRC had inadequate safety standards and criteria for licensing nuclear power plants.[32] Furthermore, in 1977, when the JCAE was disbanded and its authorization and oversight responsibilities were divided among five other committees in the House and three in the Senate, the agency's Senate authorization committee (Environment and Public Works) held hearings on certain charges made by a local environmental coalition against the NRC.[33] Members of this committee's Subcommittee on Energy and the Environment listened to the allegations that the NRC staff delayed notifying the licensing board of a geological fault underlying the nuclear power plant site of North Anna, Virginia.[34] During that same year, oversight hearings were held before the House Subcommittee on Energy and the Environment of the Committee concerning Interior and Insular Affairs on the adequacy of the seismic design and earthquake resistance of Diablo Canyon nuclear power plant in California.[35]

All in all, during the agency's annual authorization hearings in the late 1970s, the message from the House and Senate committees to the NRC commissioners and senior officials was one of caution and safety in their regulatory mission. Congressman Edward Markey badgered the agency for shirking its responsibility to protect public health and safety.[36] At another time, the senate authorization committee suggested to the NRC chairman that the Advisory Committee on Reactor Safeguards should be able to pick and choose which safety issues to review so that "it could focus on real safety problems."[37]

Meanwhile, moderates, such as Chairman Morris Udall of the House Interior and Insular Affairs Committee, displayed a healthy skepticism over the "rosy picture" presented by the current NRC chairman on safety problems.[38] During the agency's authorization hearing in 1977, he frankly stated,

> I get something of the feeling that you are presenting a picture that gives a different impression than would result from a hard look at the facts. There is little indication of the kinds of things that must trouble you and your fellow Commissioners. I would be much less apprehensive if you had come to us and said: "Look, there are certain situations out there that bother us. Here they are—A, B, and C and this is why I am concerned, and we plan to do X, Y, and Z to fix things."
>
> Instead we are given the impression that there is little there that troubles you very much and that you are exceedingly confident that the difficulties will be satisfactorily resolved.
>
> First on my list is the pipe crack at Duane Arnold. I would like to know whether you consider this an isolated incident or whether this might be something common to boiling water reactors and if so, what the significance of that might be.
>
> Next is the steam generator problem. I gather that steam generators at some of the plants need to be replaced. This seems to be a costly operation that might result in substantial radiation exposures to workmen....[39]

Udall further urged the NRC to attend to safety concerns, even if these were costly, before the nation became too dependent upon nuclear energy.[40] Indeed, one committee member suggested to the NRC chairman that there should be a moratorium on plant licensing until the agency decided upon ways to handle the problem of nuclear waste.[41]

Clearly, in contrast to NASA, the NRC was receiving safety-oriented pressures from the White House and Congress. The White House used its appointment powers to steer the agency in a safety-oriented direction while the agency's congressional overseers displayed a keen interest in the NRC's attentiveness to safety concerns. Yet, perhaps the most important players among the agency's safety oriented forces were the various interest groups that believed they represented the growing antinuclear sentiment among the general public. Generally speaking, the goal of the antinuclear movement was to produce a phase-out of nuclear power plants while urging use of other, environmentally safer (and less expensive) alternatives such as solar energy. In the process of achieving this goal, the public had to be informed of the radiation hazards from nuclear power plant operations and from nuclear waste disposal. It was also incumbent upon the groups to highlight shortcomings in the NRC's regulatory policy, to alert the public to safety problems regarding power plants either under construction or already in operation, through legal, administrative, and legislative channels, and, when necessary, even to confront the authorities through direct action.

Antinuclear Interest Groups

Energetic, but loosely organized, groups at the national, state, and local levels challenged the NRC and the industry in the operation and development of nuclear power. These were largely composed of environmental preservation and conservation groups, consumer groups, and a minority of scientists and engineers.[42] Other, more marginal groups in the antinuclear movement included student organizations, labor union locals—fearful of radiological hazards from the work environment—state political party organizations, as well as farmers', womens', and religious groups.[43] Environmentalist and preservationist interests, for example, were represented by the Sierra Club, the Audubon Society, the Wilderness Society, Friends of the Earth, and the public interest law firm that is known as the Natural Resources Defense Council (NRDC); consumer interests included representation by Ralph Nader's organization, Public Interest Research Groups (PIRG)—an offshoot of Public Citizen; and a small but conspicuous group of scientists and engineers formed the Union of Concerned Scientists (UCS).

These groups generally had representatives in Washington, D.C., and very actively voiced their presence in the regulatory policymaking arena as a counterpoint to the nuclear power industry.[44] Ralph Nader's organization—PIRG—researched and published a newsletter called *Critical Mass,* which existed to expose the vested interests of the nuclear power industry and the promotional bias of the NRC.[45] Nader also encouraged networking among environmental groups on Capitol Hill—advocating the interests of safety and fighting any legislation favorable to the nuclear power industry.[46]

There were also very conspicuous environmental and regional citizen's groups, such as the New England Coalition on Nuclear Pollution (NECNP)—which later became the Clamshell Alliance in New England—and People For Proof, the Western Bloc, and the Abalone Alliance in the West that were important players in the nationwide push for a moratorium on the construction of any additional nuclear plants.[47] They also fought against the building and licensing of nuclear plants through litigation—often with the help of the Natural Resources Defense Council—and through airing their concerns in the public hearings before the licensing boards. When these avenues for protest failed, direct action through demonstrations and arrests outside nuclear plants was often the next tactic.

In 1976, for example, the NECNP (consisting of small groups of citizens and scientists from southern Vermont and western Massachusetts) concentrated on preventing construction of two large nuclear reactor units at Seabrook, New Hampshire. It received help from the Audubon Society of New Hampshire, the Forest Society of New Hampshire, and the Seacoast Anti-Pollution League while economic, engineering, and environmental experts testified against granting a construction permit.[48] When the NRC still granted a construction permit, the NECNP formed itself into the Clamshell Alliance and embarked on direct action against building the reactors. As one commentator stated, "A new stage of the antinuclear movement began, and civil disobedience became the major tactic. For the next three years, arrests and mass demonstrations were commonplace at Seabrook, although the demonstrations remained nonviolent."[49] All of this naturally garnered much media attention and only added to the adverse publicity that the NRC and the industry were receiving.

Yet, despite all the activity focused on the insensitivity of the NRC toward safety concerns, the issue is whether these forces unearthed the insensitivity of the NRC toward one particular safety issue—the operator error of misinterpreting the pressurizer level. It was the single feature that caused the incident at the Davis-Besse plant and formed a segment of the Michelson Report in the autumn of 1977, but both of these occurrences enjoyed low visibility and failed to receive public airing. This is not to say that the role of human factors in causing plant accidents did not fall within the full range of concerns that safety-oriented forces raised with the NRC.

On the contrary, certain agency insiders resigned from the NRC in 1976, listing human factors as one area of agency laxity. Robert Pollard, formerly a project manager in the division of Nuclear Reactor Regulation (NRR) and now the president of UCS, alleged that the NRC practiced a general neglect of human factors in its regulatory policy. He spoke not only of the agency's lack of concern for control room design, but also of its complete disinterest in the role of operator behavior in plant operations:

> Every technology is replete with tales of human error. Nuclear technology is no exception—except for the immeasurably greater impact that the nuclear accident, from whatever cause, has on our society.[50]

He proceeded to cite seven instances in which mistakes by the people operating the hardware had caused serious accidents at nuclear facilities, especially the Brown's Ferry fire, where human error "narrowly missed causing a melt-down of the core."[51] His conclusion was that:

> The issue is not the fact of human error—but the realization that despite nuclear reactors being designed to account for human error, innumerable events have occurred where human error has seriously jeopardized plant and public safety.[52]

It would seem, however, that the antinuclear groups and congressional overseers either were not alert to this particular human factors problem, or were simply not made aware of it through agency leaks. The latter, of course, is difficult to conceive, if we draw from the evidence in Chapter 7. In other words, had the NRC officials not recognized the risk, how could any of them have leaked the problem to the safety-oriented forces agitating outside the agency? One could argue, however, that, left to its own devices, the agency could have simply ignored the problem in an effort to get plants on line as quickly as possible. Let us explore the extent and nature of the promotional forces that were diverting the NRC from a safety-oriented focus.

The Promotional Pressures on the NRC

Labor groups fought vigorously to vote down the numerous statewide initiatives for a moratorium on the construction and operation of nuclear power plants.[53] That such labor groups joined the California organization

Citizens for Jobs and Energy indicated that they were more worried at the prospect of massive job losses than the radiological hazards of their work environment.[54]

Meanwhile, the industry and certain groups in the White House and Congress were urging the NRC to hasten the plant licensing process. The industry had heavily invested from the high capital expenditures associated with this new form of generating electricity and was still not benefiting from the anticipated low operational costs. It was obviously eager to have the plants operating as quickly as possible. In addition, for certain policymakers in the White House and Congress, the foreign oil crisis of the mid-to-late 1970s increased the attractiveness of nuclear energy as an alternative source of electricity.

The White House

Both presidents Gerald Ford and Jimmy Carter used their leadership role to send out promotional signals to the NRC. As one scholar writes, "Many individuals within the commissions may give great weight to the president's policy positions, not because he wields rewards and sanctions, but simply because he holds the office of president, and in their minds has the right to expect compliance."[55]

President Ford made it very clear in his State of the Union Speech on February 26, 1976, that he strongly advocated the development of nuclear energy.[56] Similarly, in the summer of 1977, even President Carter, whose sympathies seemed to lie more with the NRC's safety-oriented constituency, unveiled his energy plan to meet the current energy crisis.[57] One of his proposals was to speed up the licensing process. Although Carter had emphasized the importance of plant safety, in 1978 he introduced a bill "welcomed by the industry and denounced by the environmental community."[58]

Indeed, the NRC's budget experienced steady gains. From 1976 to 1978 the NRC budget recommended by OMB to Congress increased from $243 million to $290 million. Most importantly, excluding the division of Reactor Regulatory Research, the money allocated to the plant licensing division—NRR—was the second highest and between $10 million to $15 million more than the I&E division.

Congress

In Congress, the promotional forces came initially from the NRC's principal overseer, the JCAE. It constantly exhorted the agency to hasten the licensing process. They believed that the agency was simply not moving quickly enough in getting plants on line within ten to twelve years. Other countries such as France were developing their nuclear power industry much more rapidly. It was argued that this snail's pace illustrated an ineptness that was a deep embarrassment for a superpower that was assuming a leadership role in the peaceful development of atomic power. In June and November of 1975, it held hearings and considered various ways for the NRC to expedite the licensing process. The bill, which ultimately was not passed, gave the NRC the authority to grant a combined construction permit and operating licenses upon completion without additional hearings.[59]

After January 1977, the JCAE was disbanded. The jurisdiction for the NRC was divided among several House and Senate committees, and the promotional force that came from the House and Senate appropriations committees drew similar conclusions about the agency's performance. Chairman Tom Bevill of the House Subcommittee on Appropriations (Public Works) continually railed at the NRC commissioners for failing to speed up the licensing process and threatened to cut the agency's budget. Bevill likened appropriating money to the NRC to "pouring money down a rat hole" because of the agency's poor performance.[60] Former NRC Commissioner Peter Bradford described Tom Bevill as a potent force among the five commissioners calling him "sinister and heavy-handed."[61] He continues, "The Commission has to be responsive to Moffett and Udall [chairmen of the House Authorization Committees], but tends to treat them as a nuisance, while Bevill is regarded as writing scripture."[62] Another commissioner stated that, although the authorization committees could phrase their bills in strong language, it was this committee that had the money.[63]

Similarly, Bernard C. Rusche, the director of the NRC bureau that is responsible for nuclear power plant licensing, was blasted by House Appropriations Committee member, John T. Myers, for the continuing licensing delays. During the agency appropriations hearings in 1978, Myers bitterly complained about the bureau's performance: "Here are NRC's own scheduled dates. And also I find, out of all these, only one instance did, you meet that target date. This is your own schedule of dates that you set. Something is going to be changed when you are taking 30 months for licensing permits."[64]

Only seven weeks before the accident at TMI, one member of the Subcommittee voiced his dissatisfaction with the NRC plant-licensing record:

I think we are all interested in developing nuclear energy and being able to cut down on the need for oil and thus be less dependent on foreign oil. Where is the bottleneck? I know the people are discouraged from filing applications because of the long delays, the court action, the time it takes to get a license, all the various things that make it economically very difficult for people to proceed.[65]

During the same hearing, one congressman vented his frustration over the endless licensing delays, while another hinted that the NRC Chairman, Joseph Hendrie, should commend those in his organization for expediting license applications.[66]

The Nuclear Power Industry

Not unlike the House and certain committees of Congress, the industry with its vast organizational resources had exceptionally strong incentives for urging the NRC to quicken the licensing process. Throughout two decades, those companies that designed and built these plants—the architectural engineers and reactor manufacturers—participated in the rapid development of nuclear energy "from a fledgling outgrowth of the Manhattan Project to a major U.S. industry."[67] This had been accomplished at an enormous cost, owing to the soaring capital costs of building the plants, and it was the utility companies that placed the orders that bore a significant portion of the cost. As one observer remarked: "By 1971, when the nation's first 21 commercial plants were completed, their capital costs were roughly twice the original estimates. The utilities absorbed much of the pain, but G.E. and Westinghouse, who lost as much as $800 million on their turn-key deals, also suffered."[68] In this way, the utility companies, in particular, were more than anxious to recover their losses by getting their plants in operation as quickly as possible. Unfortunately, from the industry's perspective, the plant-licensing process was interminably long because of both new safety requirements in plants that were nearly completed and the obstructionist tactics of public interest groups.[69] The latter seriously disrupted plant construction and operation in the pursuit of questionable safety benefits.[70]

Moreover, the energy crisis of 1973–1974 introduced additional financial problems for the industry. It resulted in a significant reduction in electricity consumption, which, along with higher oil prices, prompted the utilities to cancel orders for twenty three nuclear plants and defer plans for 143 more.[71] Although electricity consumption once again increased in 1976 and 1977, the industry never recovered its earlier plant construction pace.[72] In these circumstances, it looked nervously askance at current investors who were already unsettled by the plant cancellations and the slow process of plant licensing.

With its two powerful trade associations—the Atomic Industrial Forum (AIF) and the Edison Electrical Institute (EEI)—the industry undoubtedly would have little difficulty in conveying its viewpoint to the agency. Theoretically, it could very easily have applied indirect pressure on the agency through approaching such powerful figures as Chairman Bevill of the NRC's House Appropriations Committee.[73] In addition, the AIF and EEI also made their presence felt more formally during congressional hearings and the public hearings in the licensing process.

The industry also had a direct and most important way of using its clout from the special relations it enjoyed with the NRC staff. These, in turn, were derived especially from the shared professional values and sympathies between NRC staff and industry personnel and nurtured by the "revolving door" of agency and industry recruitment. These "close relationships and mutually reinforcing interests" that often characterize "agencies and private organizations," have been referred to by scholars as regulatory capture.[74]

The NRC as a Captured Agency

The notion of a regulatory agency becoming captured by the industry it regulates has been criticized by some as too simplistic and by others as extremely difficult to measure.[75] Nevertheless, with the NRC there are some important indicators that suggest the industry did enjoy a greater access to the NRC staff than its opposition—the antinuclear groups. This is significant because, where access is unequal, there is probably a greater opportunity for exerting influence.[76] According to one study of the NRC's regulatory bureaucracy, both the AIF and EEI were unique in that they enjoyed "working relationships" with the NRC that were characterized by "mutual trust and sympathy."[77]

The wealth of technical expertise that the industry offered to the agency induced NRC staff members to take the initiative and turn to industry representatives for information. As one representative of the EEI stated, "That's when you know you've made it and you've entered the fraternity...when they call and ask: what would the utilities think of this?"[78] The shared professional experiences between the agency and the industry also made it easier to communicate concerns. One former NRC commissioner observed that the NRC staff simply felt more comfortable with the industry representatives than with lawyers and citizen activists.[79] In other words, it was a situation where "scientists and engineers were talking to scientists and engineers."

This commonality of viewpoints was probably reinforced by the fact that the NRC staff itself had come from a strongly promotional governmental agency. It was stated earlier that the Atomic Energy Commission (AEC) was created to promote the commercial development of nuclear energy, but it was reorganized in 1974 into two agencies to separate the roles of promoting and regulating nuclear energy. Many argued that the change in mission was largely theoretical because most of the regulatory personnel from the AEC moved over, en masse, to the NRC.

Furthermore, a Common Cause study in October 1976 showed that several of these staff personnel were recruited from the nuclear power industry. It found that 307 of the 429 senior officials at the NRC were hired from private industries with heavy involvement in the energy field. Ninety percent of these came from private enterprises holding licenses, permits, or contracts with the NRC. Seventy of these came from the five largest reactor manufacturers—Babcock & Wilcox, Combustion Engineering, Gulf Atomic, General Electric, and Westinghouse.[80]

This same study found clear evidence of high-ranking NRC personnel moving into regulated industries. Two NRC program directors took jobs with the AIF—a major industry lobbying group—while other senior officials found jobs in the industry and with law firms that represent clients before the NRC.[81]

The preceding evidence may indicate a well-established "coziness" between the NRC staff and the industry, because it demonstrates the salient indicators of agency capture that are present in the literature.[82] There are, however, some important qualifications that should be recalled. The nuclear power industry was not the only clientele group of the agency. Although public interest groups were fledgling organizations and greatly outfinanced by the nuclear power industry, they were still a force for the NRC to reckon with. In addition, when the NRC was created, the most logical place for hiring technically experienced regulators was from the industry itself and from the regulatory side of the AEC. Finally, as one scholar points out, officials joining the industry's employment rolls have motives other than "to receive payoffs for services rendered."[83] For example, they are hired by the industry simply because of their thorough working knowledge of how the agency organization operates.[84]

Nevertheless, the NRC officials did enjoy a close rapport with the industry, and with such a relationship one could argue that the NRC staff would be sympathetic toward the industry's case. They could easily have been persuaded by the industry alone, not to mention the additional pressures coming from the White House and Congress, to get on with the job of licensing plants and ignore the early warnings.

Indeed, it has been established that the early warnings did penetrate NRR, which is the actual NRC program office that grants construction permits and operator licenses to utilities. Officials that dealt with plants under construction were warned several times of the need to address the operator error. Why, therefore, did they not insist that new plants adopt corrective procedures for this problem? The powerful White House and congressional pressures operating on the agency to hasten their licensing activities may have induced the NRC staff to drop the idea of "bothering the industry on this matter." The industry itself could have gained access to these officials and stated its case against solving the problem of the operator error. It could have argued that any new regulatory requirements for fixing the problem were simply too time-consuming and would only add to the interminable licensing delays that already existed.

Similarly, the previous chapter demonstrated that the program office of I&E that deals with the safety of plants already in operation was also warned about the operator error. This was handled through various inspection reports and a joint program office briefing between NRR and I&E on the plant accident at Davis-Besse that virtually mirrored the accident at TMI. Yet, no I&E Bulletin was issued requiring the utilities, especially those that had reactors manufactured by Babcock and Wilcox (B&W), to implement the corrective operator procedure. In this case, the industry simply could have met informally with these officials, or even talked with them over the phone, and stated that the cost of implementing the corrective procedures was unconscionable. Because this safety issue had low visibility and was completely unknown to the industry's opponents, the safety problem could have been very easily and satisfactorily resolved with the NRC official during an informal meeting or a phone call.

Yet, the assumption in this argument is that the industry would have had a very strong incentive to pressure the agency to avoid licensing delays and costly changes. This is where the argument falls down. In the first place, these changes were of procedure rather than of hardware, which means that they were not time consuming. Moreover, with regard to those plants already in operation, there was no cost incentive for the industry and its like-minded regulators to ignore the early warnings, as one industry spokesman remarked, "Hardware changes are probably more costly than operator changes. With changes in the primary system, we're talking about millions of dollars."[85] Even if they had been costly changes, the NRC might very well have alerted the industry to fix them. After all, in other situations cost factors had not daunted the staff from responding to early warnings on hardware problems. The NRC's annual reports are replete with evidence that the agency responded to safety problems by alerting those power companies affected and mandating specific corrective action.[86]

Furthermore, these procedural changes were long-lasting fixes and relatively easy, so they presented no threat to the continued production of nuclear energy from plant shutdowns. Thus, it would seem that there was really very little incentive for the industry to take such pains to persuade the NRC to ignore the early warnings. Indeed, there was every reason to adopt the corrections because, in terms of cost and political payoff, it would vindicate their own and the agency's tarnished image of treating public safety as secondary to the promotion of nuclear energy.

However, the most important argument against the notion that the NRC was pressured into ignoring the early warnings is that the industry already knew about the problem and had recognized its generic implications. It was already established in the last chapter that the utility, Toledo Edison, fixed the operator error at the Davis-Besse plant in September of 1978. The industry, however, went beyond this. It had attempted to solve this problem at all nine of the B&W operating reactors. It was shown in the earlier chapter how Joseph Kelly and Bert Dunn, individuals within the B&W organization, recognized the generic implications of the operators' behavior at the Davis-Besse plant on September 27, 1977. They concluded "the incident points out that we have not supplied sufficient information to reactor operators in the area of recovery from a LOCA [a loss of coolant accident that occurs when the reactor core is leaking]."[87] They recommended that new operator guidelines be written to prevent this scenario from happening again.[88]

Kelly and Dunn devised new guidelines by and believed that they had been forwarded to those plants with B&W reactors. Thus, they had truly thought that the problem had been addressed well over a year before the accident at TMI occurred. It was only after the accident that they discovered the memo had not been sent.[89]

Unfortunately, the guidelines had not been sent because of problems internal to the organization, and not because of cost considerations. This was a story of poor communication and ineffective follow-through by the B&W management. The memo that contained the concerns and the recommendations of these engineers circulated back and forth from one manager to another through the organization. By the time the accident occurred at TMI, the new procedures had still not been distributed to the appropriate utilities.[90] Furthermore, not only had one utility fixed the problem and a reactor manufacturer attempted to fix it, but there also appeared to be no contrary evidence to suggest that the industry was pressuring the NRC staff to ignore it.

Naturally, the NRC staff, influenced by the external promotional pressures, may have anticipated the negative reaction from industry and simply decided not to "bother" the industry by requiring new procedures in all the B&W reactors. Again, for the reason already presented, requiring a fix would not have exacerbated the licensing delays, nor were the costs that burdensome. Thus, they had little apparent incentive for ignoring the early warnings. Indeed, if the NRC had fixed early warnings on hardware problems that were far more burdensome to industry, then why would it find it so difficult to fix this less burdensome safety problem?

In sum, the evidence in this chapter tends to indicate that external forces played no role in explaining this particular organizational failure. It probably was neither the promotional pressures on the agency nor the agency's anticipating the industry's reaction that influenced the NRC staff when they received the early warnings.

All three of the hypotheses have now tested for explaining the accident at TMI. Before assessing the findings, however, we will briefly examine the internal and external changes that occurred after the accident.

Notes

1. Steven L. Del Sesto, *Science, Politics, and Controversy: Civilian Nuclear Power in the United States, 1946–1974* (Boulder, Colo.: Westview Press, 1979), p. 28; see also, George T. Mazuzan and J. Samuel Walke, *Controlling the Atom: The Beginnings of Nuclear Regulation, 1946–1962* (Berkeley, Calif.: University of California Press, 1985); The American Assembly, *The Nuclear Power Controversy*, Arthur Murray, ed. (Englewood Cliffs, N.J.: Prentice-Hall, Inc., 1978).

2. Ibid. For a fascinating account of the relationship between the JCAE, the executive branch, and Congress until the early 1960s, see Harold P. Green, *Government of the Atom* (New York: Atherton Press, 1963).

3. Ibid., pp. 82–85.

4. K.S. Shrader-Frechette, *Nuclear Power and Public Policy: The Social and Ethical Problems of Fission Technology* (Boston: D. Reidel Publishing Company, 1980), p.11.

5. Steven L. Del Sesto, *Science, Politics, and Controversy*, p. 84.

6. Ibid., p. 85.

7. Elizabeth S. Rolph, *Nuclear Power and the Public Safety: A Study in Regulation*

(Lexington, Mass.: Lexington Books, DC Heath and Co.), 1979, p. 79.

8. Steven L. Del Sesto, *Science, Politics, and Controversy*, p. 91. Del Sesto takes pains to mention that turnkey plants were not the major reason for the "great order surge." He lists four further reasons on pages 91–92.

9. Ibid., p. 79.

10. Elizabeth S. Rolph, *Nuclear Power*, p. 79–99.

11. Peter Stoler, *The Decline and Fail: The Ailing Nuclear Power Industry* (New York: Dodd Mead and Co., 1985), p. 14.

12. Steven L. Del Sesto, *Science, Politics, and Controversy*, p. 133.

13. Steven Ebbin and Raphael Kasper, *Citizen Groups and the Nuclear Power Controversy: Uses of Scientific and Technological Information* (Cambridge, Mass.: MIT Press, 1974), pp. 5–6.

14. Ibid., pp. 106–107.

15. *Staff Report to the President's Commission on the Accident at Three Mile Island, The Nuclear Regulatory Commission* (Washington, D.C.: GPO, 1979), p. 1.

16. Elizabeth S. Rolph, *Nuclear Power*, p. 155.

17. Interview # 37, November 1, 1987.

18. Interview # 28, May 5, 1987.

19. Ibid.

20. Louis M. Kohlmeier, Jr., *The Regulators: Watchdog Agencies and the Public Interest* (New York: Harper and Row, 1969), pp. 37–38.

21. Interview # 37, November 1, 1987.

22. John E. Chubb, *Interest Groups and the Bureaucracy* (Stanford, Calif.: Stanford University Press, 1983), p. 119.

23. Ibid., p. 129

24. "Curious Goings-on at the Nuclear Regulatory Commission," *National Journal*, July 27, 1978, p. 841.

25. Ibid.

26. Ibid., p. 842.

27. John E. Chubb, *Interest Groups and the Bureaucracy*, p. 120.

28. Ibid.

29. Joel D. Aberbach, *Keeping a Watchful Eye: The Politics of Congressional Oversight* (Washington, D.C.:The Brookings Institution, 1990), pp. 14, 48–75.

30. U.S. Congress, Senate, Joint Committee on Atomic Energy and the Committee on Government Operations, *Joint Hearing before the Joint Committee on Atomic Energy Congress of the United States and the Committee on Government Operations, Nuclear Regulatory Commission Action Requiring Safety Inspections which Resulted in Shutdown of Certain Nuclear Power Plants*, 94th Cong., 1st sess., 1975, pp. 1–226.

31. U.S. Congress, Joint Committee on Atomic Energy, *Joint Hearing before the Joint*

152

Committee on Atomic Energy, Congress of the United States, Nuclear Regulatory Commission Fiscal Year 1975 Supplemental Authorization Request, 94th Cong., 1st sess., 1975, p. 24.

32. U.S. Congress, Senate Committee on Governmental Operations, *Hearing before the Senate Committee on Governmental Operations, Nuclear Regulatory Commission's Reactor Safety and Licensing Procedures,* 94th Congress., 2nd sess., 1976.

33. The five committees in the House were Interior and Insular Affairs, Armed Services, Energy and Commerce, Foreign Affairs, and Science and Technology; in the Senate they were Energy and Natural Resources, Armed Services, and Environment and Public Works. For a description of the congressional politics surrounding the demise of the JCAE, see J. Dicken Kirsch, "Is Doomsday at Hand for the Atomic Energy Committee?" *National Journal,* November 20, 1976, pp. 1658–1665.

34. U.S. Congress, Senate Committee on Environment and Public Works, *North Anna Nuclear Power Station, Hearings before the subcommittee on Nuclear Regulation of the Committee on Environment and Public Works,* 95th Cong., 1st sess., 1977.

35. U.S. Congress, House Committee on Interior and Insular Affairs, *Hearings before the Subcommittee on Energy and the Environment, Oversight on Diablo Canyon Nuclear Generating Plant,* 95th Cong., 1st sess., 1977.

36. U.S. Congress, House Committee on Interstate and Foreign Commerce, *Nuclear Regulatory Commission Authorization, Fiscal Year 1980, Hearings before the Subcommittee on Energy and Power of the Committee on Interstate and Foreign Commerce,* 96th Cong., 1st sess., 1979, pp. 254–255.

37. U.S. Congress, Senate Committee on Environment and Public Works, *Nuclear Regulatory Commission Authorization, Fiscal Year 1979, Hearing before the Subcommittee on Nuclear Regulation of the Committee on Environment and Public Works,* 95th Cong., 2nd sess., 1978, p. 6.

38. Morris Udall described his position on nuclear energy as follows: "My own position is one of little enthusiasm for nuclear power tempered with the recognition we will probably have to live with it for the immediate future." See U.S. Congress, House Committee of the Interior and Insular Affairs, *NRC Appropriations Authorizations, Fiscal Year 1980, Hearing before the Subcommittee on Energy and the Environment of the Committee on Interior and Insular Affairs,* 95th Cong., 1st sess., 1979, p. 1.

39. U.S. Congress, House Committee of Interior and Insular Affairs, *Nuclear Regulatory Commissions Authorizations, Fiscal Year 1980, Hearing before the Subcommittee on Energy and the Environment of the Committee on Interior and Insular Affairs,* 96th Cong., 1st sess., 1979, p. 2.

40. Ibid., p. 2.

41. Ibid., p. 27.

42. According to Kay Lehman Schlozman and John T. Tierney in their book *Organized Interests and American Democracy* (New York: Harper & Row, 1986), such groups could loosely fall within the label of public interest groups because they attempt "to take up the cudgel on behalf of what might otherwise be the underrepresented side of the question" (p. 32). See also pages 28–35.

43. See Jerome Price, *The Antinuclear Movement*, rev. ed. (Boston:Twayne Publishers, 1990), pp. 172–176.

44. Joseph P. Tomain, *Nuclear Power Transformation* (Bloomington: Indiana University Press, 1987), p. 7.

45. Jerome Price, *The Antinuclear Movement*, 47–48.

46. Ibid.

47. One hundred and fifty antinuclear groups signed a petition supporting a moratorium. Later, they placed this antinuclear moratorium before twenty-two state legislatures "either by an initiative or in the form of a bill" but were unsuccessful. See James G. Phillips, "Energy Report/1976 Is the 'Go or No Go' Year for Nuclear Industry," *National Journal*, January 24 1976, pp. 91–98.

48. Jerome Price, *The Antinuclear Movement*, p. 89.

49. Ibid., p. 88.

50. *Hearing before the Senate Committee on Government Operations Nuclear Regulatory Commission's Reactor Safety and Licensing Procedures*, p. 551.

51. Ibid., p. 552.

52. Ibid.

53. James G. Phillips, "Energy Report/1976 Is the 'Go or No Go' Year for Nuclear Power Industry", p. 94.

54. Ibid., p. 95.

55. Terry M. Moe, "Regulatory Performance and Presidential Administration," *American Journal of Political Science*, vol. 26 (May 1982), p. 201.

56. John E. Chubb, *Interest Groups and the Bureaucracy*, p. 118.

57. "Carter's Energy Plan: A Test of Leadership," *Congressional Quarterly*, April 23, 1977, pp. 727–731.

58. John E. Chubb, *Interest Groups and the Bureaucracy*, p. 119–120.

59. U.S. Congress, Senate Joint Committee on Atomic Energy, *Proposed Nuclear Power Plant Siting and Licensing Legislation, Hearing before the Joint Committee on Atomic Energy*, 94th Cong., 1st sess., 1975, pp. 25–30.

60. Susan Tolchin and Martin Tolchin, *Dismantling America* (New York: Oxford University Press, 1983), p. 209.

61. Ibid.

62. Ibid.

63. Ibid.

64. U.S. Congress, House Committee on Appropriations, *Hearing on the Appropriations Bill, 1978, before the Subcommittee of Energy and Water Development of the Committee on Appropriations,* 95th cong., 1st sess., 1977, pp. 510–511.

65. U.S. Congress, House Committee on Interstate and Foreign Commerce, *Hearings before the Subcommittee on Energy and Power of the Committee on Interstate and Foreign Commerce Fiscal Year 1980,* 96th Cong., 1st sess., 1979, p. 262.

66. Ibid.

67. Peter Stoler, *Decline and Fail,* pp. 13–14.

68. William Lanouette, "Nuclear Power in America," *The Wilson Quarterly* (Winter 1985), p. 118. Lanouette further remarked that "the big plants required so much capital (and produced so much power) that utilities often had to combine forces to purchase them."

69. Peter A. Bradford, former commissioner, U.S. Nuclear Regulatory Commission, "Nuclear Hearings, Nuclear Regulation, and Public Safety: A Reflection on the NRC's Indian Point Hearings," Speech before the Environmental Defense Fund Associates, The Sheraton Russell Hotel, New York, October 7, 1982, p. 10; see also, William Lanouette, "Nuclear Power in America," p. 118.

70. Peter Stoler, *Decline and Fail,* p. 97.

71. John E. Chubb, *Organized Interests and the Bureaucracy,* p. 96.

72. Peter Stoler, *Decline and Fail,* pp. 13–14.

73. Susan J. Tolchin and Martin Tolchin, *Dismantling America* (New York: Oxford University Press, 1983), p. 209.

74. Schlozman and Tierney, *Organized Interests,* p. 339.

75. Ibid., p. 346; See also, Paul J. Quirk, *Industry Influence in Federal Regulatory Agencies* (Princeton: Princeton University Press, 1981), chap. 1.

76. See the discussion in Schlozman and Tierney, *Organized Interests,* pp. 343–346; Paul J. Quirk, *Industry Influence,* chap. 1.

77. John E. Chubb, *Organized Interests and the Bureaucracy,* p. 107.

78. Ibid., p. 108.

79. Interview # 37 November 1,1987.

80. U.S. Congress, House Committee on Interstate and Foreign Commerce, *Authorization Fiscal Year 1979, Hearings before the Subcommittee on Energy and Power of the Committee on Interstate and Foreign Commerce,* 95th Cong., 2nd sess., 1978, p. 5. The Common Cause study was called *Serving Two Masters: A Common Cause Study of Conflict of Interests in the Executive Branch* (Washington, D.C.: Common Cause, 1976).

81. Ibid.

82. See Schlozman and Tierney, *Organized Interests,* pp. 339–343.

83. Paul J. Quirk, *Industry Influence,* p. 166.

84. Ibid.

85. Interview # 31 May, 1987.

86. The NRC's annual reports are replete with clear examples where the agency responded to safety problems by alerting those power companies affected. For example, the NRC was informed of a flaw in the "Mark I" reactor containment design. Not only were the other utilities alerted about this, but they were also required to increase their margin of safety by decreasing the stress load on the containment structure.

87. U.S. Nuclear Regulatory Commission Special Inquiry Group, *Three Mile Island, A Report to the Commissioners and to the Public* (Washington, D.C.: GPO,1980), p. 159.

88. Ibid.

89. Ibid.

90. Ibid., p. 60.

9

The Aftermath: Internal and External Changes

The accident at TMI produced a bureaucratic and political environment that was more focused on safety than it previously had been. A thorough analysis of how well the NRC responded to the ensuing multitudinous recommendations is beyond the scope of this research topic. It is certainly legitimate, however, to highlight the major changes in the organization's recovery and to consider briefly the postaccident conditions outside the NRC, especially as they relate to the agency's ability to compensate for its professional bias.

Internal Changes

It is clearly evident that the NRC made significant strides in compensating for the particular shortcomings that caused the accidents. The most significant improvement to result from TMI was probably the time and energy devoted to experimental research on small-break LOCAs and to upgrading the role of human factors in reactor safety. In the latter case, especially, this was one of the most conspicuous changes resulting from TMI.[1]

A New Emphasis on Human Factors

A new operator procedure was implemented that anticipated the scenario that caused so much confusion at TMI. Moreover, the NRC demanded significant improvements from the industry in writing, reviewing, and monitoring of plant procedures.[2] As one agency official remarked: "When you get right down to it, operator procedures are the most important since if they can't fix it nobody can."[3] In particular, the emergency procedures were significantly upgraded: a new type of "function-oriented" procedure was devised for ensuring a safe emergency shutdown of the plant even if the operator had not correctly identified the problem at hand. Thus, whatever specific procedure is chosen to correct the perceived problem, other operators focus on making sure the following actions have been completed: the reactor is shut down, the core is covered with water, the decay heat is removed, and the containment building is maintained.

In addition, the NRC demanded a general upgrade in the technical expertise of the operators and supervisors and the adoption by the industry of higher standards in both its recruitment and training programs. Major improvements in the control-room design were also required by the NRC to enhance operator performance. The NRC also made other organizational and procedural changes which, although precipitated by the accident, actually had no direct relationship to the accident.

Other Organizational and Procedural Improvements

The list of general improvements in agency regulatory policymaking was exhaustive and included such things as upgrading its inspection and enforcement program. Safety inspections were more rigorous, and there was a significant increase in both the number and the dollar amount of fines levied against the industry.[4] The NRC also expanded and accelerated its resident inspection program, increased civil penalties of rule violations, focused more attention on the quality assurance programs of the licensees, and considered additional safety features in the reactor design. Other changes for enhancing the actual management of the agency were also made on the assumption, no doubt, that such change would also contribute to the future enhancement of safety. Within the NRC, new powers were given to the commission chairman and the executive director of operations to provide some central direction to the day-to-day management of the agency and to assume control of the agency from the five highly compartmentalized bureaus.[5]

Also, efforts were made to overcome the physical isolation and improve the communications among the bureaus at headquarters by consolidating the scattered offices into fewer buildings in the suburbs around Washington, D.C. The divisions of NRR and I&E in particular were only a short distance from each other in Bethesda, Maryland. Finally, in the spring of 1988, most of the agency was housed in one building at White Flint, Maryland.

All of these changes that in one form or another were geared toward improving the safety of nuclear reactors were simultaneously symbolic of a chastened organization that was trying desperately to regain its credibility with the public. Yet, there were other changes that reflect even more directly on the organization's fundamental change in attitude toward excessive risk taking.

Resolving the Attitudinal Problem

More than anything else, the accident at TMI compelled the NRC to acknowledge that serious plant accidents can, indeed, happen. Nowhere was this more apparent than in the new regulatory rule requiring that states and localities establish emergency evacuation plans for the geographic area within a ten-mile radius of nuclear plants. This plan must be approved by the Federal Emergency Management Agency before the operation of any plant. Before the accident, the agency had not really been concerned about such things. In fact, only two days before TMI, the NRC had disagreed with a General Accounting Office (GAO) recommendation that it not grant an operating license without an adequate state and local emergency response plan. The commission argued that the GAO had exaggerated the problem and that such plans were not essential to determining whether nuclear power plants were an undue risk to public health and safety.[6]

Furthermore, the NRC set about creating new procedures so that it could predict potentially serious accidents. Before TMI, there was no systematic review of the Licensee Event Reports (LER) that were filed with the agency. The chairman of the President's Commission on TMI remarked that

> They also had no systematic way—I mean that absolutely literally and I am repeating sworn testimony by senior NRC officials—of learning from experience. It was an agency convinced that the equipment was so foolproof that nothing bad could possibly happen; they therefore honestly believed that whatever they were doing was sufficient to assure safety.[7]

Now, an Office for Analysis and Evaluation of Operational Data (AEOD) rectifies this deficiency as it analyzes long-range trends and patterns of safety problems from LERs. In this way, by early 1980, a total of fifteen people from the office were reviewing the operating experience of seventy-two reactors over the last sixteen years. Most important, this office would coordinate its efforts with similar organizations in NRR and private industry.

Similarly, new procedures were created so the agency could react quickly in an emergency. In 1978, the agency had created a well-equipped emergency response center at I&E headquarters in Bethesda called the Incident Response Center (IRC). It had made no provision, however, for filtering the mass of incoming information that poured into the IRC on the status of the TMI-2 reactor. Moreover, the actual telephone links with TMI were grossly inadequate. They were indirect—operating through the regional level. They were also insufficient because the telephone lines became so overburdened from the incoming calls that at one point headquarters lost communications with its contact man in Region 1.

After TMI, the NRC installed "dedicated" telephone lines between the IRC and the actual control rooms of all seventy-two operating reactors in the country. In addition, the NRC significantly upgraded the reporting procedures of licensees to headquarters. First of all, the licensee must immediately report an "event" at the plant to headquarters and regional management, whereas previously this had to be done merely within three days. The time permitted for a written LER, however, is still three months after the event. All incoming calls are screened by professional operations officers who are on duty twenty-four hours a day at the IRC. These are highly qualified and rigorously trained individuals whose job is to assess accurately the seriousness of the problem. If the event is serious, an emergency team headed by the commission chairman is set up and personnel are brought from various parts of the agency to assist and advise the licensees and state authorities. For less serious problems, a conference call takes place among officials in NRR, I&E, and regional management, and the appropriate action and follow-up work is undertaken. Weekly, one-hour briefing sessions with senior managers from NRR, I&E, and the AEOD discuss the week's conference calls. Thus, the offshoot of upgrading the emergency response was that the agency effectively monitors the operational status of all the power plants in the nation. Thus, it maintains a day-to-day pulse on what is happening at the nuclear power plants. One agency headquarters official remarked after TMI: "Prior to TMI, immediate action [after a plant incident] was done solely by the regional offices. [They] were the primary actors [and] a lot of things were not reported. Now we know every time a plant has 'tripped'.[8]

Actually, the industry was greatly shaken by the accident at TMI and embarked on reforms of its own. For example, it established the Institute for Nuclear Power Operations (INPO) to police the utilities' management of the nation's nuclear plants. Its aim was to establish "industry-wide benchmarks for excellence in nuclear power operation and to conduct independent evaluations to assist utilities in meeting the benchmarks."[9] In particular, one of the five divisions of INPO would review the training and education process of plant operators and certify instructors, assisting "in their training and the development of teaching skills."[10]

In sum, it is clear from even such a cursory review of the organizations that these accidents produced an extensive array of technical, regulatory, structural, and procedural changes aimed not only at fixing the immediate causes of the accidents but also at alleviating a variety of other problems highlighted as safety hazards by the various investigations. At the same time, these changes were intended to convince external forces of the agency's rededication to safety so that normal agency relations could resume. Let us explore further the nature of the NRC's relations with its external environment during the first two years after the accident.

External Changes

The safety-oriented forces did not gain significantly more momentum at the expense of the promotional forces. Actually, both sides of the nuclear energy controversy simply became more firmly entrenched in opposition and intensified their attacks on the NRC. As one observer remarked:

> One band of critics scorns the commission as too reluctant to regulate and too sympathetic to the nuclear power industry. And the industry feels that the agency, eager to prove its toughness, has imposed safety demands that have driven up the cost of atomic energy.[11]

In this way, external forces continued to reflect the ambivalent attitude of the nation toward the development of nuclear energy, and the NRC was the whipping boy.

On the one hand, the poor public standing of both the agency and the nuclear power industry only provided additional incentives to the various antinuclear groups to advocate a shutdown of all nuclear power plants and a moratorium on future nuclear plants. Organizations such as Public Citizen capitalized on the negative publicity surrounding the NRC. They reiterated various long-standing grievances with the agency, such as the unresolved safety issues that the agency was still neglecting, and even raised new ones.[12] Within Congress, the agency was subjected to rigorous scrutiny by its oversight committees as embarrassing organizational shortcomings, before and during the accident, were exposed. In an exchange with Sen. Gary Hart, during a postmortem on the causes of the accident, Chairman Joseph Hendrie felt obliged to tell the senator that the agency was "not bright enough" to see the seriousness of the situation.[13] Senator Hart continued to make things uncomfortable for Hendrie when he asked the NRC chairman whether it had occurred to the agency that the sequence of events that took place at a B&W plant might also happen at the sixty other plants made by other manufacturers. The chairman was noncommittal.[14]

On the other hand, although the accident riveted the nation's attention upon the horrifying potential of the incident, the promotional forces appeared not to miss a beat in and outside Congress: their advocacy of more plants on-line was as strident as ever. Nuclear power was presented to the public as the way to "insulate our citizens" from "future oil embargoes directed at the United States for political reasons."[15] President Carter personally led the way in a news conference only two weeks after TMI, when he said, "There is no way for us to abandon the nuclear supply of energy in our country, in the forseeable future," and he reiterated the need to hasten the licensing process.[16] (Yet, it is noteworthy that there have been no new contracts for nuclear power plants since the accident at TMI.)

Similarly, in Congress the same message comes forth during the hearings of the agency's appropriations subcommittee one year after the accident at TMI. The opening statement by Sen. Bennett Johnston was about the seriousness of the energy crisis: "Gentlemen, the energy problem we have today is much more serious than the average American dreams of. The President has said we need nuclear power; the Congress has said we need nuclear power; the Secretary of Energy has said we need nuclear power."[17]

He continued by saying that although the committee has provided the NRC with the necessary financial resources to "insure safe operation of existing nuclear power plants and to continue licensings activities without unnecessary delays," there had been no evidence of this. He proceeded to launch into the problem of these delays and the subsequent cost to the consumer.

In sum, although the agency itself was most definitely more safety-oriented, the tension between safety concerns and the drive to speed plant licensing only increased. Promotional and safety-oriented forces became even more pressing, thereby intensifying the agency's old dilemma of balancing safety with providing the nation with energy. In 1980, Chairman Hendrie articulated this difficulty: "We are continually faced with the question of how to balance a necessary and appropriate level of safety against what seems to me the obvious underlying public interest in being able to use technology and to have its benefits."[18]

Conclusion

In conclusion, the accident at TMI undoubtedly produced a greatly increased safety awareness, and effected changes that resolved certain agency and industry shortcomings prevalent before the accident. It is questionable, however, whether the NRC has been able to maintain the benefits derived from the accident as well as the same level of enthusiasm and alertness that characterized the first several years after the accident. The accident at TMI occurred more than a decade ago, and, as yet, there has been no other accident of the same magnitude in the United States. This does not necessarily mean, however, that the agency has maintained the same level of safety consciousness that existed immediately after the accident. According to one former commissioner, the attitude at the NRC was beginning to change as early as 1983: "The NRC staff certainly senses a different mood: some of the very same senior NRC officials who were outdoing each other three years ago in proposing new safety require-ments are now competing to eliminate such requirements."[19]

By 1983, citizen groups were already arguing that the proindustry sympathies of the Reagan administration had encouraged the NRC to revert to its earlier lax regulatory attitude—euphemistically described as industry self-regulation. More recently, there have been highly critical accusations from several oversight committees on the agency's coziness with the industry. At the same time, one of the agency's own commission-ers accused his colleagues of adopting a cost-benefit analysis on potential regulations that was overly weighted against safety. Also, there were allegations that the top management of the agency was trying to "muzzle" its own special investigators who probe wrongdoings at reactor plants.[20]

If citizen groups and their compatriots in Congress are correct in their assertion that an insensitivity toward safety concerns has returned to the NRC, then perhaps the reason is that the lessons from the accident were not truly assimilated in reshaping the agency's regulatory tasks. Peter Bradford, an NRC commissioner during the early 1980s, remarked:

The NRC and the utilities' commitment to learn from the [TMI] accident has waned as the memory of the accident fades. That tendency has been exac-erbated by the excessive and unfounded diversion of NRC attention and energy to the question of licensing delay.[21]

In any case, it is beyond the scope of this research enquiry to assess the long-term effects of the accident at TMI. The NRC and the nuclear power industry obviously responded to the problem once the risk associated with the operator error was recognized. The other evidence suggesting that the agency has become increasingly lax in later years needs much additional research and analysis. Nevertheless, the compelling question here is whether organizations such as NASA and the NRC can find ways to "police" themselves so that in the future they are able to perceive accurately the risks from safety problems that surface within their organizations. This issue is examined more thoroughly in the conclusion, which follows the summary of findings that appears in the next chapter.

Notes

1. Robert S. Budnitz, "The Response of the NRC to the Accident at TMI," *Annals of the New York Academy of Sciences*, vol. 365 (1981), pp. 203–209.

2. *NRC Lessons Learned Task Force: Implementation of Short Term Recommendations* (NRC Public Documents Room, Washington D.C., Appendix A, p. A42–A56; Appendix B, p. B–6.)

3. Interview # 9, August 15, 1986.

4. Joseph P. Tomain, *Nuclear Power Transformation* (Bloomington: Indiana University Press, 1987), p. 127.

5. John G. Kemeny, *Report of the Presidential Commission on the Accident at Three Mile Island, The Need for Change: The Legacy of TMI* (Washington: GPO, 1979), p. 21.

6. U.S. General Accounting Office, Report to the Congress by the Comptroller General, *The Nuclear Regulatory Commission: More Aggressive Leadership Needed*, EMD–80–15, January 15, 1980, pp. 11–12.

7. John G. Kemeny, "Political Fallout," *Society* (July-August 1981), p. 6.

8. Interview # 24, March 18, 1987.

9. U.S. Congress, House Committee on Interior and Insular Affairs, *Hearings before the Subcommittee on Energy and the Environment of the Committee on Interior and Insular Affairs, Industry's Response to the Accident at Three Mile Island*, 96th Cong., 1st sess., Sept. 21, 25, 1979, p. 65.

10. Ibid., p. 69.

11. "Nuclear Agency Seeks to Strengthen Its Role in Promoting Safety," *Wall Street Journal*, August 7, 1979, p. 1.

12. U.S. Congress, Senate Committee on Environment and Public Works, *Three Mile Island Nuclear Powerplant Accident. Hearings before the Subcommittee on Nuclear Regulation of the Committee on Environment and Public Works*, 96th Cong., 1st sess., 1979,

pp. 335–357.

13. Ibid., p. 28.

14. Ibid., pp. 25–26.

15. Senate Committee on Environment and Public Works, *Three Mile Island Nuclear Powerplant Accident*, p. 379.

16. Ibid., p. 377.

17. U.S. Congress, Senate Committee on Appropriations, *Energy and Water Development Appropriations for 1981, Hearings before a Subcommittee of the Committee on Appropriations*, 96th Cong., 2nd sess., p. 454.

18. Ibid., p. 571.

19. Robert Pollard, "At NRC It's Safety Last," *The Nation*, vol. 236 (May 7, 1983), p. 569.

20. U.S. Congress, House Committee on Interior and Insular Affairs, *NRC Coziness with Industry, An Investigative Report, Subcommittee on General Oversight and Investigations of the Committee on Interior and Insular Affairs*, 100th Cong., 1st sess., 1987, pp. 19, 36.

21. Pollard, "At NRC It's Safety Last," p. 571.

10

Summary of the Findings

An effort has been made to explore three possible explanations for these two organizational failures— that the early warnings were blocked by structural or procedural deficiencies so that key people were not alerted; that these two organizations fell prey to promotional forces in their environment that resulted in a diminished regard for safety concerns; or that, through a process of selective attention, NASA and the NRC officials downplayed them simply because they did not recognize the early warnings for what they were.

NASA

The evidence in Chapter 2 showed that the early warnings on the flawed seal joint reached key people in the shuttle organization. The shuttle managers at Marshall were continually reminded of the seal erosion when presented with the evidence after post-flight inspection of the solid rocket boosters. The upper levels of the organization were shielded from the seriousness of the seal joint problem in that, in many instances, the problem with the joint was simply not included in the Level I briefings. Moreover, on the rare occasions when the problem was raised, the information on the joint was minimal. Nevertheless, information on the detailed problems with the joint still made its way to Level 1. Irving David's memorandum in July 1985 and the subsequent headquarters briefing a month later are cases in point.

The evidence in Chapter 3 suggested that there were great pressures to keep the shuttle flying. In the first place, the agency had overcommitted itself based upon the capabilities of the shuttle program to survive in a radically altered external environment from that of the Apollo days.

NASA had achieved its mission of placing a man on the moon, and public interest seemed to have diminished. In addition, a more fiscally conservative White House and Congress were focusing upon domestic problems. In NASA's struggle to survive, the administrator, James C. Fletcher, sold the shuttle as an operational, rather than as a research and development, program. He asserted that the vehicle would pay for itself with frequent flights. Years later, when the shuttle was operational, the agency found itself striving to achieve an unrealistic flight rate with insufficient agency resources.

Meanwhile, there were too many cheerleaders in the agency's external environment and no countervailing pressures urging the agency toward increased caution on safety matters. Congress, the White House, and the media, for self-interested reasons, encouraged the agency to achieve its overly optimistic flight schedule. They were simply not sufficiently critical of NASA's ridiculous claims. At the same time, the agency's attentive interests simply assumed that the agency was adequately concerned about safety matters.

Similarly, although the Aerospace companies naturally provided a promotional push for NASA, there were no organized groups exerting a counterpressure on the agency. Thus, in the space policy arena, there was an absence of groups oriented toward safety concerns. The manned space program had always been extremely popular in the United States. In addition, the financial cost of the manned space program is shared by all American taxpayers so that their perceived self-interest is ambiguous. Therefore, people have little incentive to organize against the program. At best, people associate it with a strong sense of national pride; at worst, they are indifferent.

It was only after the Challenger accident that the seal joint problem was finally recognized and corrected. Taking its cues from its external environment, the agency also engaged in addition, extensive improvements in other safety areas, and an internal reorganization upgraded safety offices and aimed at greater centralization of the shuttle program. Meanwhile, NASA's overseers became more vigilant in scrutinizing the agency's handling of safety problems.

The NRC

With the NRC, the early warnings reached key people in the organization through formal and informal channels. An incident at the Davis-Besse plant, a reactor with the same manufacturer as the unit at TMI, and a research report called the Michelson Report, warned that under certain conditions the plant operators could inadvertently turn off vital emergency pumps for keeping the reactor core cool. This was especially serious because the operator, untrained for this scenario, misinterpreted a pressure gauge and was unaware that the reactor core was leaking. This information was conveyed to several NRC staff who were capable of alerting those plants with B&W reactors and requiring them to implement corrective operator procedures.

One memorandum was lost, which may have happened because of the poor horizontal communication flow between the headquarters program offices. They were notorious for their isolationism and rivalry. The fact that the entire headquarters was housed in various offices scattered around the Washington, D.C., area probably only exacerbated this problem. In any case, the lost memorandum was trivial because it related to the problem at only a single plant, which was corrected a year later by the efforts of James Creswell. In addition, although the NRC was hampered by the lack of any systematic evaluation of safety problems at nuclear plants, enough people within the NRC were warned, innumerable times, about the inappropriate operator behavior.

Most important, although the incident at Davis-Besse created great concern among NRC officials, very few of them actually recognized the significance of the operator's error. The regional inspectors' reports to the inspection and enforcement bureau at NRC headquarters, therefore, failed to capture completely the significance of operator error although their reports indicated that there was a leak and that the operator turned off the emergency pumps several minutes before the leak was secured. They focused on the hardware problems associated with the incident. Furthermore, most of the headquarters officials were guilty of the same omission.

The NRC officials had great difficulty in recognizing not only the operator error, but most important, its generic implications, which were crucial if the organization was to avert, or at least obviate, the accident at TMI. Creswell, for example, was persistent in having the operator problem resolved at Davis-Besse, but the evidence does not seem to indicate that he went further and raised the possible generic implications of the problem. In all fairness to Creswell, as a regional inspector his responsibilities were more narrowly focused than his superior' at headquarters. Moreover, it seems that his total energies were expended in eliciting a response from his superiors concerning poor management and operational problems at Davis-Besse. The operator problem was only one aspect of many serious shortcomings.

When Gerald Mazetis reported the Davis-Besse incident, he raised the operator error, but neither he nor his boss, Denwood Ross, apparently considered it a generic problem. Even when Sanford Israel actually recognized the generic implications in a memorandum to his subordinates in his office, he did not circulate this information to other parts of the headquarters organization where action conceivably could have been taken on plant safety in operation. He justified this omission by saying that he believed the problem was already resolved. In other words, there were procedures already in place that covered such a contingency. (If this was the case, which, by the way, he did not apparently verify, why did he write the memorandum in the first place?)

Such a lack of response from the NRC could be explained by promotional forces bearing down on the agency and pushing it away from safety considerations. Chapter 8 demonstrated that although safety-oriented groups were important in the nuclear regulatory policy arena, promotional forces enjoyed a significant edge over their opponents in influencing the NRC staff. This was particularly true of the nuclear power industry. The industry enjoyed superior organizational resources and sported strong ties with the NRC staff, which resulted from sharing the same professional and employment background. These close links were probably reinforced by the prospects of future employment in the private sector. In this way, "officials take care of clients so that clients will take care of them."[1]

With such important ways of exerting leverage, it would seem that, in all likelihood, the agency yielded to industry demands and ignored the early warnings. Although there is no direct evidence to illuminate this question, it was probably not the case. Closer scrutiny revealed that circumstantially it was probably unlikely that the industry played a significant role in pressuring the agency to ignore the early warnings on the operator error. The costs of fixing the operator error were relatively inexpensive in comparison with hardware changes. But, most important, the industry had already attempted to correct the problem conveyed by the early warnings. Toledo Edison, for example, implemented new operator procedures at its Davis-Besse plant in late 1978, while the manufacturer of the reactor—B&W—had engineers who believed that a similar remedy had already been applied to all the B&W plants in the nation. Therefore, why would an industry that was voluntarily attending to the problem pressure the NRC to ignore it?

Chapter 9 details the agency's approach in correcting its previous shortcomings in relation to human factors. Moreover, attention was given to upgrading other areas in the agency's regulatory policymaking, and important efforts were made to give the commission greater coordination and control of plant operations as well as of its own organization. In the agency's external environment, there appeared to be no noticeable change in that the external forces continued to reflect the tensions between pro-nuclear and antinuclear sentiment.

Given this summary of the case studies, the following chapter evaluates the findings to achieve a better understanding of these two outcomes. Most important, it concludes by examining the issue of avoiding these kinds of failures in the future.

Notes

1. Kay Lehman Schlozman and John T. Tierney, *Organized Interests and American Democracy* (New York: Harper & Row, 1986), p. 342.

11

Causes and Concerns

Public organizations often either fail to achieve or fall short of the expectations of political institutions and the public-at-large. Moreover, the nature of the failure can vary greatly—from the inability of the State Department to maintain security for its embassies, to the failure of the Social Security Administration to implement effectively its new supplemental security income program.[1] The Challenger accident and TMI raised questions of laxity in safety. Two organizations—one managing, and the other regulating, a complex technology—were forewarned of critical safety problems, but they ignored them.[2] The twofold goal of this chapter is that of reaching some final conclusions about the findings presented in the preceding chapters and examining the prospects for organizations such as NASA and the NRC for achieving a long-term organizational commitment to safety.

The three possible explanations that have been presented for these two organizational failures are that the warnings did not reach key people in the organization because of a blockage from organizational structures and procedures; the true risk of the early warnings was not "received" properly because of perceptual problems (in other words, there was a "gap 'twixt cup and lip"); and external forces pressured officials into sacrificing safety concerns for those of production. In the preceding chapter, which summarized the findings, it was evident that only two of the explanations seemed to illuminate these failures. Agency officials appeared to exhibit perceptual problems with the incoming information and, in the case of NASA, they were also experiencing very strong pressures from the external environment to keep the shuttle flying. These findings will be explored further beginning with NASA.

An Explanation of the Findings

The misperception of risk at NASA was one in which the shuttle managers downgraded the risk. There was clearly a "gap 'twixt cup and lip," because the shuttle managers should have rated the information they received as an unacceptable risk and grounded the shuttle. Instead, they persisted in offering various spurious rationales that justified flying the shuttle as an acceptable risk—even after a team was assigned to redesign the seal joint in the spring of 1985.[3] Drawing from Festinger's theory of cognitive dissonance, one could argue that the shuttle managers were striving to achieve a consonance between the dissonance created by two cognitive elements—the incoming warnings that something was seriously wrong with the design and the incontrovertible fact that the shuttle kept returning. The mounting evidence showed that the shuttle returned despite the serious problems and previous flirtations with catastrophe.

Thus, the excessive risk-taking at NASA was triggered by the reassuring return of the shuttle for twenty-four consecutive flights. During the actual launches, there were no visible signs of seal deterioration. The erosion was discovered only when the Solid Rocket Boosters were dismantled after each successful launch. Indeed, the successful launches themselves became one of the dubious rationales for justifying the next flight. Instead of becoming more alarmed as more flights showed evidence of erosion, the agency fell into a mindset that the seal joint was an acceptable risk, which was easy to do because there was really nothing to jolt it from the track it was on. As the former chairman of NASA's own Aerospace Safety Advisory Panel reflected:

> I have one thing about (NASA's) single-event success syndrome...It pervades the agency. 'We've done it, so it's got to be good.'...NASA was no less safety conscious from the standpoint of not wanting anything to happen, but it doesn't take long for human nature to dull its senses.[4]

If the shuttle had exhibited serious problems on the television screen during the launch—black smoke, for example, that miraculously did not develop further—the shuttle managers probably would have been jolted into reality. Moreover, embarrassing questions from the media and its congressional overseers may have prompted the organization to ground the shuttle and give the joint the serious attention it deserved. None of these situations occurred, however, to break this patterned response of downgrading the seal joint erosion.

In sum, the shuttle managers held dearly to their initial assessment that the risk associated with the seal joint was acceptable, despite new information that contradicted their initial judgment. They adopted a view of their plight that they could live with and accepted the dubious condition of the seal joint as a reasonable risk.

If downplaying the risk was owing to the safe return of the shuttle, then what role did external pressures play in this case of excessive risk-taking? The launch pressures were clearly an exacerbating factor and contributed to the shuttle managers' resistance to the notion of grounding the shuttle. The downgrading would have occurred, however, even without launch pressures and would have continued if the Challenger accident had not occurred because the crucial factor in accepting the risk associated with the flawed seal joint was the safe return of the shuttle.

Actually, no one will ever really know what the shuttle managers thought as they were informed of the erosion data and were also trying to meet an ambitious launch schedule. One can only conjecture.

In contrast to NASA, the evidence in the NRC case study suggested that there were no promotional pressures inducing the regulators to ignore the seriousness of the operator error. There were, of course, extremely strong promotional pressures in the agency's environment—pushing for such things as expediting the licensing process and relaxing regulations. In this particular instance, however, it would appear that the presence of promotional forces—especially those from the industry—apparently provided no explanation for the reason that officials failed to realize the generic significance of the operator error.

It was also evident, however, that when the officials received the information about the operator error, there was a "gap 'twixt cup and lip." This was the inability of the NRC regulators to recognize the significance of the operator error by raising it as a generic issue. Once again, it is virtually impossible to determine the thinking of these regulators when they received the information of the operator error. One can, however, infer certain things from the way they behaved. None of the NRC officials raised the issue of the operator error as a generic concern. The inspectors did not even bother to include the error in their report. They overlooked it. Headquarters officials took note of it, but their response did not indicate that they truly comprehended the operator error as a serious risk to the overall safety of the plant.

And so, it would seem that this inability to recognize the significance of the operator error was rooted in the professional training of the NRC officials. As engineers, they clung to the belief that hardware safety systems alone were sufficient to prevent serious accidents. In other words, any problem that was not hardware automatically received less consideration because they believed that any consequences of human error created in the complex interaction of a plant "event" would be automatically handled by the emergency core cooling systems. Operator behavior and operator procedures were not considered an integral part of the technological systems—that is, plant operations. Indeed, there was very little regulatory oversight of this facet of plant operations, which, in itself, indicates the degree of importance that the NRC attached to it. Thus, unlike the shuttle managers who were receiving continuous feedback of the data and then underestimating the risk, the NRC officials simply failed to realize that there was any possibility of serious risk in the first place. Moreover, this regulatory overconfidence was probably reinforced by the fact that no previous accident had spiraled out of control and shaken the regulators' confidence.

Had this situation been different, any action of the operators that jeopardized the integrity of the emergency core cooling systems would have alerted the regulators to the generic implications of the safety problem. They surely would have alerted the utilities with Babcock and Wilcox reactors (including the two at TMI), and additional procedures would have been developed.

The root cause of these two operational failures in NASA and the NRC was an organizational overconfidence in the performance of technological hardware. In both cases, the reliability factor (whether it was of an individual component or an entire technological system) was overestimated, and the risk of a serious accident with catastrophic consequences was underestimated. In one case, the agency was informed repeatedly of a critical malfunction in a hardware component; yet, it persisted in rating the risk as an acceptable one. In the other case, the human-factor component was not even recognized as a serious risk; therefore, the overall reliability of the reactor system was overestimated because not all of the pertinent factors were included. The mistake was one of omission rather than commission.

These conclusions reinforce the findings of scholars focused upon risk measurement techniques for entire technological systems.[5] Quantifying risk through fault-tree and event-tree analysis are forms of probability risk assessment (PRA), and they are an attempt to ascertain more precisely the probability of serious accidents in such systems as nuclear power plants or chemical manufacturing plants. Analysts quantify the failure rate of each component and experiment with the ways a serious chain reaction—a "pathway to disaster"—can develop from a single component failure "to a major system failure."[6] Among the difficulties of compiling such a pathway is the one where the risk analysts are "prone to omission," especially when it involves "human error or misbehavior."[7] In addition, according to the work of Amos Tversky and Daniel Kahneman, risk analysts tend to overestimate the reliability of the system as a whole, because they exhibit an initial preconception that is overly confident about the reliability of each individual component.[8] As a result, the overall chance of failure is underestimated when, in fact, "the probability of an overall failure can be high if many components are involved."[9] Thus, risk measurement techniques share the similarities with these two case studies judging the acceptability of risk—because human perception is involved, and the risk perception is susceptible to an overconfident bias.[10]

Some argue, however, that quantifying risk can, nevertheless, contribute to the goals of safety and reliability because it forces organizations to face risk-taking in a more realistic light by helping to pinpoint uncertainties.[11] Before the Challenger accident, NASA chose not to follow this method of measuring risk. Instead of using the technique of PRA that quantifies the failure rate of each component to calculate the overall failure probability of the spacecraft, it opted for a qualitative risk assessment called Failure Modes and Effects Analysis.[12] Although all of the possible failures, and the consequences of each, are listed, the probability of failure for each component is not assigned—"except perhaps to categorize it as highly unlikely, possible, or probable."[13] Thus, the overall reliability of the system cannot be calculated. The argument given is that there is just too much uncertainty to be able to quantify: "Space vehicles, even unmanned ones, confound risk analysis because of their very complexity."[14] Yet, others argue that this is all the more reason to do so.

One view is that without the quantitative risk-assessment method, "the safety and reliability staffs do not seem to command the same respect in the space program...as they do in the nuclear industry. As a result, there is a lack of clout in the decision-making process at the program level."[15] Another commentator believes that the lack of a quantitative risk assessment indicates agency disinclination to face "the inevitable uncertainty of a strict quantitative estimate of risk," because the costs (both economic and political) of such knowledge would be too high for the agency.[16] According to this source, during the Apollo program, a quantitative estimate of the overall failure of the spacecraft was completed, and engineers found that there was roughly one chance in twenty of catastrophic failure.[17] As one engineer recalled, "They showed that number to the administrator, and it was so ridiculously low that he said, 'Bury that number, disband the group, I don't want to hear about anything like this again.'"[18] A contemporary agency official, however, stated that PRA was not adopted during the Apollo moon program because it produced "mixed results."[19]

After the Challenger accident, an independent scientific panel investigating various aspects of the shuttle risk management process criticized it on several counts. One of these was for its subjectivity, while another alluded to the "fragmented picture" in the way it "looks at each component separately."[20] By using data that measured the past performance of the seal joint—including its past failures at sealing—the panel was able to calculate the failure rate of the joint; from this it was able to determine the risk of catastrophic failure. According to one source, it recommended that NASA adopt PRA, stating that if the "managers had had this analysis [PRA] before the Challenger launch, they 'probably' would have stopped the launch."[21] The same source, however, stated that the director of safety in the Office of Space Flight at NASA headquarters, believed PRA was "extraordinarily difficult to do well" because of the lack of available past data.[22] Apparently engineers "had recently tried it in limited trial runs" but "using it extensively would involve more time and money than the program has."[23]

One interesting finding from the Challenger case study is that the misperception of risk was more pronounced among the line managers who, as with the risk analyst, were not close to the actual workings of the individual component. It was the engineers—in the early testing days of the joint and on the eve of the Challenger flight—who tended to show a more realistic perception of the risk with the seal joint. They were the ones who were willing to adapt or change their initial preconception about the joint and perceive it as an unreasonable risk. Let us elaborate further on this point.

Engineers and Risk-taking

The data from both within NASA and its contractor, Morton Thiokol, clearly indicated that certain engineers at various times were the ones least inclined to take a risk with the seal joint. (There was the one exception with the NASA and Thiokol line managers—Allan McDonald—a Thiokol manager who argued against launching the Challenger in the early morning cold temperatures). During the early testing days of the shuttle, a NASA engineer told his managers that they had serious reservations about the viability of the joint.

In addition, on the night before the Challenger launch, several Thiokol engineers urged Marshall managers to delay the launch, and later dramatically exhorted their own line managers to remain with their initial unanimous recommendation to postpone the Challenger launch. Their initial rejection by the Marshall managers, on the basis that their data were not "hard" enough, did not deter at least two engineers from pushing their case very forcefully with their own company managers.[24]

This discrepancy in the attitude toward risk-taking that occurred between the engineers and the line managers is intriguing. It could be, for example, that the technical staff is allowed the luxury of making decisions solely on the basis of its technical expertise, whereas line managers are more susceptible to the political pressures that ripple through the line offices.[25] The difference between the engineers and line managers in their perception of risk was also noted by Dr. Richard P. Feynman, one of the commissioners on the Rogers Commission. During the postaccident investigation, he found that there was a significant discrepancy in the probability of mission failure through the failure of a main engine. Estimates ranged from roughly 1 in 100 to 1 in 100,000. The higher figures were from working engineers, and the very low figures from management.[26] This led Feynman to conclude that "the management of NASA exaggerates the reliability of its product to the point of fantasy."[27] One other interesting observation is that the voices of caution— the engineers—are heard only at the very beginning and, after a long hiatus, at the very end of the pre-Challenger shuttle program period. It could be that these people simply became tired of vocalizing their concerns in an unsympathetic environment and realized that there was no longer any incentive to do so. It was only when unprecedented cold temperatures prompted NASA to call a teleconference that they spoke up.

These findings raise fascinating questions and are ones that deserve thorough research. The tentative message from the NASA case study is that the technical staff can be a force for caution in the organization because it is likely to have a more accurate perception of risk than the line managers. If further evidence from future research indicates that technical staff are less susceptible to underestimating risk, then the implications for avoiding future disasters are clearly significant: with the right kind of agency leadership, the technical staff should be given sufficient incentives and opportunities to present a counterbalance to those forces in the organization that are more susceptible to underestimating the risk.

This last point raises the general concern of whether or not these kinds of organizational failures can be avoided or at least minimized over the long term.[28] Achieving this goal within NASA or the NRC would be justification enough for such a line of inquiry. However, a brief review of technological failures in the United States and abroad indicates that such occurrences of misperceived risk-taking are by no means freak incidents and are therefore added reasons for pursuing this question.

Other Cases Where Early Warnings Were Ignored

The Aberfan disaster in the United Kingdom that occurred in 1966 appears to share similarities with the NRC case. A portion of a colliery tip on a mountainside at Aberfan, South Wales, slid down into the village and engulfed the village school. One hundred and forty-four people were killed, including one hundred and fourteen schoolchildren. This catastrophe probably could have been avoided, if early warnings about the dangers of coal-tip slides had been heeded by the National Coal Board and the coal industry. Certain professional engineering groups within the British National Coal Board discounted a memorandum anticipating the tip slide and suggesting ways of stabilizing the problem.[29] Apparently, their professional antennae were tuned to only the actual safety problems within the mines rather than the potential hazards that existed outside them.

The U.S. Department of Energy's (DOE) most recent crisis with its nuclear weapons plants seemed to have fallen into the same pattern as NASA in that its officials downgraded safety problems and were also experiencing very powerful production pressures.[30] The crisis was precipitated by an accident at the Savannah River (nuclear weapons) Plant in August 1988, which resulted in the shutdown of the nation's seventeen nuclear weapons plants. When several reports describing the serious safety problems associated with running the nation's nuclear weapons plants were brought to the attention of the administrator, Dr. James B. Edwards, in 1981, he apparently discounted them as inaccurate. Meanwhile, he reduced the budget and staff for safety programs by 22 percent while resources were channeled to complete the goals for materials production. In addition, oversight on the safety aspects of the nation's nuclear weapons program was virtually nonexistent, as one observer remarked, "Congressional experts...are unable to recall the last time the Armed Services Committee, which has primary oversight of weapons production, held a hearing examining safety concerns in warhead production."[31]

Other cases of organizational failures were recently recorded by the Atomic Energy Authority in the United Kingdom (AEA).[32] From a total of ten cases, five were attributed to early warnings on safety problems. Two of these—the Challenger accident and the Aberfan disaster—are already known to us, but the AEA added two others that occurred in the United Kingdom—a chemical explosion at Nypro (U.K.) Ltd. in Flixborough in 1974. When a crack was found in one of the chemical reactor vessels, a bypass pipe was installed so the problem could be investigated without shutting down the plant. Unfortunately, the pipe was poorly designed and exhibited early warnings of safety problems, but they were not responded to, and the pipe ruptured, causing a massive explosion that killed twenty-eight people and injured thirty-six.[33] The Clapham Junction Rail Crash occurred in 1988, when a commuter train collided with a stationary train on the same track. Thirty-five people were killed, sixty-nine were seriously injured, and 415 received minor injuries.[34] The accident was owing to a signaling failure on the track; such a failure had occurred several times previously on other British Rail lines, but "the potentially disastrous consequences of such signalling failures were not fully appreciated and the lessons were not learned."[35]

These findings offer promising possibilities for further research into organizational misperception of risk, especially with regard to postaccident organizations and their ability to ward off future disasters. Yet these current case studies still afford us with an opportunity to speculate along these lines.

Learning from Failure

Chapters 5 and 9 describe the extensive measures taken by both agencies to rectify the technical and organizational deficiencies highlighted by the Challenger accident and TMI. These accidents provided NASA and the NRC the opportunity to redress the imbalance between caution and risk-taking in these organizations. In other words, the organizational cultures, meaning "the persistent and patterned way of thinking about the central tasks and human relationships," were affected so that the approach to these particular tasks—be it operating the US manned space program or regulating the nation's nuclear power plants—was redefined.[36] Only a catastrophe or near-catastrophe provided the jolt that broke through the old and characteristically obstinate preaccident "patterned way of thinking" that lead to these two organizational failures. However, our primary concern is how well the lessons from the accident can be sustained in the future history of these agencies.

Thus far, there have been no reoccurrences of a serious plant accident precipitated by human factors and on the scale of TMI, but charges of the agency's becoming overly promotional and lax on other safety issues, were just as common ten years later in the late 1980s as they were at the time of the accident.[37] Nevertheless, it could be that the agency and the industry have learned from their mistake of neglecting human factors in the pre-TMI era. It may also be owing to pure good fortune. Additional research on how well the agency has overcome this "selective attention" of its preaccident regulatory culture could offer important insights for other regulatory organizations. In addition, there may still be other safety areas that are invisible to the engineering perspective. It is noteworthy that, by 1988, a new professional group of psychologists was penetrating the ranks of the agency professionals, although this was an extremely small number in comparison with the overwhelming dominance of the engineering and science grades.[38] Broadening the professional base of its outside advisory committee—the Advisory Committee on Reactor Safeguards—or even creating a new outside oversight panel from various professions might help to minimize the likelihood of a professional "blind spot" from reoccurring at the agency. Such a panel could monitor the agency and devise a checklist of things that the agency must consider.

During the six years since the Challenger accident, NASA received mixed reviews in rectifying the imbalance between caution and risk-taking that existed before the accident. After the accident, the catchword at the agency was epitomized in the words of James F. Herrington, director of space shuttle operations at the Kennedy Space Center: "We want to fly, and we're going to fly, but we're not going to fly until we're ready, and the key word is ready."[39] Since then, there have been scores of delays for safety reasons, and an unprecedented grounding during the summer and most of the fall of 1991 of the three space shuttle fleets because of hydrogen fuel leaks in two of the older orbiters—Columbia and Atlantis.[40]

Meanwhile, the agency has been embarrassed by serious disclosures of safety laxity. The hydrogen leaks, for example, were apparently owing to poor quality control in the past. Moreover, several weeks after the shuttle was grounded, one of the primary mirrors of the recently launched $1.5 billion Hubble Space Telescope was discovered to be flawed because of a grinding error by the contractor—Perkin-Elmer Corporation. The finished products were not rechecked by NASA after they were made in the late 1970s and early 1980s.[41] Although these safety problems were the result of poor quality control in the pre-Challenger era, the agency has more recently exhibited similar laxity in monitoring its contractors.[42]

The ideal situation for this postaccident organization would be to have assimilated the lessons learned so that the number of occasions for exercising caution are minimized by producing a quality product. If the agency must accept responsibility for launch delays, let it be owing to circumstances beyond its control, such as bad weather or unforeseen and understandable glitches. In all fairness, it has been six years of tumult for NASA, with its difficult recovery period of two and one-half years (ending with the launch of the Challenger replacement, Discovery, in June 1988). In addition, the agency experienced three leadership changes in a turbulent external environment regarding the long-term goals of the agency.[43] (Admiral Richard H. Truly, who succeeded James C. Fletcher during the recovery period, resigned in March 1992 and has been replaced by Daniel S. Goldin—an aerospace executive from TRW corporation).

It may be that NASA has yet to achieve what scholars variously describe as a "sense of mission," or, "essence," or "distinctive competence" in pursuing a manned space program.[44] In other words, the lessons of the Challenger accident—of balancing caution and risk-taking—have not yet passed the litmus test of becoming both "widely shared and warmly endorsed" throughout the organization."[45] An outside task force that was examining the long-term direction of the space program seemed to suggest this when it stated:

> There is no more important task for managers at all levels of NASA and its contractors than to nurture a culture of excellence; of *complete dedication* to product quality and safety; and to total teamwork in achieving that goal...For its part, management at all levels must create a culture in which people are actively encouraged to disclose even minor anomalies, to put problems squarely on the table. Equally important, it must be clear that management and workers alike will not for a moment tolerate those who would intentionally undermine this culture of excellence, since to do so is to nourish an organizational cancer.[46] [author's emphasis]

In this way, achieving a sense of mission could not only minimize the downplaying of safety concerns, but also result in the refinement of risk assessment techniques, and the reduction of other forms of safety laxity (for example, sloppy work and poor quality control) that can cost the agency dearly. Managers oversee a work environment that encourages— through incentives and rewards—verbalizing safety concerns and communicating them to higher levels for appropriate resolution. Ideally, engineers and technicians who design, maintain, and repair the hardware and who oversee contractors would be so committed and dedicated to the idea of what the agency symbolizes that the need for outside safety watchdog groups and managerial safety incentives and rewards would be minimal.[47]

The presence of a substantial agency autonomy along with sustained charismatic leadership that has "a strong personality and a forcefully expressed vision of what the organization should be," are two fundamental prerequisites for a sense of mission to prevail.[48] These were very much in evidence when past agency executives, Gifford Pinchot of the Forest Service and J. Edgar Hoover of the FBI, for example, headed these agencies.[50]

Without this postaccident "sense of mission," eventually overconfidence could very well creep back into the organization's risk-taking—especially if the program is functioning smoothly. The telltale indications of such a contingency would be not only relative inattention to safety concerns, but also reduction in resources for ensuring its strong presence within the organization.[51]

A tendency to minimize these problems may be especially acute when a program is ostensibly running smoothly—setting the stage for another possible crisis and a series of reforms. Perhaps the Challenger accident was the beginning of a second cycle that jolted NASA from inattentiveness toward safety. The first cycle began almost twenty years earlier on January 27, 1967, when the agency was only nine years old, with the Apollo launchpad fire. NASA had been warned several times previously about the dangers of using a pure oxygen environment for the Apollo space cabin. There were earlier fires in the space cabin simulators that caused serious injuries in some cases.[52] In addition, a space study highlighted this risk three years before the Apollo fire but concluded that "the relative simplicity of such a system made it acceptable."[53] A crisis cycle proves a compelling notion when juxtaposed against the life cycle theory of organizations, and warrants further research.[54]

In any case, a catastrophe may be the only real restraint on excessive risk-taking. It may be that safety awareness in high technology organizations is driven by crisis, because it is only then that neglected safety problems are brought to the attention of the bureaucrats, their overseers, and the public.[55] In the final analysis, there really is no guarantee that postaccident remedies for these kinds of organizational failures will be effective. One can "tirelessly tinker" with various remedies both inside and outside the organization, and hope to prevent future disasters.[56] Or one can make a value judgment, decide that the costs of these tragedies are too prohibitive, and kill the programs. This may prove difficult to do because of vested interests or political expediency—the public has become so dependent on the technological benefits of modern life that people are unwilling to make the kinds of tradeoffs in the services they receive to enhance safety. If there is no fail-safe protection of the public interest against organizational failures, society has, nevertheless, made its choice; it is willing to accept the risks and the costs of controlled accidents that cause limited deaths or destruction, or both, in exchange for the benefits they enjoy from these advanced technologies.

Notes

1. James Q. Wilson, *Bureaucracy, What Government Agencies Do and Why They Do It* (New York: Basic Books, 1990), pp. 93-95; Martha Derthick, *Agency under Stress* (Washington D.C.: The Brookings Institution, 1990).

2. Thus, the safety concerns that brought on these failures were not the result of the usual "sins" against safety—cutting corners or sloppy monitoring of component manufacturing and assembly. (Although postaccident investigations by the government and the media did unearth strong evidence that NASA, in particular, was seriously negligent on both these counts.) Stuart Diamond, "NASA Wasted Billions, Federal Audits Disclose," *New York Times,* April 23, 1986, p. 1; Stuart Diamond, "NASA Cut or Delayed Safety Spending," *New York Times,* April 24, 1986, p. 1.

3. This occurred when the primary O-ring had failed in April 1985, but the secondary O-ring held. (NASA declared the secondary O-ring no longer completely reliable.)

4. "Success Relaxed NASA's Vigilance," *Washington Post,* May 26, 1986, pp. A1, A10.

5. See Baruch Fischoff, "Cost Benefit Analysis and the Art of Motorcycle Maintenance," *Policy Sciences* vol. 8 (1977), pp. 177–202.

6. Ibid., p. 181.

7. Ibid.

8. Amos Tversky and Daniel Kahneman, *Judgement under Uncertainty: Heuristics and Biases* (Cambridge: Cambridge University Press, 1988), pp. 15–16.

9. Ibid. These researchers based their conclusion on their research on gambling choices. They found that individuals will show an overconfident bias in their prediction of outcomes of compound events. Their bias is rooted in their overly optimistic belief in the success of each event so that their final estimate of success tends to be overly optimistic.

10. Literature that focuses on examining the serious difficulties of resolving the acceptable risk problem with modern technologies includes Paul Slovic, Baruch Fischhoff, and Sarah Lichtenstein, "Rating the Risks," *Environment* (April 1979); Baruch Fischhoff, Paul Slovic, and Sarah Lichtenstein, "Weighing the Risks," *Environment* (May 1979); Baruch Fischhoff, Sarah Lichtenstein, Paul Slovic, Stephen L. Derby, and Ralph L. Keeney, *Acceptable Risk* (New York: Cambridge University

Press, 1983); William W. Lowrance, *Of Acceptable Risk* (Los Altos, Calif.: William Kaufman Inc., 1976).

11. "Panel Concludes NASA's Risk Management Still 'Fragmented,'" *Washington Post*, May 19, 1988, p. A6.

12. Kevin Mckean, "They Fly in the Face of Danger," *Discover* (April 1986), pp. 49–58.

13. Ibid., p. 49.

14. Ibid., p. 51.

15. B. John Garrick, "The Approach to Risk Analysis in Three Industries: Nuclear Power, Space Systems, and the Chemical Process," in *Risk Assessment in Setting National Priorities*, James J. Bonin and Donald E. Stevenson, eds. (New York: Plenum Press, 1987), p. 71.

16. Kevin Mckean, "They Fly in the Face of Danger", p. 58.

17. Ibid., p. 48.

18. Ibid.

19. "Panel Concludes NASA's Risk Management Still 'Fragmented,'" p. A6.

20. "NASA's System for Assessing Risks is Faulted," *Boston Globe*, March 5, 1988, p. 4. The independent panel was the Committee on Shuttle Criticality Review and Hazard Analysis Audit of the National Research Council, chaired by General Alton Slay. See U.S. Congress, House Committee on Science, Space and Technology, *Space Shuttle Recovery, Hearings before the Subcommittee on Space Science Applications*, 100th. Cong., 1st. sess., vol. 1, 1987, pp. 2–9, pp. 283–288;

21. Ibid.

22. "Panel Concludes NASA's Risk Management Still Fragmented," *Washington Post*, March 5, 1988, p. A6.

23. Ibid.

24. This last point appears to contradict the statement made by James Q. Wilson in *Bureaucracy* (pp. 62–63) that the "anxieties" of the engineers "were not as forcefully expressed as they might have been because they were perceived as hunches, not facts or numbers." The two Thiokol engineers, Arnie Thompson and Roger Boisjoly, forcefully objected but ultimately gave up.

25. See, for example, Barbara S. Romcek and Melvin J. Dubnick, "Accountability in the Public Sector: Lessons from the Challenger Tragedy," *Public Administration Review*, May-June 1987, p. 231.

26. William P. Rogers, *Report of the Presidential Commission on the Space Shuttle Challenger*, vol. 2, Appendix F (Washington: GPO, 1986), p. F-1.

27. Ibid.

28. Scholars, such as Joseph G. Morone and Edward J. Woodhouse in *Averting Catastrophe* (Berkeley: University of California Press, 1986), have devised strategies for agencies to reduce the hazards of the complex technologies they regulate by improv-

ing the management of them. For example, better containment of the effects of ca-
tastrophes and "prohibiting the action or technology that poses the potential for
uncontainable catastrophe." Banning fluorocarbon aerosols is an example they give.
Other types of failures in complex organizations can result from operator errors, and
much has been written on ways to avoid or reduce them. See for example, Todd R.
LaPorte, "The United States Air Traffic System: Increasing Reliability in the Midst
of Rapid Growth," *Institute of Government Studies* (University of California at Berkeley, June 1988); "The Self-Designing High-Reliability Organization: Aircraft Carrier
Flight Operation at Sea," *Naval War College Review* (Autumn 1987), pp. 78–91.

29. Barry A. Turner, "The Organizational and Interorganizational Development
of Disasters," *Administrative Science Quarterly*, vol. 21 (September 1976), p. 385.

30. "Defects in Nuclear Arms Industry Minimized in Early Reagan Years," *New
York Times*, November 7, 1988, pp. A1, B12.

31. "After 40 Years the Silence Is Broken on a Troubled Nuclear Arms Industry,"
New York Times, October 16, 1988, p. E4.

32. A.M. Jenkins, S.A. Brearley, and P. Stephens, *Management at Risk*, (London:
SRD Association, HMSO, 1991).

33. Ibid., p. 83.

34. Ibid., p. 73.

35. Ibid., p. 74.

36. Wilson, *Bureaucracy*, p. 95. See also, Howard E. McCurdy, "NASA's Organizational Culture," *Public Administration Review*, March/April 1992, p. 189, who states
that "Within organizations, cultures are often expressed as assumptions—beliefs
that define 'the way we do things.'"

37. "Critics Say That NRC Is Watchdog Without Teeth," *Boston Globe*, February 22,
1987, pp. A1, A14; "Nuclear Agency Said to Lag in Seeking Out Crime," *New York
Times*, January 31, 1988, p. 30; "NRC Bows to Industry, Panel Says," *Washington
Post*, December 21, 1988; "Cozying up to the Industry at the NRC," *Boston Globe*,
April 13, 1987, p. 17.

38. There were 10 psychologists, 1,369 engineers, and 80 scientists in metallurgy,
meteorology, chemistry, and so forth. See *NRC Count of Employees in Select Occupational Groups*, May 5, 1988, NRC Personnel Office.

39. "Delay Is a Part of the Routine for the Shuttle's Next Flight," *New York Times*,
August 1, 1988, pp. A1, A13.

40. "NASA Casts Wary Eye on Threatening Weather," *Washington Post*, December
1, 1988, p. A3; "Shuttle Roared through Cloud Gap after a Cliffhanger Count-
down," *New York Times*, June 5, 1989, pp. A1, A17; "NASA Postpones Telescope
Launch to Replace O-Rings," *Washington Post*, January 19, 1990, p. A7; "Faulty
Power Unit Delays Space Telescope Launch," *Washington Post*, April 11, 1990, p.
A4; "NASA Schedules Shuttle Launch for April 25, a 15 Day Delay," *Washington*

Post, April 3, 1990, p. A3; "Leak Eludes Shuttle Team; Liftoff Date Uncertain," *New York Times,* May 31 1990, p. D22; "NASA Grounds Space Shuttle Fleet," *Milwaukee Journal,* June 30, 1990, pp. 1,7; "Leak Eludes Shuttle Team; Liftoff Date Uncertain," *New York Times,* June 31, 1990, p. D22; "Hopes Rise on Fixing Shuttle Leaks So the Fleet Can Resume Flying," *New York Times,* July 14, 1990, p. A7; "Shuttle Liftoff Delayed 11 Days," *New York Times,* September 7, 1990, p. A16; "Leak Scrubs Shuttle Launch Again," *Washington Post,* September 18, 1990, p. A3; "Space Shuttles' Leaks Fixed; Atlantis Launch Set Nov. 9," *Washington Post,* October 31, 1990, p. A2; "Space Shuttle Launching Delayed by Navigational Equipment Flaw," *New York Times,* 2, June, 1991; Cracks in Shuttle Door Hinges Could Delay Mission a Month," *Washington Post,* February 20, 1991, D2.

41. "NASA Was Curbed in Checking Mirror," *New York Times,* July 19, 1990, p. A15.

42. "House Panel Examines NASA's 'Midlife Crisis,'" *Washington Post,* August 2, 1991, p. A4.

43. The agency, for example, was placed on the defensive over its cost estimates of the highly controversial space station—Freedom. In addition, it was at the center of the debate over what constituted an economically and scientifically sound space policy program for the twenty-first century. See "Higher estimate for Maintaining Station in Space," *New York Times,* July 11, 1990, p. A7; "NASA Defends Space Station Cost Estimate," *Washington Post,* May 2, 1991, pl A4: "NASA Reduces Cost and Role of its Orbiting Space Station," *New York Times,* March 5, 1991, p. A1; "En Route to Space Goal, Groups Diverge," *Washington Post,* December 11, 1989, p. A13; "Ground NASA and Start Again," *New York Times,* March 16, 1992, p. A17; "Coalition of Scientists Decries Space Station," *Washington Post,* July 10, 1991, pl A3; "Space Yes, Space Station No," *New York Times,* June 6, 1991, p. A24.

44. See, for example, Wilson, *Bureaucracy,* pp. 236–266. Michael H. Halperin, *Bureaucratic Politics and Foreign Policy* (Washington: The Brookings Institution, 1974), p. 28; Philip Selznick, *Leadership in Administration* (Evanston, Ill.: Row, Peterson, 1957), pp. 42–56.

45. Wilson, *Bureaucracy,* p. 95.

46. Norman R. Augustine, chairman, *Report of the Advisory Committee on the Future of the U.S. Space Program* (Washington: GPO, December 1990), p. 16.

47. Ibid., p. 95.

48. Autonomy in this context refers to the agency's ability to protect its turf and handle the myriad political constraints on an agency executive so that "its jurisdiction is coterminous with the tasks that must be performed and the resources with which to perform them." See Wilson, *Bureaucracy,* p. 187. For further explication of the concept of agency autonomy see *Bureaucracy,* pp. 383–404; Michael H. Halperin, *Bureaucratic Politics,* pp. 51–54.

50. Wilson, *Bureaucracy*, pp. 95–99. In addition, we know from other studies of agency behavior how other, more recent studies have cited several agency executives who have made a tremendous impact on the agency they led. They exhibited uncommon personal and special leadership qualities that made the difference between success and failure. Most important, they had the ability to abandon routine behavior of the past and adopt a new set of attitudes and beliefs. See also James W. Doig and Erwin C. Hargrove, eds., *Leadership and Innovation*, abridged edition (Baltimore: The Johns Hopkins University Press, 1987), p. 10; Edgar H. Schein, *Organizational Culture and Leadership: A Dynamic View*, 1st ed. (San Francisco, Ca.: Jossey-Bass Publishers), 1985.

51. Ibid., p. 101

52. "4 Burned Critically in '62 Oxygen Chamber Test," *New York Times*, January 31, 1967, p. 24; "Space Fires Reported in Past by Scientists," *New York Times*, January 30, 1967, p. 3.

53. "4 Burned Critically in '62 in Oxygen Chamber Test."

54. Anthony Downs, *Inside Bureaucracy* (Boston: Little Brown and Company, 1966).

55. See Martin Landau, "On the Concept of a Self-Correcting Organization," *Public Administration Review*, Nov./Dec. 1973. He states that the oversight of agencies is really taken seriously by Congress only after an organizational crisis, p. 536.

56. Gilbert Y. Steiner, *The State of Welfare* (Washington, D.C.: The Brookings Institution, 1971), p. 31.

Appendix

Pre-Accident Organization and Communication Flows

NASA—The Pre-Challenger Accident Organization

NASA was created in 1958 by the National Aeronautics and Space Act to manage and promote the research and development of aeronautics and space technology. More specifically, it was mandated to manage and direct "aeronautical and space activities" and research, which involves the research and development of space and aeronautical vehicles, the operation of a space shuttle system, and other "activities as may be required for the exploration of space." In addition, the agency must engage in "scientific measurements and observations" in space.[1] Thus, although safety is an important requirement for fulfilling the agency's mission, it is not, as with the NRC, an explicit goal of the agency.

NASA is an independent agency. It does not belong to any executive department. It does, however, have important presidential constraints. For example, its single executive can be dismissed peremptorily by the president, who also appoints him. Independence does not, however, preclude NASA from the scrutiny of various oversight committees.

Figure A–1 shows the organization chart of NASA as of January 1986. The administrator is aided by a deputy administrator and a general manager. Below these are a series of staff and support offices, followed by six line offices, each of which is headed by an associate administrator: Space Science and Applications, Aeronautics and Space Technology, Space Flight, Space Station, Space Tracking and Data Systems, and Management. The associate administrators of the six program offices report to and receive overall guidance and direction from the administrator.

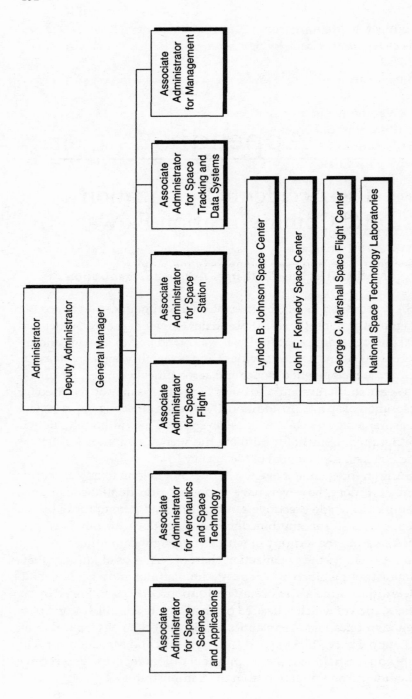

Figure A–1 Major NASA Headquarters Divisions and Space Centers, January 1986

Source: William P. Rogers, *Report of the Presidential Commission on the Space Shuttle Challenger*, 5 vols. (Washington, D.C.: GPO, 1986), 1:226.

Three of these program offices have field installations. The Office of Space Science and Applications has two (the Jet Propulsion Laboratory and the Goddard Space Flight Center); the Office of Aeronautics and Space Technology has three, all of which are research centers (Ames, Langley, and Lewis); and the Office of Space Flight has four (Lyndon B. Johnson Space Center, John F. Kennedy Space Center, George C. Marshall Space Flight Center, and National Space Technology Laboratories). This study, however, is concerned with the organization of the Office of Space Flight at the time of the Challenger accident. This office, located at headquarters and at its three space centers, forms the core of the shuttle program. Although the headquarters office oversees the program, it is at the space centers that the nuts and bolts of the program are located: Marshall Space Flight Center at Huntsville, Alabama, is responsible for the Solid Rocket Booster (SRB), external tank, and the shuttle main engine, while the Johnson Space Center at Houston, Texas, is responsible for the orbiter and the training of the astronauts. Finally, the Kennedy Space Center, at Cape Canaveral, Florida, assembles and launches the shuttle.

More precisely, the shuttle program has an elaborate management structure that consists of four levels, (see Fig. A–2). The lowest is Level 4, which consists of the private contractors who design and produce the shuttle hardware. Level 3 incorporates the various program and project managers from the three space centers. They are responsible for the development, testing, and delivery of all shuttle hardware to the launch site, that is, the orbiter, the SRB, the external tank, and the shuttle main engine.

Level 2 is located at the Johnson Space Center, which is the "lead" center for the National Space Transportation System (NSTS) of which the shuttle program is an integral part. The manager of the NSTS provides the necessary technical oversight as he coordinates and integrates the various elements of the shuttle program. Level I is the Office of the Associate Administrator for Space Flight at headquarters. It consists of the associate administrator, two deputy associates, one assistant administrator, and their staff. The associate administrator for Space Flight, who is directly accountable to the NASA administrator, oversees the budgets for the three space centers and is responsible for the overall policy and "top-level technical matters" of the shuttle program.[2]

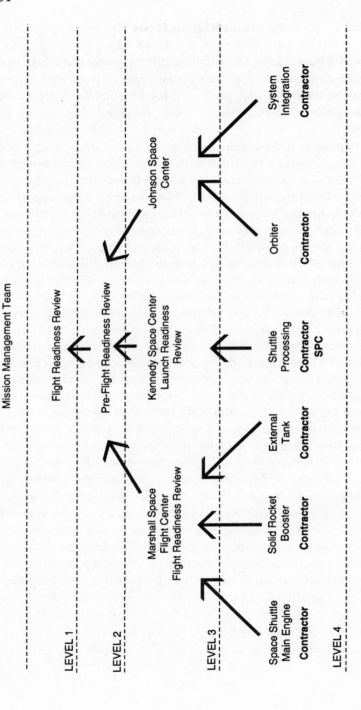

Figure A–2 Flight Readiness Reviews in Shuttle Program Management Structure, January 1986

Source: *Report of the Presidential Commission on the Space Shuttle Challenger*, 1:83.

Communication Flows

Now that the pre-Challenger organization has been described, it is easier to understand the various formal communication channels within the organization. One of the most important channels is the Flight Readiness Review (FRR) Process.

The Flight Readiness Review Process

The flight readiness of the shuttle hardware is reviewed no fewer than eight times before each shuttle launch. The FRR takes place through each of the four levels of the shuttle management structure; it is one of the major channels through which safety problems of the shuttle hardware are communicated throughout the shuttle organization.

The scope of these reviews follows a comprehensive set of prescribed guidelines from a NASA Program Directive.[3] In particular, project and program managers must follow an agenda that includes the "status and issues in areas such as...unexplained anomalies (unexplained events or unexplained departures from past experience), hardware failures, prior flight anomalies..."[4]

Figure A–3 best illustrates the elaborate reporting process that the Challenger SRBs would routinely pass through. In particular, it shows that any safety item on the Shuttle element or activity would probably surface at the first three briefings because it is there that detailed reviews are conducted by the project managers. The final briefing at Level 3 is conducted by the Center Director, and extends to all the Shuttle program elements for which the Space Center is responsible. At Marshall, for example, this would be the SRB, the external tank, and the shuttle main engine.

At Level 2, the review expands to the shuttle hardware in its entirety along with the ground support. It is at Level 1 that the actual flight readiness of the shuttle is decided in a conference chaired by the associate administrator, as "all activities/elements for safe and successful conduct of the launch, flight, and post-landing operations" are assessed.[5] Beyond this point, a mission management team, called L-1, is established to investigate any problem associated with the oversight of the final launch preparations. "It is standard practice of Level 1 and Level 2 officials to encourage the reporting of new problems or concerns that might develop in the interval between the Flight Readiness Review and the L-1 meeting and between the L-1 meeting and launch".[6]

Level	Date	Reviewing Office	Scope of Review
4	12/11/85	Thiokol Wasatch	Conducted by Thiokol Solid Rocket Motor Program managers in preparation for presentation to Marshall Space Flight Center (MSFC)
3	12/17/85	SRM Office	Conducted by Larry Ware, Mgr., of Solid Rocket Motor Program Office, MSFC. Material presented by Thiokol personnel.
3	1/3/86	SRB Project Office	Conducted by Larry Mulloy, Mgr., of the Solid Rocket Booster Project Office. This is a combined briefing on the SRM and the elements making up the booster assembly when integrated make up the Shuttle Solid Rocket Boosters.
3	1/9/86	Shuttle Projects	Conducted by Stanley Reinartz, Mgr., Space Shuttle Projects Office, MSFC. This review discusses all elements of the Shuttle managed by Marshall.
3	1/13/86	Center Board	Conducted by Dr. William Lucas, MSFC Director. Final discussion of Marshall hardware in preparation for review by the Space Transportation System Program Manager.
2	1/14/86	STS Program	Conducted by Arnold Aldrich, Space Transportation System Program Manager. First review dealing with the flight vehicle and associated ground support in its entirety.
1	1/15/86	Space Flight	Conducted by Jesse Moore, Associate Administrator for Space Flight. Remaining items that impact launch are discussed and assigned for disposition. Certificate of Flight Readiness is signed.
1	1/25/86	L–1 Review	Meeting of the Mission Management Team to receive reports on action items remaining from the Flight Readiness Review. All Action items should be closed by this time.

Figure A–3 Challenger Flight Readiness Reviews

Source: U.S. Congress, House Committee on Science and Technology, *Report of the Committee on Science and Technology: Investigation of the Challenger Accident,* H. Report 1016, 99th Cong., 2nd Sess., 1986, p. 46.

Other Communication Channels

In addition to this painstaking process, safety information can also be transmitted through the numerous ad hoc meetings and telephone conferences that characterize NASA's shuttle management.[7] There are also routine "special" meetings and telephone conversations that take place at an appointed time. For example, every day at noon Central time, a teleconference, called the Level 2 Program Requirements Change Board meeting, is held among all managers of the shuttle program elements from the three space centers. Level 1 also participates in the noon teleconference where "Program status, urgent problems, and program requirements are brought up...."[8]

Furthermore, NASA has its own organizational "watchdog" in the form of a "loose confederation" of Safety Reliability and Quality Assurance (SR&QA). They are located among the three space flight centers and the agency's private contractors and have an agencywide responsibility for flight safety. There are two SR&QA reporting devices that document and transmit safety information. The Problem Tracking Assessment System identifies and reports on hardware reliability to the NASA and contractor project managers. Also, a Critical Items List on the various shuttle elements is circulated to inform the shuttle management of just "how serious the failure of a particular item or system would be."[9]

These examples do not exhaust the list of possibilities. Undoubtedly, informal communication channels play a role in transmitting safety problems through the NASA organization. Furthermore, beyond the routine FRR's it is quite feasible for Center managers and engineers to contact Level 2 or their program office at headquarters to inform them of a particular safety problem. In addition, as with the NRC, NASA has an independent statutory watchdog advisory committee whose input on safety problems may also provide another avenue through which the agency is alerted. This is the Aerospace Safety Advisory Panel, which was created in 1968 as a result of the Apollo spacecraft fire in January 1967.

The NRC—The Pre-TMI Organization

The Nuclear Regulatory Commission (NRC) was created by the Energy Reorganization Act of 1974 as an independent regulatory commission to license and regulate nuclear facilities and the handling of nuclear materials. Actually, the Act was "coupled with the still-existing Atomic Energy Act of 1954, with all its amendments," because these functions were essentially transferred from the extinct Atomic Energy Commission (AEC).[10] The AEC was abolished by the Act and its conflicting responsibilities of promoting the growth of nuclear energy and regulating it were separated into two new agencies: the Energy Research and Development Administration and the NRC. Thus, through its powers of licensing, the agency was to "provide adequate protection to the health and safety of the public."[11]

This particular regulatory agency has a plural executive of five commissioners, which demonstrates the point of view that a diversity of perspectives is better suited for rulemaking than an organization headed by a single administrator.[12] Furthermore, the staggered terms of the five-member commission would give more continuity and expertise than a single administrator in the administration of the agency's regulatory programs.[13] There are those, however, who entirely disagree with this form. They argue that "There is little or no evidence to support these contentions which are wishful thinking, and that there are substantial advantages from having a single administrator."[14] (It is interesting to note that seven of nine health and safety regulatory agencies are under the direction of single administrators.)[15]

The NRC is also independent in the same sense that it is more removed from the president's control than other parts of his administration. Although the commissioners are appointed by him, only three can be of his own party, and none of them can be removed by the president before their term of office has ended. These arrangements are undoubtedly justified by the need to have fairness and impartiality from the Commission, especially when performing its quasi-judicial role.[16] (Yet, the NRC is still not so autonomous that it can escape Congress's own oversight powers.)

Figure A-4 shows the NRC organization at the time of the accident at Three Mile Island. The commission heads the organization and has been described as a collegial executive in which the chairman is simply the "nominal" chief executive.[17] The commission sets overall policy for the agency, is the final "appeal court" on licensing questions, supervises its own staff, directs emergency response activities, and administers funds.[18]

The commission is flanked by various commission staff offices and advisory and licensing panels, but below it is the Office of the Executive Director for Operations (EDO). He "coordinates the development of policy options for the Commission" and also coordinates and directs the day-to-day running of the agency among five program offices and support staff.[19]

The five program offices are headed by program directors appointed by the commission and constitute the "thick" middle of the organizational hierarchy. Each office or division is of a substantial size, broken

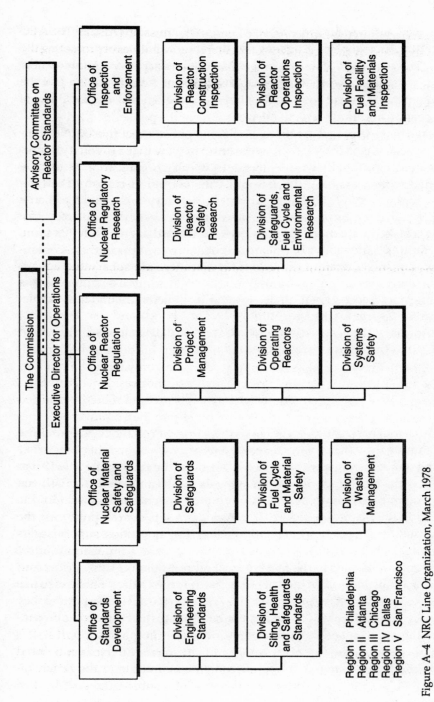

Figure A-4 NRC Line Organization, March 1978

Source: U.S. Nuclear Regulatory Commission, 1975 Annual Report (Washington: GPO, April 1976).

down into its own divisions, subdivisions, and branches or sections; taken together, they depict the agency's wide range of regulatory responsibilities. They are the Office of Nuclear Material Safety and Safeguards, the Office of Nuclear Regulatory Research, the Office of Standards and Development, the Office of Nuclear Reactor Regulation (NRR) and the Office of Inspection and Enforcement (I&E).[20]

Two of these program offices—NRR and I&E—are of special relevance to the accident at TMI. If there were any forewarnings of TMI, these two bureaus undoubtedly would have been involved. They are directly concerned with overseeing the safe construction and operation of nuclear power plants. While NRR grants the construction permits and the license applications for the operation of nuclear power plants, however, it is I&E that is tasked with monitoring the safe operation of nuclear power plant operations.[21] Indeed, I&E's major responsibility was to inspect the construction and operation of nuclear facilities for safety violations of the license provisions and commission regulations.[22] It accomplished this through its five regional offices located in Philadelphia, Pennsylvania; Atlanta, Georgia; Chicago, Illinois; Dallas, Texas; and San Francisco, California. If the licensee is found to be remiss in its responsibilities, then I&E takes the appropriate enforcement action.[23]

Communication Flows

This brief description of the NRC provides a convenient framework for examining the various ways in which safety problems would be reported to the senior management at the NRC headquarters during the late 1970s. Two of the most important ways were through channels in the I&E enforcement program office and through the "open door policy." I&E Inspection Reporting Procedures The major headquarters source of safety information at operating plants is through the inspection reports of the regional I&E inspectors. These are the linchpin in this communication flow and are located at the five regional offices. Some of these inspectors were actually located on the operating plant site with the phasing in of the new resident inspector program in 1977. Although the I&E inspectors rely heavily on the licensee "to report, analyze and correct safety problems," they themselves have important responsibilities in this respect.[24]

For example, the inspector can report the licensee's performance by telephone or by memo to the appropriate I&E official at headquarters. It is through written reports from routine and reactive inspections, however, that safety information is documented and transmitted to headquarters at I&E.

Routine inspections of the power plant are conducted periodically,

> Throughout preconstruction activities, construction, preoperational testing and startup, operation and decommissioning of nuclear power plants....[During a routine inspection,] an inspector determines the effectiveness of quality assurance systems, 'by observing the work in progress, checking records, interviewing people, and where appropriate, making direct measurements.'[25]

Reactive inspections, however, are prompted by notifications of a safety problem at the plant from any number of people—the licensee, a vendor, a licensee employee, and even members of the public.[26]

During 1977, the licensees alone submitted 3,000 reports to the NRC describing various occurrences at powerplants.[27] They may also be induced by an "event of safety significance" at the plant such as excessive releases of radiation or overexposure to radiation.[28] In this case, immediate or twenty-four hour reports are required. The plant personnel first telephone the nearest of the NRC's regional inspection and enforcement offices "which take action on a case-by-case basis in accordance with established response procedures."[29] A detailed written follow-up report must be submitted within fourteen days. In the case of a less serious safety problem such as equipment failures during tests or the licensee failure to perform required surveillance, a time period of thirty days is allowed.[30]

The Licensee Event Report (LER) describes the event and the corrective action taken or the proposed corrective action. The inspector oversees the whole process and makes his own evaluations of the safety problem. If necessary, he prescribes his own course of action for the licensee to achieve the necessary compliance.[31] A General Accounting Office report gives a detailed description of this function:

At the NRC regional offices, inspectors are required to assess each licensee event report for (1) the appropriateness of licensee corrective action and the need for a follow-up inspection effort; (2) the event's generic importance to other components, systems, or activities within the powerplant or at other powerplants in the region; and (3) possible reporting to the Congress as an abnormal occurrence. Staffs of the three NRC headquarters offices assess each report for its safety importance at the powerplant, its applicability to all other power plants, and its potential for reporting as an abnormal occurrence. An important part of this assessment is the identification of potential safety-related problems needing further evaluation and perhaps action in the form of new regulatory requirements.[32]

There was no provision at the time of Three Mile Island for the systematic evaluation of the operating data from these LER's and the inspection reports. Copies of these reports, however, were sent from the regional offices to a distribution office at the NRC headquarters, established in 1978, which routed them to the appropriate staff office, the Office of Management and Program Analysis.[33]

Because program directors may communicate directly with the individual commissioners, then theoretically the I&E or NRR director could take any problem that had surfaced from an LER or an inspection report to the commission itself. In reality, the NRC ex parte rules apparently dampened any inclination by the directors and their staff to communicate with the commission for fear that the issue might appear before them in their adjudicatory role.[34] This agency rule strictly limits communication between the commissioners and the NRC staff, license applicants, or other parties on any substantive issues in active public hearings because the commissioners can, though rarely do, exercise the right to review appeal board decisions, and they must remain strictly impartial.[35]

The "Open Door Policy"

The "Open Door Policy," is the second major channel for communicating safety problems through the provision for whistle-blowers.[36] It encourages all employees of the agency to air their complaints "regarding NRC operations and activities," with the commission itself.[37] This provision is probably by far one of the most expeditious ways of transmitting information because it bypasses the middle level of the organization, thereby reducing the likelihood of the blockage or filtering of information. Nevertheless, it is probably rarely used because of the employee's fear of recrimination by his superiors. Indeed, during the year before TMI, one of the commissioners was most concerned about making the "open door" policy more of a reality "both in concept and in practice."[38]

Other Communication Channels

This list by no means exhausts all of the possibilities for information on safety problems to penetrate the organization. One must not, for example, discount the importance of informal communication channels in which friends can pass along information from one part of the agency to another or even from one agency to another. One must also acknowledge the presence of an independent "safety watchdog," the Advisory Committee on Reactor Safety (ACRS). It is described as "a statutory committee of 15 scientists and engineers advising the Commission on safety aspects of proposed and existing nuclear facilities, and on the adequacy of proposed reactor safety standards and performing such other duties as the Commission may request."[39] Information about safety problems could quite feasibly emanate from this committee and flow in any number of directions to the commission, the Atomic Safety Licensing Boards, and the bureaus of NRR and I&E.

Notes

1. National Aeronautics and Space Act of 1958, Public Law 85-568, pp. 4-5.

2. William Rogers, *Report of the Presidential Commission on the Space Shuttle Challenger* (Washington: GPO, 1986), p. 102.

3. U.S. Congress House, Committee on Science and Technology, *Report of the Committee on Science and Technology: Investigation of the Challenger Accident,* H. Report 1016, 99th Cong., 2nd sess., 1986, pp. 207–208.

4. Ibid. p. 208.

5. Ibid. p. 207.

6. *Rogers Commission Report,* 83.

7. *Investigation of the Challenger Accident,* p. 171.

8. Ibid. p. 171.

9. *Rogers Commission Report,* 152.

10. Joan Aron, "The Reorganization Syndrome, The Nuclear Regulatory Case," *Southern Review, Public Administration,* Winter 1982 p. 465.

11. Ibid.

12. Patty Dale Renfrow, "The Establishment of the New Regulatory Agencies: Independent Commission versus Executive Department Agencies" (Ph.D., Rice University, 1982) p. 7.

13. Ibid., p. 6.

14. U.S. Congress, Senate Committee on Environment and Public Works, *Hearings on Proposals to Reorganize the Nuclear Regulatory Commission before the Subcommittee on Nuclear Regulation of the Committee on Environment and Public Works,* 100th Cong., 1st sess., 1987, p. 45.

15. Ibid., p. 44.

16. Renfrow, *The Establishment of the New Regulatory Agencies,* p. 7.

17. *Staff Report to the President's Commission on the Accident at Three Mile Island: The Nuclear Regulatory Commission* (Washington: GPO, 1979), p. 22.

18. Ibid., p. 21.

19. Ibid., pp. 23–24.

20. Ibid., pp. 19–20.

21. Ibid., p. 20.

22. U.S. Nuclear Regulatory Commission, *1978 NRC Annual Report* (Washington: GPO, 1979), NUREG-0516, p. 223.

23. Ibid.

24. Ibid.

25. Ibid., p. 97.

26. Ibid.

27. U.S. General Accounting Office, *Reporting Unscheduled Events at Nuclear Facilities, Opportunities to Improve Nuclear Regulatory Oversight*, EMD-179-16, January 26, 1979, p. 3.

28. Ibid., p. 4.

29. Ibid.

30. U.S. Nuclear Regulatory Commission Special Inquiry Group, *Three Mile Island, A Report to the Commissioners and to the Public* (Washington: GPO, 1980), p. 151.

31. U.S. General Accounting Office, *The Nuclear Regulatory Commission: More Aggressive Leadership Needed*, EMD 80-17, January 15, 1980, p. 4.

32. Ibid.

33. *President's Commission on the Accident at Three Mile Island*, pp. 24–25.

34. U.S. General Accounting Office, EMD 80-17, pp. 36–37.

35. *1978 NRC Annual Report*, p. 223.

36. Ibid.

37. Ibid.

38. *1984 NRC Annual Report*, p. 191.

39. Ibid.

About the Book and Author

How bureaucracies perceive and respond to technological risk is the subject of this study in organizational theory. The author offers evidence from primary sources such as the testimony of agency officials; agency memoranda; and extensive interviews in Congress, the bureaucracy, and the White House to explain the organizational failures leading to the Three Mile Island and Challenger accidents. She examines the implications of these organizational failures in terms of how organizations communicate about and cope with potential risks to public safety—in hopes of avoiding such disasters in the future.

Maureen Hogan Casamayou received her Ph.D. at Boston College and is an assistant professor of political science at Mount Vernon College in Washington, D.C. Her teaching interests are primarily in the fields of public administration and American political institutions.

Index